"Working predominantly within high-performance sport Monica was able to make the key existential themes come to life within a context that I was able to relate both personally and professionally.

"Through reading Monica's books and attending her 'Existential Coaching' training I know my practice as an Executive Coach within the corporate world has shifted to a deeper existential philosophical approach.

"Monica has taught me the importance of being at one with the client where I feel more attuned to their needs and the challenges, uncertainties and dilemmas we experience as part of the human condition, relinquishing a desire to drive a performance orientated agenda.

"What Monica does exceptionally well, often leaving me in awe is the simplicity in which she tunes in then gently challenges the client to open up a new sense of perspective providing the clarity to move towards meaningful and purposeful change.

"Existential coaching is an art form that dances between the philosophical and the psychological. It gives the practitioner the bandwidth to adapt and flex rather than abide to a one shoe fits all approach. You will learn how to create a mutually collaborative relationship that enables your client(s) to reflect and commit to meaningful and purposeful action fully aligned to their values.

"The only warning I will give upfront is that you will not be able to put it down as lightbulbs and deep reflections will be happening as you flick through every page!"
Ian Guyah Low, *EMCC Certified Coach, BASES Accredited Sport and Exercise Scientist (Performance Psychologist), Accredited Mindflick Practitioner (London, UK)*

"Culture in mediation is the much-needed and nuanced compass for navigating difficult conversations. As an immigrant, I experience the daily reality of otherness. As a professional, I recognise the immense potential for understanding and bridging the conflict gaps between us through active listening and empathy. We're looking for maps and how-to guides when all we need is a sturdy compass.

"Monica's approach to culture in mediation provides such a reliable compass, guiding us through the conflict intricacies of our global village. While not a traditional how-to guide, this book offers valuable insights and instruments to help one better navigate the challenges brought upon by mediation."
Andra Vlaic, *Leader, Coach, Mediator, and Trainer (London, UK)*

"Conflict is multi-layered and complex, and emotions are at the very basis of every conflict. Monica's refreshing approach of psychologically informed mediation and conflict resolution proves that if no space is created for these emotions to be expressed and let go of, the resolution of the dispute can be nearly impossible. In this book Monica continues to give further psychological insight into conflict adding culture as a force to be reckoned with. Understanding the role culture can play as a source of conflict, or an obstacle to conflict resolution, should be a key tool in every mediator's skillset toolbox. While applying that skill, the mediator should not forget to confront their own cultural heritage, as it can equally be a tumbling block in resolving conflict! Having attended several of Monica's advanced trainings over the past years, I have come to known her as one of the most influential facilitators cultivating a refreshingly new approach to mediation and conflict resolution. With this book, Monica not only continues to share her expertise but also gives mediators a distinct advantage helping resolving disputes."

Bart Gorissen, *Legal & Business Consultant, CMC Accredited Mediator (Amsterdam, The Netherlands)*

"In her new book, Monica reveals the importance of culture in mediation – a phenomenon that all professionals notice, but only the rare and brave name and describe. A great book, which, while reading, I shouted out loud: 'That's right! Exactly.' Culture and multiculturalism will increasingly influence the mediation process, so now is the right time for every professional mediator to read Monica's new book."

Dana Rone, *PhD. Dana Rone, sworn attorney at law, certified mediator in Latvia, associate professor of Law Faculty of Turiba University (Latvia)*

"Monica is one of the leading experts who masterfully applies existential philosophy and psychology to various areas of practical interest. She is also well known in the field of conflict resolution through her training courses and her practical experience.

"In this book she delves deeper into the specific aspects of the role of culture in mediation, drawing on theory and on her own experience as a mediator and trainer of mediators in the UK and beyond. She looks at how we can come to grips with what might be meant by 'culture', understood as a specific mode of what existentialists might call being-in-the-world, individual, political, familial, ethnic, sexual, geographical, spiritual, etc. She gives insights into the historical, global and cultural particularities before posing the fundamental question of whether or not a culturally influenced approach is a worthwhile endeavour, exploring whether it helps to be culturally informed or even influenced as a mediator, or is it better to take a step back and adopt a phenomenological approach relying on what we might call the shared uniqueness of what it means to be human. I honestly recommend her new book to find orientation in these questions."

Dr. Georg Martensen, *Logotherapist, Existential Coach, Supervisor (Brunswick, Germany)*

"An existential understanding of culture in mediation requires recognising deeply rooted values, beliefs, and identities of the parties. This enables mediators to build trust, address identity needs, and understand cultural contexts to promote long-term, respectful solutions. Phenomenology, which focuses on direct and conscious experience, complements this approach through empathic listening, understanding subjective meanings, and contextualising experiences. Both approaches allow for a deeper consideration of the conflict, taking into account cultural and existential needs, promoting sustainable, integrative solutions. In her new book on the role of culture in mediation, Monica Hanaway draws on her diverse experience and describes the importance of an existential perspective on cultural issues in conflicts. Unlike psychologising concepts, it addresses the essential core issues of human existence. The key to resolving many conflicts lies in people's existential experiences, which reveal more similarities than cultural differences suggest. This book completes Monica's significant body of work on existential thinking in our time."

René Märtin, *Logotherapist, Existential Coach, Supervisor, Author (Osnabrück, Germany)*

"Monica can always be trusted to make the case for her chosen subject. Utilising her profound understanding, she delivers a detailed consideration of the material that is supported by worked examples. In her latest publication *Culture in Mediation* she once again provides an outstanding exploration of a topic that is of the utmost importance to both practitioners and participants. Readers familiar with her literary canon will not be disappointed."

Bob Cree-Hay, *CEDR/MII Accredited Mediator, Dispute Negotiator, Supervisor (Belfast, UK)*

Exploring the Role of Culture in Mediation

This new book explores the historical development of mediation (conflict resolution) from a cultural and existential perspective, and considers the cultural challenges involved for a mediator.

The author, Monica Hanaway, has been mediating disputes across cultures for several years. She sets the scene for exploring the role culture plays in conflict and its resolution by explaining what mediation is and what we understand by the word 'culture'. From there she explores what mediators need to keep in mind when considering culture in the context of mediation. Within this, she covers such topics as the merits of using interpreters, and the pros and cons of using mediators from the same culture as the disputants. The final section of the book comments on what mediation professional and training bodies need to do to raise the profile of the cultural aspects in conflict.

Written by an experienced practitioner, *Exploring the Role of Culture in Mediation* will be of particular interest to all mediators, coaches, and psychologists, those interested in applying philosophy to resolving conflict, and those considering mediation.

Monica Hanaway is a mediator, mediation trainer, executive and leadership coach and consultant, and an existential psychotherapist. She is the author of several books on mediation, coaching, and leadership, and regularly speaks on these topics at international conferences. She mediates a variety of disputes including in the corporate sector, across gangs, and in families. She runs regular courses on mediation, coaching, and leadership. She passionately believes that an understanding of existential and phenomenological philosophy has much to offer on a practical basis on how we navigate life in these uncertain times.

Exploring the Role of Culture in Mediation

An Existential Approach for Mediators, Coaches, Psychologists, and Organisations

Monica Hanaway

LONDON AND NEW YORK

Designed cover image: © Monica Hanaway

First published 2025
by Routledge
4 Park Square, Milton Park, Abingdon, Oxon OX14 4RN

and by Routledge
605 Third Avenue, New York, NY 10158

Routledge is an imprint of the Taylor & Francis Group, an informa business

© 2025 Monica Hanaway

The right of Monica Hanaway to be identified as author of this work has been asserted in accordance with sections 77 and 78 of the Copyright, Designs and Patents Act 1988.

All rights reserved. No part of this book may be reprinted or reproduced or utilised in any form or by any electronic, mechanical, or other means, now known or hereafter invented, including photocopying and recording, or in any information storage or retrieval system, without permission in writing from the publishers.

Trademark notice: Product or corporate names may be trademarks or registered trademarks, and are used only for identification and explanation without intent to infringe.

British Library Cataloguing-in-Publication Data
A catalogue record for this book is available from the British Library

ISBN: 9781032867335 (hbk)
ISBN: 9781032867328 (pbk)
ISBN: 9781003528890 (ebk)

DOI: 10.4324/9781003528890

Typeset in Times New Roman
by Newgen Publishing UK

Contents

Acknowledgements — xi

PART ONE
Overview of What We Understand by 'Mediation' and 'Culture' — **1**

1 Introduction — 3

2 Mediation Today — 22

3 Different Mediation Styles — 27

4 The Mediation Process — 40

PART TWO
Psychologically Informed Mediation Using an Existential-Phenomenological Approach — **49**

5 Why a Psychologically Informed Approach is Needed in All Mediation but Particularly in Culturally Sensitive Disputes — 51

6 Key Existential Concepts for Mediation — 61

7 Existential Dimensions — 75

8 Key Relevant Phenomenological Concepts for Mediation — 78

9 The Process of Psychologically Informed Mediation — 81

PART THREE
Bringing Together Thoughts on Culture and Mediation, Exploring the Issues for Mediators and the Need for Change   **91**

10 What is 'Culture'   93

11 The Cultural History of Mediation   108

12 Current Responses to the Use of Mediation   117

13 Key Considerations and Skills for Working with Cultural Difference   123

14 Considerations and Implications for the Mediation Profession   138

15 Conclusion – To Return to the Existential and Phenomenological   147

Bibliography   *153*
Index   *161*

Acknowledgments

I would like to thank all those students who took part in the first 'Role of Culture in Mediation' Course which took place at Jesus College, Oxford University, in February 2024. This book is a culmination of the research I undertook to write the course, plus the fruit of the fascinating discussions which took place on the course.

Part One

Overview of What We Understand by 'Mediation' and 'Culture'

Chapter 1

Introduction

What Do We Mean by Mediation and Culture?

I am hoping that you have not misread the title of this book and like many people mistaken 'mediation' for 'meditation'. It may be easier to think about the role of culture in meditative practices such as yoga or mindfulness, than in a practice such as mediation which is still linked in many people's minds with legal processes. If you are here by mistake, I fear you will at first feel disappointed but if you continue you may find some surprising similarities, as my own approach to mediation is psychologically informed and looks at the worldview of everyone involved including all aspects of how they relate to the world, including their values and beliefs and spirituality.

To properly consider what role culture plays in a mediation, we first need to explore what we understand by 'mediation', and what we include when we speak of 'culture'.

What Do We Mean by Mediation?

It is not just 'meditation' which gets confused with 'mediation' which is very understandable given the similarity of the spelling, but people also regularly confuse mediation with negotiation, so before going on to look in some depth at what mediation is, it is worth briefly looking at how it differs from negotiation.

Negotiation

All mediators need some understanding of negotiation. Some participants in a mediation may choose to bring their lawyers with them. For many such lawyers they still see their role as to negotiate on behalf of their clients and will automatically adopt this stance. This will usually mean focusing on the 'facts' and on material or concrete aspects of the dispute and will not look at identifying or working with underlying emotional, moral, or other issues. This can cause problems in a mediation, particularly if only one side has come with legal representatives. The mediator needs to be alert to when parties may be moving prematurely from a mediation approach to a negotiation, and gently move the process back into the more fruitful area of exploration and the opening of debate rather than a premature attempt to close down discussion and 'get to an agreement' no matter its relevance or meaning.

However, it is inevitable that in the latter stages of a mediation some element of negotiation will legitimately enter the process during the drawing up of the Heads of Agreement document. The mediator needs to have the skills to know when they have enough information about the worldviews of the parties, the emotions evoked by the issue and the meaning of the dispute and any settlement agreement. Mediation is not therapy (although when done well will have therapeutic effect) so to keep trying to 'dig deeper' is not the aim of mediation; the mediator needs to use the knowledge of what is important to the different parties to facilitate an agreement which will be 'good enough' for everyone and in line with the values and needs of each person. In this part of the mediation there is a degree of negotiation, but it is focused on finding a place of agreement which is meaningful to both parties and with which they both can live, rather than one where one party feels they have won out over the other.

Below I outline some of the key differences between negotiation and mediation to resolving disputes.

To put it simply, negotiation is often directly between the parties in dispute, although each side may choose to involve a lawyer, or indeed delegate the whole process to the lawyer to negotiate on their behalf. Mediation involves a neutral third party to facilitate discussion between those in dispute, involving any other people which both parties are willing to have present.

Negotiation generally focuses on the expressed presenting issues and adopts a 'problem-solving' approach using reason and logic to negotiate against norms or standards, rather than individual meaning. It may use an approach which is termed 'Principled Objective Bargaining' or a contrasting one known as 'Positional Bargaining' which Wilks, a mediator and negotiator, in a presentation for an M&D training course, describes as 'a position of will, stubbornness, personal agenda ... typically due to lack of experience, lack of leverage or, conversely, misguided view of surplus leverage (i.e. someone who thinks they hold the cards).' She differentiates between what are termed 'value claim' deals which aim for a win/lose solution and 'value create' deals which are aiming for a win/win outcome.

Negotiation is a more structured approach than mediation with those involved more focused on the original desired outcome, moving between the Least Most Desired Outcome (LDO) to the Most Desired Outcome (MDO) using an agreed, although not necessarily overt set of 'game rules', aiming to move the parties from their individual territories to what is termed the Zone of Mutual Agreement (ZOMA) (Figure 1.1).

For an observer there may appear little difference in mediation and negotiation, yet careful listening will see they employ a completely different philosophical approach. In line with its legal origins, negotiation will try to narrow down discussion to 'the point in hand' and have a clear view of where it wants things to

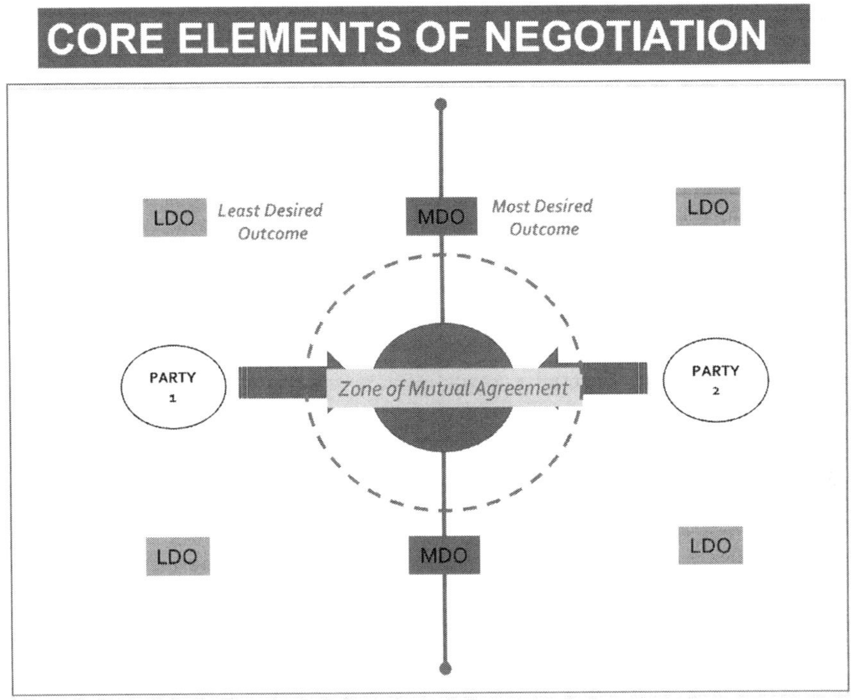

Introduction 5

CORE ELEMENTS OF NEGOTIATION

Figure 1.1 Course Elements of Negotiation
Kelli Wilks (2020) presentation for Monica Hanaway course

go. This may be evidenced by the use of more controlling language such as closed questions and a desire even from the start to keep things 'firmly on track'. There will be little or no interest in finding underlying meanings or motivations or giving time to exploratory discussion about things which may appear to have no bearing on the presenting problem. This approach will be more attractive to some cultures than others.

As a mediator, I would show a preference for mediation over litigation and negotiation. In Table 1.1, I offer some of the reasons for this.

Having given a brief view of what is understood by negotiation I wish to move on to give a more detailed description of what I mean when I speak of mediation.

Mediation

There are several different forms of mediation, also known as alternative dispute resolution (ADR) and I shall introduce some of these later. Many are still rooted in legal and negotiation practices, while the newer approaches are more psychologically informed. In this newer approach to mediation there is an interest not just

6 Exploring the Role of Culture in Mediation

Table 1.1 Differences between Litigation and Mediation

Litigation	Mediation
Can take years	Quick (often just a day)
Expensive	Cheap
Binding judgment	On a without prejudice basis
Formal	Informal
Open to public and press	Strictly confidential
Confrontational and competitive	Active involvement from the parties to seek a solution
Uncertain outcome	70%+ successful
Dispute has escalated	Dispute solved *before* it escalates
Lose/lose outcome	Win/win outcome
Focus on wants and differences	Conciliatory and focus on needs
Destroys relationships	Preserves relationships

in process, goals, problem solving, and reaching an agreement, but in the uncovering of and seeking to understand the worldviews of all parties to the dispute, and so sitting within a more transformative tradition. It would seem self-evident that this approach takes account of culture in a deeper and more relevant way than a more legalistic approach does. As I intend to show, this approach can be used in all kinds of mediation, whether corporate, with street gangs, or indeed everything in between.

However, before we can mediate, we must have a dispute or conflict to work with. Conflict is always personal, relational, tied in with our self-esteem, and therefore emotional. The most effective way of finding a meaningful and lasting solution is to address the underlying (usually non-factual) causes and motivations together with the emotional response to the situation. To do this requires us first to look at the nature of conflict.

What Is Conflict?

> At present, most of us hate conflict; we are usually in conflict with the very idea of conflict and don't want to think about it.
>
> Mindell, 2017: xiii

However conflict averse we are, we cannot avoid conflict. Some conflict is small and internal – shall I resist that cheesecake or give in and eat it? If I decide I shall leave it in the fridge, is that the end of the matter? Probably not, thoughts of that cheesecake may take up my thoughts long after I have made my decision. A bit of a silly example, I know, but I would suggest that if we try to ignore conflicts of any size, we almost certainly build up more problems for ourselves, and are probably merely putting off a difficult conversation which is likely to develop into a more challenging confrontation. We may then find that in addition to the original disagreement we will need to deal with a conversation heightened by feelings of not being heard, ignored, and disrespected. In my mediation work I am often faced with situations, which if addressed early, would never have developed into a full-blown dispute. Clearly it takes courage to address different options, and some cultures are more likely to sweep things under the carpet and hope they go away than other cultures where there is an expectation of speaking up early and directly.

Of course, we all have different responses to conflict. How we respond may be laid down in our family history where we will have seen how our parents addressed or attempted to ignore conflict. This blueprint will either be challenged or reinforced by our subsequent experiences of disagreement. If robust discussion was a regular thing in our families as we grew up, we are more likely to respond early and clearly to disagreement, whereas in families where children see no evidence of disagreement, they can feel very unskilled and inexperienced later in life when other people choose to address things head on.

When I am training mediators, I often ask them just to reflect on the word 'conflict' and to note down their immediate response to the word. Responses will often include nouns such as 'war' or 'fight', but will usually elicit emotional responses, with people describing feeling 'afraid', 'angry', or even 'excited'. They may also describe embodied reactions such as temperature change, 'butterflies in the stomach', 'feeling nauseous' or 'shaky', or even fear that they may faint. Very few people have a neutral response to conflict. Their intuitive response, created through their prior experiences, will inform how they behave when confronted with a conflict.

Although we have different responses to being in conflict, Glasl (1999) suggests that any conflict goes through several identifiable stages.

Hardening
Initially, a person will try to make their views known to the other person/s. However, if they feel that they have not been listened to, they may then become more rigid and determined to stick to their own views. This may result in people grouping behind each viewpoint in a standoff situation 'the standpoints attract adherents, and groups start to form around certain positions' (Glasl 1999:56) and develop 'habitual behaviour patterns' (ibid). These patterns usually start with verbal sparring, before moving to a position where neither party believes in the humanity of the other, or the possibility of resolution, but instead chooses to experience the other as 'alien' and so unlike themselves that they have no hope for a mutual dialogue.

Debate and polemics
From there, disputants become '*locked into inflexible standpoints*' (ibid), moving away from the lived experience of the initial incident. They begin to focus on their perception of the intrinsic personality of the other, particularly focusing on perceived negative traits. In this stage disputants become more and more removed from the commonalities they share as human beings making it more difficult to identify shared common goals.

Actions not words
By the third stage parties are often refusing to speak to, or even acknowledge each other; 'see themselves as being held captives by external circumstances they cannot control. They therefore deny responsibility for the course of events. An increasing part of their own actions are regarded as necessary responses to the behaviour of the other' (ibid).

Images and coalitions
In the fourth stage identified by Glasl, the parties continue to reduce the other to fixed archetypes, by now 'the negative images are screens that occupy the field of vision whenever the parties meet each other' (ibid), *thus* denying the potential for change.

Loss of face
In this fifth stage, the stereotyping develops to leave both sides seeing the other as bad and as being on the side of the devil whilst they are firmly on the side of the angels, thus experiencing the other as Fanon's 'uncivilised savage'. In this phase the biggest fear is the loss of face, which may occur when moving from any expressed 'bottom line' to more of a compromise position. The party are still far from trusting each other and are concerned that showing any hurt or vulnerability will result in the other party seeing them as weak and using that against them. In trying to guard against these feelings of vulnerably an individual may try to defend themselves by acting in a way which may be perceived as 'arrogant'. Aggression is often a defensive response to fear and in 'macho' cultures may be the only culturally 'acceptable' response if they wish to retain respect from their social group.

Strategies of threats/Limited destructive blows/Fragmentation of the enemy
When a person is aware of their vulnerability, Glasl suggests that the conflict moves to the next stage, creating 'a pressure to act rapidly and radically', with the desire to 'eliminate/destroy' the other. Their primary desire at this stage is to survive, and they may hold a belief that in order to do so they may need to destroy the other and have their view be validated by the mediator and the other's view denied.

Together into 'the abyss'
This final stage, in which the need to destroy the other becomes paramount, can lead both parties to forget what they originally wanted as a resolution, and instead to descend into what Glasl terms 'the abyss' together. They become intent on a fight with the aim being to defeat the other person. This creates a situation where no-one wins, and everyone loses.

Although Glasl offers these as universal stages, how these stages are experienced by different people will differ, and not all stages will be identifiable. Kilmann (2023) developed five different conflict resolution behaviours or strategies which they identified as ways in which people handle conflict. These include avoiding, competing or defeating, compromising, accommodating, and collaborating.

Competing or defeating is an uncooperative assertive approach where the individual considers the conflict as a competition resulting in an outcome with a winner and loser. This approach requires an individual to pursue their own concerns at the other person's expense. It is a power-oriented model in which the disputant will attempt to overpower the other person, both their argument and their confidence. It can mean using whatever power they can muster (including status, their comparative comfort and skill in arguing a point, power to impose sanctions or economic power, not caring what the other thinks of them, not being concerned about upsetting the other, etc.) in an unscrupulous manner to ensure their own position remains unchanged, and eventually is agreed to by the other person. Competing has a positive side meaning that people stand up for their rights or defend a position which they believe to be correct, or morally right. A mediator must be watchful that a competing person does not attempt to bully the other person into submission. They will need encouragement to engage at all with opposing positions.

Accommodating is almost the opposite of competing. It is an unassertive and cooperative approach. The accommodating individual tends to neglect their own concerns and prioritise the concerns of the other person. This can be negatively constructed as adopting a martyr-likeor self-sacrificing position. An accommodating person can offer selfless generosity or charity but may tend to go along with an opposing view to avoid conflict, or annoying or upsetting the other person. In mediation a mediator must be careful that such a person does not simply 'roll over' to get out of the conflict situation

Avoiding is also unassertive but unlike accommodating it is uncooperative. The person seeks to avoid conflict at all costs. An avoidant person will attempt to sidestep an issue. They hold a false belief that by postponing addressing an issue in the moment, there will a better time to do so in the future ... usually that better time never arrives. They can be very adept at spotting conflict and getting out of the way of it as quickly as possible. This avoidance can frustrate the other person, their anger will grow and when the conflict does come to a head it will be much more combative than it would have been if addressed at an earlier point. A mediator will often have to deal with an avoidant person's over-willingness to apologise and run, rather than engage in any difficult discussion.

Collaborating is the opposite of avoiding in that it is both assertive and cooperative. A collaborative person will want to work with others to find solutions which satisfy everyone's concerns. There is a willingness to enter into exploring what lies below the initial presenting issue in order to discover the real, and often unstated, underlying needs and wants of the parties in disputes. They are interested in the way everyone sees the situation and are willing to explore creative ways forward. Any mediator who finds themselves with collaborators on either side is very lucky.

Compromising can be both assertiveness and cooperativeness, sitting between competing and accommodating. Although compromise may carry some negative associations for some, a compromising party looks to find a realistic and mutually acceptable solution that is acceptable to both parties. The mediator needs to take care that a compromising individual does not rush too quickly to offer a solution which is devoid of any understanding of motivation, emotional attachment, or self-esteem needs. This may be by offering to split the difference, exchange concessions, or find a quick middle-ground solution. Both parties will need to be willing to compromise on something but only after understanding what really matters to each of them, so that the compromise does not go against key values and beliefs, and addresses to some extent the needs rather than the wants of both.

Kilmann's thesis seems to assume that people choose to what extent they will be cooperative or assertive in a conflict. However, it could be argued that in such a heightened stress situation people do not always have a rational considered reaction but may be led by a more primary and basic neurological response. The more insecure the individual the more likely it is that they will have a predetermined strategic game plan which they hope they can keep to in order to achieve the outcome they want. If the mediator uses a psychological approach to find a way through this defensive front (which may be presented as a confident, assertive front), then both parties are more likely to find a solution which is meaningful to them both, and so has a greater chance of being sustained.

As suggested above, conflict is an emotional experience which will be received in different ways by different individuals. Our response to conflict is essentially emotional rather than rational. If there was a logical answer, clear to all, there would be no conflict.

Whether we enjoy conflict or abhor it, our emotional reaction will be signalled by a physical reaction. The release of adrenaline is attractive to some but frightening to others. When stressed, we may experience what is often termed an 'amygdala hijack'. This term was first used by the psychologist Daniel Goleman in his 1995 book; 'Emotional Intelligence: Why it can Matter More than IQ'. In this, he describes how an ancient structure in the brain, a small almond shaped segment, the amygdala, is designed to respond to a physical or psychological threat. When someone disagrees with us it is a threat to our thoughts, beliefs, values, and self-esteem. The amygdala originally served a very important function allowing us to make a split second, non-reflective response to a perceived threat. This results in us taking one of three options fight-flight-freeze. This has an important function in places like the battlefield where a moment's hesitation may result in our demise, but in today's modern world the threat is more likely to be a psychological one.

Wherever the threat comes from it triggers a bodily response which may be expressed as fear, anger, loss of control, depression, etc. This can happen very quickly. Think of a time when you have quickly read an email which has annoyed you, this can quickly be experienced as a threat to status or bring forth feelings of being disrespected or misunderstood. In turn this can make us feel angry or threatened by the perceived challenge. When this happens, our emotions take precedence over our actions. The emotional part of the brain, the amygdala, overrides the thinking part of the brain, the neocortex, in response to any perceived threat. This compromises the ability to reason and think logically. An important thing to remember when trying to mediate.

In the immediate moments following the perceived threat the brain sends a message to the adrenal glands, which begin a process involving a release of hormones including adrenaline. The purpose is to prepare the body for emergency action. Non-essential processes are immediately switched off. If the body is in the process of digesting food, this stops immediately and may cause a feeling of churning or 'butterflies' in the stomach or feeling nauseous or sick. The body seeks to rid itself of anything which may slow it down, and so glucose and fats are released into the bloodstream. These are fuel for the muscles, so oxygen is needed to burn them. Breathing increases and may cause breathlessness. The body needs to get fuel and oxygen to the muscles quickly, causing the heart to beat faster, sometimes experienced as palpitations. Blood pressure rises, and some people notice feeling hot or cold, or begin sweating as the body attempts to dissipate the heat generated by the vigorous muscular activity for which the body is preparing. As muscle tension increases a person may shake or become restless, or experience chronic headaches or backache.

As all this is happening in the body, there are two important changes in the neurology. As reflexes speed up, so does the thinking process, leading to some people noticing racing thoughts and an inability to focus. The blood supply to the frontal parts of the brain, which are responsible for the higher levels of reasoning, is reduced, and the blood supply to the more primitive parts, near the brain stem, which are responsible for automatic, instinctive, or impulsive decision making, and behaviour, is increased. This may result in a stressed person becoming more prone to impulsive thinking and behaviour which they may regret later. Trying to work with conflict in a rational and logical way when parties do not have access to the logical part of the brain, can result in them feeling misunderstood or dismissed. One needs to find creative ways to work with the emotional part of the brain, taking it through a process where at the right time more logical thinking can be accessed and work can begin to take place to find a workable, realistic solution which addresses not just material and concrete requirements, but also the psychological needs of the parties.

An individual's response will be a 'lived experience' unique to them, flowing from their past experiences and general personality. So, what do we find if we look beyond the individual to more universal understandings or definitions of conflict?

The Merriam Webster dictionary offers definitions that include 'competitive or opposing action of incompatibles: antagonistic state or action (as of divergent ideas, interests, or persons)' and 'mental struggle resulting from incompatible or opposing needs, drives, wishes, or external or internal demands'. These definitions draw our attention to the fact that conflict can be internal as well as external.

Collins dictionary also gives an internal and external definition. It defines external conflict as a 'serious disagreement and argument about something important'. If two people or groups are in conflict, they have had a serious disagreement or argument and have not 'yet reached agreement'. It places emphasis on the seriousness and importance of the disagreement, but it does not define whether it is the parties who deem it serious, or whether it would be seen as serious by most external observers. We have all seen fights where people can no longer remember what they are about. I once mediated a dispute between two high powered executives which had stemmed from one failing to give a birthday present to the other's wife! What was relevant was the importance placed on this by one party, and the seriousness lay in the potential negative outcome whereby they would cease to work together and make many people redundant. The Collins dictionary also sees conflict as 'a state of mind in which you find it impossible to make a decision', it sees such a conflict as stemming from 'a serious difference between two or more beliefs, ideas, or interests'. Such a definition does of course lead us into the arena of cultural differences.

So, different definitions emphasise the seriousness of the dispute whilst others look more to the time taken up by it. Encarta defines conflict as a '**continued** struggle or battle, ... open warfare between opposing forces; disagreement clash between ideas, principles, people; a psychological state resulting from the often unconscious opposition between simultaneous but incompatible desires, needs, drives, or impulses; opposition between characters or forces in a literacy work'.

Shantz (1987:285) drew a critical distinction between short-term disputes and long-term conflicts. He defines conflicts as '**time-distributed** social episodes' consisting of a series of discrete components that include issues, oppositions, resolutions, and outcomes'. Burton (1990) also distinguishes between conflict and dispute by time and by the issues involved. Interestingly, he differentiates conflict and dispute differently, speaking of short-term disputes, which he sees as relatively easy to resolve, and long-term conflicts which may contain seemingly resistant non-negotiable issues involving moral or value differences, vulnerability of self-esteem and the need to dominate, in addition to more concrete material matters. It is for this reason that people often remain in conflict for years. It can even get to the point where the original dispute is forgotten or no longer relevant but the process, with the almost inevitable attacks on each party, escalating the dispute further, so the primary objective moves from the original issue of contention to the need to dominate, beat, or even annihilate the other person and be declared 'the winner'.

The Cambridge dictionary offers several definitions of conflict, some of which contain what I would see as cultural aspects. These include 'an active disagreement between people with opposing views or principles'; 'fighting between two or more groups of people or countries'; 'a situation in which beliefs, needs, facts etc. are very different and cannot easily exist together or both be true'; 'a situation in which there are opposing demands or ideas, and a choice has to be made between them'.

Although we are counselled not to look to Wikipedia, my preferred definition is to be found there, in the description of conflict as being 'when two or more parties, with perceived incompatible goals, seek to undermine each other's goal-seeking capability'. The reason I am drawn to this definition is that when speaking of '**perceived** incompatible goals' it introduces the understanding that conflicts are not about facts but about perceptions. More of this later. This gives mediators hope, as we cannot change what has happened (generally but incorrectly referred to often as 'the facts'), whereas we can enable a change of perceptions.

Although Shantz, who I referred to earlier, distinguishes between conflict and disputes, in referring to conflict I am including disputes within this. However, some theoreticians have sought to make meaningful distinction between the two. Costantino and Merchant (1996) define conflict as fundamental disagreement between two parties, of which conciliation, conflict avoidance, capitulation, or dispute are possible outcomes. This would seem to indicate that dispute is a result of conflict. This may only be their disinclination to treat 'conflict' as a noun and 'dispute' as a verb. This distinction supports Yarn's statement (1999:115) that 'a conflict can exist without a dispute, but a dispute cannot exist without a conflict.' Yarn saw conflict as a state, rather than a process, involving people with opposing values or needs being in a state of conflict, which may be latent or manifest and may develop into a dispute.

However we choose to define conflict and dispute, and I shall not necessarily differentiate between the two, my own understanding is that both conflicts and disputes are the results of perceptions and therefore essentially psychological in nature. If this is the case, then any attempt to resolve the conflict calls for a psychological approach which focuses on the underlying psychological motivators for starting or maintaining the dispute. These motivators may, or may not, be consciously known by those in dispute. Even when they are known to the individual, they may be reluctant to admit them to themselves or others.

A psychological approach to conflict resolution will look to unearth those motivators through an exploration of the individual's value systems, emotional language, and worldviews. The mediator will understand the sensitivities involved and attempt to do this whilst seeking to preserve or even enhance self-esteem by working with the fundamental human psychological needs for respect, recognition, identity, and security. Strasser and Randolph (2004:27) developed just such an approach to mediation. They stress the need to uncover these psychological elements present in both disputes and conflicts. 'One of the most important elements is the exploration of the covert reasons for the dispute, as well as the overt. The parties will have developed rigid belief systems as their overall strategy for survival in an uncertain world'. These psychological factors are not just evidenced in the cause of a dispute but can also cause the dispute to become entrenched. People often stay in what looks like an easily resolved conflict do so because they are afraid to 'roll over' and so be seen as weak. Even when they have changed their mind an individual will argue their point long after they have stopped believing it because to do so would be seen as having got something wrong. If we understand that a conflict is primarily psychological then there is little point in focusing on what each party insists are the 'facts' of the case, as they are only ever the perceptions of each individual. It is perceptions which are in conflict although the argument will be made that they are arguing over 'facts. If facts were indeed truly facts, there could be no argument and therefore no conflict. There would be nothing to argue about, but as stated earlier, it's our emotional reaction which informs our perception of events and through which we develop our own 'facts'.

Another writer who explored conflict through a psychotherapeutic lens was Totton (2006:30) who suggested that the debate on conflict has focused on questions of aggression. He considered whether 'aggression is an innate human trait, or is it the product of specific conditions? Is aggression wholly negative, or does it have positive aspects and expressions?' He was interested to explore whether 'therapy (can) contribute either to minimising aggression or to supporting its positive aspects?' People's response to being in conflict is always emotional and often manifested as anger and aggression. If we feel threatened by another person, even if the threat is just to our perception of an event or our self-esteem, rather than a physical threat, we feel the need to defend ourselves or at least to win them over to our view of the world, our values and beliefs. This suggests that the response to being in conflict is more about self-defence, rather than aggression. When faced with aggression most people's response is to try to minimise any aggression, or even to try to subdue any emotion which is being expressed. There is a widely held belief, although I would dispute it, that to resolve a conflict we must quickly remove the emotional response and bring some logic to the situation. This is disrespectful to the importance of the conflict in a person's life, and we are in danger of missing the point of the conflict. You may successfully negotiate a 'logical' agreement, but it may have little meaning to the individual, the underlying emotional conflict remains, and a settlement will be hard to maintain.

How people express the depth of their feeling differs. It may be demonstrated through, experienced as, and perhaps even acknowledged as 'aggression' where others will describe similar feelings as 'passion' and express them from that understanding. It is easy for a third party to confuse these emotions and respond instinctively. Even in the mediator role there may be a feeling that we need to defend ourselves from the perceived aggression by becoming submissive or through trying to assert our imagined authority by matching, or even going beyond, the other's 'aggression' or trying to shut them down. If we experience the other's communication as passionate rather than aggressive, we are more likely to be interested in what they have to say and so instead of adopting an attitude of closing down, we are more likely to invite an opening up.

This negative response to perceived aggression is shared by many thinkers and writers. Some see aggression as an innate instinct common to us all, others that it is learned behaviour. As we have seen earlier it can be regarded as a neural and hormonal response to a perceived threat which stimulates the amygdala. The suggestion that high testosterone levels also cause aggression is often cited but has also been refuted. Higley et al. (1996) reported that those with elevated testosterone levels may exhibit signs of aggression but rarely commit aggressive acts. This leads them to suggest that cultural, social, and cognitive factors play a mediating role in any subsequent behaviour.

As a psychotherapist as well as a mediator, I have looked to psychotherapeutic writers to see what can be learnt from their different responses to conflict, and perceived aggression. Freud saw aggression as innate, and as essentially dangerous; he does not write of the creative function of aggression and surprisingly little about its triggers, but does point to our collective vulnerability when we experience a threat, he believed that 'men are not gentle creatures who want to be loved ... they are, on the contrary, creatures among whose instinctual endowments are to be reckoned a powerful share of aggressiveness ... In consequence of this primary mutual hostility of human beings, civilised society is perpetually threatened with disintegration' (1985:111).

Reich disagreed with Freud, seeing human beings as essentially possessing 'natural decency, spontaneous honesty, mute and complete feelings of love', and presenting a more neural and biological viewpoint, seeing aggression as 'the life expression of the musculature, or the system of movement' (1973:186). Suttie (1936), building on Reich's work, took a very psychoanalytical approach seeing hate and destructiveness as secondary reactions to threatened primal love. Melanie Klein spoke of an innate conflict between love and hate, which had to be dealt with through projecting one's destructiveness into others and adopting the depressive position to address the task of reparation. However, for many therapists and others, aggression and conflict are essential parts of our internal human nature, and so to understand someone it is important to be curious about their unique emotional response and the lived experience which caused it. A mediator will be faced by emotional parties. It is impossible to feel neutral and calm when someone is disagreeing with you, as they are effectively threatening your worldview and within that not just your perception about the dispute but often your core values and beliefs. The degree to which a person will openly express their emotions is heavily influenced by their culture. Some people will come from a family, a community, or a geographical culture where it is considered unacceptable to express emotions, whereas others will have grown up in contexts where immediate emotional responses were expected, encouraged, and not feared. The mediator will bring their own cultural heritage regarding emotional experience into the mediation dynamic and must find a way of recognising that the other people may be more or less comfortable with the level of emotional discharge than they themselves are. When working with parties from different cultures there is the likelihood that there are at least three cultural scripts in play, all with different levels of emotional tolerance.

Other writers, taking a wider view than those from the therapeutic community, have focused more on the social aspect of conflict. Samuels took a political stance, seeing aggression as lying at the heart of a pluralistic approach to politics, 'often masking the deepest need for contact, dialogue, playback, affirmation' (1993:198). He presents a more positive view, more in line with my own, in which conflict is accepted as a precursor or even a necessary component to growth and change. If we have no internal or external conflict, then why change? Even though we may accept it as necessary it does not make it easier to sit with.

This understanding is reflected in the work of scholars who have focused more on conflict. When I first came across the work of Mindell it was quite a challenge to my personal culture. His calling for us to 'Value trouble. Accept nature. Make peace with war' (1995:241) did not initially fit comfortably with my worldview. Surely, we should try to stop trouble and end war. I slowly realised that what I needed to do by 'valuing' trouble was to learn to welcome expressions of trouble, to not quickly seek to calm the waters. To do so would be disrespectful to the depth of feeling which had been evoked in the individual by the dispute. If I considered their reaction to be out of proportion, or frightening, then that was my problem as I was failing to sufficiently understand them and therefore potentially undermining their experience. Such a mismatch would make it impossible to develop the trusting working alliance needed for successful resolution. The work of Totton, who focused on therapy, offered a similar personal challenge as it called for therapists to 'affirm aggression, support conflict, speak up for competition – while also affirming, supporting and speaking up for the victims of alienated and destructive expressions of these qualities' (2006:36). As we shall learn later, the identification of 'victim' and 'aggressor' may not always be what it first seems.

Discussion about what conflict is, and our different responses to it, has fascinated many thinkers, and although their thoughts differ, it would be fair to say that most acknowledge that we can never be without conflict and so it is an essential element to our lives, which can be used negatively or positively. We need to find ways of embracing positive conflict because without conflict there is little incentive to move from the status quo. Indeed, if we are comfortable and everything feels fine, where is our incentive to innovate and change, with all the challenges which change brings on a psychological and concrete level? Conflict can bring challenge and creativity into the mix. One quest is to find a way of working with conflict which does not make one party feel they have 'won' and leaving the other devastated.

Because it is ever present in human existence it is not surprising that we see its central role in most literature, songs, and film. Indeed, we find stories of conflict at the heart of most religious texts too. This may be just the struggle between good and evil, but we see it played out in narratives of conflicts between individuals and groups. Foster-Harris claimed that all plots stem from conflict. He describes this in terms of what the main character feels: 'I have an inner conflict of emotions, feelings... What, in any case, can I do to resolve the inner problems?' (1881:30). Whatever the external conflict presented as the cause, it is important to remember that an internal emotional struggle will almost inevitably accompany it, and that it is this internal battle which may rage more fiercely than the external one.

Whatever the nature of the dispute, conflict is always relational. It may focus on a relationship with another person or group of people, or on an intra-psychic relationship within an individual, it may even focus on our relationship with the environment or objects within it. The culture from which those in dispute come will likely have a hierarchy of validity for these, and some cultures will readily engage with the idea and importance of an inter-psychic struggle, whilst others will downplay this with comments such as 'don't be so self-orientated', 'stop thinking about things', 'just get on and sort them', or the wonderfully British 'keep a stiff upper lip'. With these responses they aim to take a pragmatic and logical approach to resolving a dispute and not want to 'waste' time considering any psychological or moral aspects which they would consider to be mere unhelpful side-issues. Other cultures will honour a conflict which stresses the relationship between humankind and the environment as central to the existence of humanity, whereas other cultures will not see the relevance. For example, the philosopher and writer Ayn Rand (2000) argued that man against nature is not a conflict because nature has no free will and thus cannot make choices. This is a view which may be challenged in some cultures, such as that of indigenous Australians, who have a stronger view of the equality between humans and nature, seeing themselves as living components required by the environment with each dependent on the other in order to thrive, meaning the land is part of them and they are part of the land. Even in more Western and capitalist cultures we are experiencing an increasing focus on the importance of the environment with groups such as Extinction Rebellion, and Climate Change Deniers such as the Acton Institute of the Study of Religion and Liberty (they would deny that this was their mission, although this is how they are identified by Greenpeace), providing strong yet opposing views. We have an emotional and psychological reaction to the way we relate to nature which may be present in disputes which on the surface seem to be about something very different.

Another section of conflict can revolve round what Rand termed the fourth basic conflict; 'man against society', where man stands against a man-made institution or against the government or commercial powers. 'Man against man' conflict may shade into 'man against society', with the need to remove the uniqueness and humanity of the person we are in conflict with, and instead experience them as a thing or part of an oppressive group. One's cultural background will impact on the extent to which you may start with a more individual or collective view of the world and therefore of conflict. Dai and Chen (2023:34) suggest that 'the ethics of concern only for self are egocentric. "Being for the other" is more desirable, but it tends to sacrifice one's own interests and rights. Hence it is not an ethical principle either.' The cultural influences on us and our own life experience may mean we are drawn to one end of this continuum. The mediator needs to be alert to this, or a party can easily slip into the role of unselfish victim or selfish aggressor in the eyes of the other and even of the mediator.

My apologies for the masculine gender-based terminology in Rand's writing, reflecting the time in which they were written, for as we know, all genders experience conflict. How they experience and express the conflict may be influenced by cultural expectations of normative gender behaviour. A mediator must be prepared to experience behaviours which test their own gender perceptions and experience. Whatever the gender identity of a party, when in conflict against individuals and/

or society people are forced to make moral choices and may through fear or a need for acceptance cling to societal norms, or be frustrated by social rules, leading to feelings of inauthenticity.

Even when the dispute appears to be between representatives of groups or organisations the individuals concerned will be affected as individuals. Their self-esteem will be at stake, and they will wish to return triumphant to the group they represent carrying aloft the outcome the group desired and allowing them to enjoy the feelings of success, instead of returning with their tails between their legs to report that they have 'failed' the group by not negotiating the settlement they wished for.

Some people might argue that some disputes are not relational and merely transactional. For example, I may have a dispute with a company who has failed to deliver what I expected them to. However, I am sure many of you will have struggled not to feel that dispute which takes place over the phone with an unnamed and unseen customer service representative is personal and relational. When I am listening to the repeated message of 'your call is important to us' or 'we are experiencing a higher number of calls than usual' or 'you are number 137 in the queue', I do not sit calmly and think 'oh they are having a busy day, how awful for them to be so overworked ... I have nothing better to do than wait my turn, I shall just hum a merry tune and wait'. I have to confess, that isn't how it is for me. I feel angry and disrespected ... is my time not important ... do they not know all the things I have to do today ... can they not experience what it is like to be without the service they have promised me'? I start by being angry and upset about the original failure for the service and this gets added to by the feeling of being treated as having no importance. Only once I am connected with a person, even if it is just their voice, can I begin to feel any empathy for their situation. Even this will be affected by my culturally informed levels of feelings of entitlement and my ability to connect and empathise with their lack of power.

Obviously, the most clearly relational type of dispute is when it is between two or more individuals, representing themselves and focused on their inability to see or incorporate the views of the other. Yet, even here, they will be carrying the hopes of their families and friends for an outcome which benefits the person they care about. So, relationships are usually more complex and layered than they at first appear. In these kinds of disputes there may be a greater wish to continue the relationship in some way beyond the mediation, giving a greater incentive to settle.

Although we can, to some extent, categorise conflicts in this way, it is important to remember that each conflict is unique to those involved in it and is experienced through the individual's filters of context, culture, values, experience, and beliefs, and is always relational. By noting these elements, it immediately becomes clear that the resolution of conflict does not rely on logic. If disputes were logical, there would be no conflict as there would be only one 'logical' solution, obvious to all. Conflicts become entrenched because they are not logical but emotional. People 'hang on' to a conflict and can become obsessed with it because it threatens something deep within them. It questions their perspective on themselves, life, and the cosmos, and so is deeply unsettling. It is of little use bringing a logic-led approach to resolving conflict if conflict is essentially emotional.

It flows from this understanding that if conflict and its resolution is essentially an emotional and relational engagement then, before we can mediate effectively, we must firstly understand ourselves and our own intuitive and emotional reaction to conflict. Although I started by quoting Mindell's assumption that most people hate conflict this is not universally the case. Some people actively enjoy it, they love, perhaps need, the adrenaline buzz which often accompanies conflict. Some may even provoke conflict as it provides the opportunity to make them feel powerful offering them an opportunity to 'win', and in so doing defeat the other. For other people fear is the overwhelming emotional response, the amygdala kicks in and they may freeze in the face of conflict, they may run from it or try to ignore it. In conflict we are inclined to look to defend our self-esteem and power and to hold tightly on to our beliefs without considering why they are seemingly not shared with those we conflict with. To openly explore our beliefs and the meaning we give to certain behaviours and thoughts challenges our self-concept calling for us to explore who we are and why we think as we do, and so can feel very scary. It may be that to change our perception and understanding may lead to us being ostracised from the group we currently belong to and so leave us isolated.

These are all psychological responses and concerns. Conflict is always psychological. It touches us at a deep level and may confront us with uncomfortable questions. Indeed, there would be no conflict if the event hadn't distressed us in some way. To bring a psychologically informed approach to mediation a mediator must welcome and be able to engage with all these aspects. Anything that is deemed significant to those involved is important in understanding the conflict and in working towards a meaningful resolution, and so must not be dismissed or side-lined. In a dispute I mediated between Mason and Markus, two high powered individuals, on the surface it seemed to be about a belief held by Markus that he worked a lot harder than Mason who he believed preferred spending much of his time at social events to which Markus was not invited. Markus wanted a redistribution of shares and assets to reflect what he considered to be the inequality of work between the two, or to end the Partnership. The absence of an invitation to a particularly glamourous event seemed to have brought things to a head. Through not trying to control the content of the mediation it became clear that Markus had previously considered Mason to be his best friend, and they had regularly socialised together outside of work. As the business became more successful this had stopped. Markus had created an internal narrative that Mason had stopped liking him and instead preferred spending time with their rich and prestigious clients. Mason was shocked to hear that this was how Markus saw things. He was able to use the opportunity to explain how much of his day was now taken up with social engagements with rich potential clients, who he did not enjoy being with. He saw these meetings as marketing events which often resulted in the company gaining profitable contracts. He told Markus that these events exhausted him and that he had to get up very early each morning for a workout in the gym to try to lose the weight he had put on due to the number of meals he had to eat each day! He would return from these meetings so tired that he went straight to bed, drawing complaints from this partner that he was never available. A parallel to Markus' complaints. Mason invited Markus to replace him at some of the functions. Interestingly Markus did not wish to do so, acknowledging that he was somewhat of an introvert and that was why they had initially agreed that Mason would do most of the customer facing work. He had forgotten this, realised that he had created a narrative of rejection and now saw the situation very differently. Together they agreed to take on another partner to share some of what Markus now saw as the vital marketing work that Mason had been doing and to book regular times to go out for a meal together like old times. As we were able to explore in the mediation this was a misperception which was relatively easy to explore, and the two parties were able to re-establish the excellent working relationship they had held previously.

So, as we have seen, if conflicts were logical people would calmly sit down and agree a rational answer based on what would be considered the only logical outcome. The truth is, conflicts are never logical they are emotional driven, often by things seemingly unrelated to the presenting dispute, and accompanied by a need to protect our dignity and self-esteem. It is natural for us to want to be proved right and for opponents to be told they are wrong. In truth we all experience events differently and so being proved 'right' is an idealised goal.

There may be no universal 'right' within the dispute, what we think we saw, heard, and experienced may differ and our reactions to a shared event will differ too. It is not the 'facts' of the event in itself which are conflictual, but our emotional and psychological response to it. Whatever happened, happened; we cannot undo history, though we can understand and experience it differently. The narratives about what happened can never really be 'the facts' but can only ever be about different perceptions of the same event. Each person creates their own set of 'facts', which they invest in believing to be 'the truth'. It does not benefit the mediator to spend a great deal of time trying to establish the 'truth' or the 'facts' of what happened, as they 'exist' only in the individual's perception of the past. All that can be changed are these resulting perceptions and attitudes. Understanding and exploring the nature and meaning of these perceptions is central to a psychologically informed approach to the mediation process, enabling the mediator to understand what is most important to each party in any resolution. To return to Mindell, who reminded us of Einstein's statement that, 'we all dance to a mysterious tune' and that our task is to learn to hear that tune. I go a little further believing that we need to hear both the treble notes and the bass notes and to give both equal importance.

In the next chapter I propose that psychologically informed mediation provides a way of incorporating all the above aspects in the conflict resolution process, and so presents a greater possibility of arriving at a resolution which is meaningful to each party, through taking account of the individuals' need for self-esteem and for solutions which remain in tune with their values. If the mediation succeeds in achieving such an agreement it is more likely to be adhered to than a solution which is offered by a third party and focuses on an evaluation of facts and logic rather than on emotions and values. One may argue that the centrality of the approach, in focusing on this attention to uncovering the beliefs and values of the parties, is especially important when we are working cross-culturally or with parties who have very clear differences, However, as I shall argue later, to some extent there are always cultural differences at play, presenting the mediator with a more difficult and subtle task when there seems to be surface commonalities between the parties.

Chapter 2

Mediation Today

Mediation today is often referred to as ADR, 'alternative dispute resolution'. Comically I have heard lawyers refer to it as an 'Alarming Drop in Revenue' as it may be seen as taking work away from legal practices!

It is a simple concept by which a neutral third party or parties assists those in dispute to work towards their own settlement. It is becoming more widely accepted as effective in a variety of disputes such as family, community, commercial, legal, diplomatic, and workplace but general awareness of it as an alternative to litigation still needs developing. People still seem to link the idea with the need to compromise and so may prefer the idea of fighting it out in court.

To resort to the court isn't a logical decision as mediation is quick (often just one day) and relatively inexpensive in comparison to legal processes. Its success rate is high and is on a steady rise with the CEDR's (Centre of Effective Dispute Resolution) 2018–19 survey reporting a success rate of 89%, with the majority of mediations completed within one day, and their 2022 audit reporting that 92% of mediations were successful. It is much harder to find similar figures for litigation, although there is a lot of material showing how lawyers calculate the likelihood of success before taking on a case. By rejecting those cases which are considered unlikely to be successful this naturally increases the eventual success rate for those proceeded with.

As the mediation procedure is quite quick, it means that it is not just the lower fee which makes it much cheaper than legal alternatives, but also the additional hidden cost savings which are made. In workplace mediations CEDR estimated that mediation saves businesses around £3billion a year in wasted management time, damaged relationships, lost productivity, and legal fees. It is easy to show companies how mediation can save them money if you ask them to assess the cost of having someone off work with stress, as is often the case, the cost of the line manager's time in dealing with the issue, the loss of productivity, the cost of HR time, and the potential costs of recruitment and onboarding of new staff should a party leave.

Another positive aspect of mediation is that, unlike court proceedings, which are open to the public and often reported in the press, mediation offers confidentiality. The only exceptions usually involve child or sexual abuse, actual or threatened criminal, violent, or dangerous acts, knowledge of dangerous goods, or concealment of proceeds of crimes

Legal procedure is based on a one size fits all, without the time or inclination to look at individual motives, perceptions, values, required time scale, and meaningful needs. Indeed, litigation is often being more concerned with wants rather than needs, with the emphasis usually being on concrete and material wants rather than psychological and behaviour changes and needs. Mediation can offer a more bespoke service based on a framework that makes sense to the individuals concerned and in which they take responsibility. This gives the parties the space, time, and opportunity to encourage creative thinking, enabling those involved to work towards a meaningful resolution tailored to their needs.

One of the main reasons people choose mediation over litigation is their concern to maintain a relationship with the person on the other side. This may be because they are family members, they work together, or are members of the same group or community. The mediator holds this need in mind and facilitates a process which is more cooperative and collaborative and so can provide an excellent choice for those disputes where people will need to maintain a relationship after the mediation. However, it is equally effective in those disputes where the parties may never need to be in touch with each other following the mediation. A mediation doesn't aim for the disputants to love or even like one another at the end of the process, it is not about seeing people dance hand in hand into the sunset from the mediation room. It aims to enable the drawing up of a 'good enough' agreement which gives the parties their lives back and allows them to move on. This is sometimes referred to as a win-win agreement where neither party loses, nor becomes the 'defeated' person. However, in reality it is often more a case of lose-lose, where each party in a mediation needs to give up some long-held belief (in reality; merely a perception) which had led to a desire to annihilate the other, financially, emotionally, morally, or in some other way. Sun Tzu in 'The Art of War' reminds us that to be a successful leader we must build our opponent 'a golden bridge to retreat across.' He understands that destroying someone's self-esteem is likely to leave the other with the feeling that they must retaliate and attempt to destroy the other. We see this on a continuous basis in world politics at the moment. Mediation can allow for all parties to leave via the golden bridge with some level of dignity intact.

There have been many changes in mediation practice since I trained more than twenty years ago. When I trained, I was one of only two students on the course who was not a solicitor or a barrister. I came to mediation from a business background and through my work as a psychotherapist. This meant that my central focus was on *why* there was a dispute and on finding a way of resolving it which transformed the understanding of those involved through an open creative process which engaged with all possibilities. For many people mediation is still seen as part of the legal process, and although many mediators no longer come from legal backgrounds, the lack of public understanding in many countries means that they may still expect, or even demand, that mediators are also lawyers. When I have been training lawyers, many at first struggle with a psychological approach which in many ways is the opposite of their training. They are being asked to take interest in meaning and motivation and to keep things as open as possible and not to ask for bottom lines or push too early for a resolution. Disputes may have legal and logical elements, but they are always emotional. Lawyers are not trained to place emotions in the foreground. Legal training tends to equip lawyers to be adversarial rather than collaborative. They are well trained to ask closed questions which aim to back the client into a corner with only a yes or no answer possible, whilst mediators will aim to use open, exploratory questions. The legal stance of never asking questions to which they don't know the answer is the opposite of what mediators aim for as it narrows down the potential for creative resolution. So, in many ways legal skills are the opposite of mediation skills. Lawyers usually find the final part of mediation easier when it is time to draw up an agreement. Some mediators coming from more psychological backgrounds can struggle at this stage as they can get lost in the party's narrative and want to keep digging deeper. For these mediators, the challenge is to know when they have enough information for them to turn their attention to working on the settlement document rather than keep exploring deeper.

Many lawyers have argued that as mediation settlement agreements are legal documents mediators do need to be legally trained. This is not the case. Most agreements call on common sense rather than legal knowledge to ensure that they are workable. If there are legal concerns, then a lawyer can check the agreement and write it up for court if need be. In some mediations a party may choose to bring a lawyer with them and may want the lawyer to take a prominent position in the drawing up of the final agreement, and this is perfectly acceptable, although the mediator has to ensure neither party is being pushed into agreeing. It is understandable that the legal profession may see mediation as competition. However, if a lawyer can please a client by introducing them to mediation, and the process is successful, it reflects well on the lawyer. The late Paul Randolph, a well-known mediator and barrister, and much missed colleague and friend, would explain jokingly how he needed to explain to lawyers that ADR, the alternative name for mediation, stood for Alternative Dispute Resolution and not for an Alarming Drop in Revenue.

Lawyers are paid to fight to get their client the best possible outcome for themselves. So, the requirement for mediators to be neutral is another challenge for lawyers who are trained to be strong advocates for one side: 'their side'. In most mediation models, it is often the competitive nature of the law that is attractive to many lawyers, and they gain professional satisfaction in winning and in so doing defeating the other side. It is not usually the role of the mediator to evaluate the strength of one side's agreement against the other and give any kind of judgement about the relative validity of one side's narrative. Having said this, there is a form of mediation called evaluative mediation which does offer such options, and I shall say more about this later. However, one of the strengths of mediation, and the source of frustration in those parties who are sure they are right, is that a mediator is not a judge. It is the role of the mediator to follow what they are told by each side and not to decide or offer what they think would be the best solution. What might look like a good solution to the mediator may not fit with the values and needs of the parties. It is not unusual for claimants to leave court with what their legal team considers to be a good settlement only to feel very dissatisfied with the result because it does not meet their emotional or ethical needs. This should never happen in mediation.

As I referred to earlier, early mediation courses were dominated by participants, usually male, from legal professions, but there has been a shift, with the genders more equally represented, and the backgrounds of those in training also more varied. One of the most impressive mediation students I taught was a dry cleaner. She had found the details of the course in the pocket of a suit she was cleaning for a barrister. She was experienced in communicating with people from many different backgrounds, dealing with complaints and explaining what was and what wasn't possible and so she demonstrated her strong natural and instinctive interpersonal skills during her training, and she is now working very successfully as a community mediator.

The main skills required of a good psychologically informed mediator are the ability to uncover and understand people's worldview; their beliefs and values, their needs rather than wants, their motivations and the accompanying meaning they are placing on the events leading to the dispute and also on the process of mediation itself. Having unearthed these key aspects, all of which can be considered to be of an existential nature, the mediator must be skilled at working with the accompanying emotions. Their first task is to make all parties feel safe through developing trusting working alliances with all involved. This includes any friends, partners, family, lawyers, trade union officials, etc. who they have chosen to bring with them and whose presence has been agreed by all parties. With diverse groups looking to mediate a wide range of disputes the time is ripe to extend diversity and a greater understanding of cultural difference within the profession. Without a sense of safety and trust in the mediator people may not feel able to express themselves emotionally and fully gain the further understanding of their own thinking and positions which provides the gateway to change. This self-exploration must happen before they can gain any real understanding of the other person's view, just as in an emergency on a plane when we are told we must sort ourselves out before looking to help others. In mediation we may think we know why we are there and what we think and may come armed to attack the view of the other party but during a process of exploration which a skilled mediator can facilitate, we may come to understand ourselves better and potentially change our perceptions.

In arguments, when feeling under pressure, people often get into 'fight, flight, or freeze' mode. They are emotional and can get angry, are afraid, or can even shut down completely. When people are upset or shut down, no amount of logic or knowledge of law is going to help. A psychological understanding of how people react to conflict is more important. A mediator needs to feel comfortable staying with the emotions rather than shutting them down. All emotions are intentional; they are always about something, and understanding and seeking to understand the underlying cause of the emotion will tell the mediator a lot about what the party needs to have a successful outcome which meets emotional as well as material needs. The disputant primarily needs to feel they are in the presence of a skilled fellow human being rather than someone skilled in playing the role of mediator. Mediation is at its heart a relational and emotional experience even when the presenting disagreement feels very unemotional.

Chapter 3

Different Mediation Styles

Even within the UK, there are different styles and structural frameworks used in mediation practices. All of these encompass the idea that a neutral third party will enable those in dispute to find a resolution they can agree to.

The role of the mediator, and the degree to which they are dominant and directive or otherwise will depend on the mediation model and the personality and skills of the mediator. My own mediation approach uses a format based on the Harvard Model, which I shall write more about later. I use this merely as a process framework onto which I can add a philosophical approach which aims to recognise the uniqueness of each person engaged in the process, whilst facilitating an uncovering of any commonality between the parties' values, meaning, and desires. This makes it a model which is very suited to working with people from different backgrounds and cultures.

I have encountered people who have been through a mediation which did not operate outside of a transactional and directive approach which personally I would not recognise as mediation and would more likely identify as a negotiation. All the different approaches are valid and carry their individual pros and cons, but it is important that those engaged in the mediation know what approach is being taken.

The different approaches could be grouped into two main styles: facilitative/transformative or evaluative/problem-solving. I have tried to point out the key differences in Table 3.1.

In the facilitative and transformative approaches, the mediator is a neutral third party who remains non-judgemental throughout the process and will hope to empower participants to take responsibility for the resolution of the dispute. If the final agreement is considered acceptable to both sides, then a facilitative/transformative mediator will ensure that the parties are aware of anything which seems strange, but will not try to change it, even if they do not think it is logical. As long as it is workable, and unlikely to break down, the mediator has done their job. By empowering those involved it is hoped that it will also be a transformative process during which the parties may change their perspective of each other and of the dispute, through a better understanding of the other's viewpoint. Evaluative mediation is different in its approach with the mediator appearing to be more active

Table 3.1 Comparison of Facilitative/Transformation against Evaluative/Problem-Solving Approaches

	Facilitative/Transformative	*Evaluative/Problem-solving*
Beliefs about conflict	Conflict is long-term and goes beyond the presenting dispute.	Conflict requires a solution to the resenting issue as quickly as possible.
Focused aims	Increase empowerment of all involved. Increase recognition of the worldview and perspectives of others.	Collaborate to identify and solve immediate issues. Maximise joint gains.
Goal	Transformation (perceptions and possible behaviours) of those involved.	Settlement agreement for presenting issue.
Role	Mediator follows the needs of the parties and facilitates their exploration of the dispute.	Mediator leads and directs, may offer evaluations and judgements.
Action	Mediator manages the process not the content. Explores the meaning of the dispute, the difference in perceptions, and the resulting emotions.	Mediator leads the process and manages and directs the content and may drop aspects which the mediator considers to not be amenable to negotiation.
Focus	Relational aspects – parties' interactions and perceptions of the dispute and each other. Needs of each party (psychological as well as material) rather than wants.	Material aspects – wants rather than needs. Focused on logic and rational rather than emotional and psychological.
Time	Timing of sessions led by the needs of the individual party. Although there will be contracted beginning and end times there is considerable flexibility with the division into private and joint sessions led by the needs and movement of the parties.	Mediator focused on moving the parties in a linear way through the stages.
Success criteria	Empowerment and recognition. Increase in parties understanding of self and others.	Mutually agreed settlement.

and analysing the individual arguments and pointing out strengths and weaknesses. Such an approach helps parties understand their legal position.

Experienced mediators will probably use a combination of these styles depending on their individual approach, as well as the specifics of the case, and the needs of the parties involved. Below I shall expand a bit more on some of these models, and offer a brief overview of the most common approaches:

Arb-Med

Arb-Med is the term which is short for a hybrid approach which mixes Arbitration and Mediation. Arbitration is a process in which an arbitrator considers a dispute which is submitted to them by the parties after which one or more arbitrators make a binding decision on the dispute.

The benefits of Arb-Med are considered to be speed, flexibility, confidentiality, choice of professional skills of the mediator, and the enforcement of the outcome. The process starts with an arbitration proceeding, after which a non-binding arbitration award is issued. Then, the parties work with a mediator to attempt to resolve their conflict.

The mediator hears disputants' evidence and testimony in arbitration then writes an award but keeps it from the parties. The mediator then attempts to mediate the parties' dispute before unsealing and issuing their previously determined binding award if the parties fail to reach agreement.

It is thought that the process removes the concern in med-arb about the misuse of confidential information whilst keeping the pressure on parties to reach an agreement. It is not acceptable for the arbitrator/mediator to change the award they drew up at the beginning of the process based on any new insights gained during the mediation.

Compulsory or Court-Mandated Mediation

In the 2018 report of The Civil Justice Council (CJC) in England's on ADR and Civil Justice it was recognised that voluntary mediation processes had low uptake and therefore some level of mandatory mediation process was considered to be the best way of increasing uptake. Unfortunately, the inherent problems with this as a cornerstone of mediation practice lies in it being a 'voluntary, consensual process'. The degree to which it is voluntary can be questioned in many cases, for example workplace disputes, where mediations are usually paid for by the employer. In these cases, participants may be told it is voluntary but may believe that if they do not engage in the process then disciplinary action will be implemented.

Some courts have raised the concern that mediation may prevent parties from gaining access to their right to trial and wish to keep mediation within their remit. This is not the case. Paul Randolph (2013) reported Lord Phillips, the former lord chief justice, as refuting these contentions at a Delhi Conference in 2008, stating that it merely briefly delays the progress to trial and does not remove any right to trial. Indeed, it aims to reduce the considerable expense of litigation, and the amount of time it takes in pursuing a legal pathway, with all the emotional upheaval that the long wait causes. Courts are under a duty to actively manage cases to further that objective.

Civil Procedure Rule (CPR) 1.4(2)(e) expressly states that courts have a duty which includes 'encouraging the parties to use an alternative dispute resolution procedure where the court considers that appropriate and facilitating the use of such procedure'. Often, the court will be willing to pause proceedings to enable a mediation to take place, indeed the court may sometimes explicitly order the parties to firstly take part in some form of ADR. The CPR pre-action protocols also require the parties to consider ADR, including mediation, or risk an adverse costs order being made against them. Legal representatives are required to confirm that they have explained to their client the need to try to settle, the options available to do so, and the possibility of costs sanctions if they refuse to try to settle. This is formalised using the 'directions questionnaire' (a court form which must be filed in most cases).

However, if the parties are forced to use mediation it is less likely to succeed, there is a danger that people may attend a mediation but not actively engage with the process. Although the CJC 2018 report strongly advocated the greater promotion of ADR and mediation, it did not support any move towards making ADR or mediation compulsory. However, it did call for any parties to litigation who were not willing to participate in mediation to be required to explain to the court why mediation was not considered suitable for their case.

E-mediation

E-mediation, also called Online Dispute Resolution (ODR) is a form of mediation which takes place online. It is considered to have many benefits for those with busy time schedules or where parties are in different countries or geographical locations or whose conflict is so strong that they cannot be in the same room.

The process may be a completely automated online dispute resolution system with no human intervention, and it will be interesting to see how this develops in the new world of AI. However, often, e-mediation is more likely to resemble facilitative mediation, only delivered from afar. It is claimed that the use of videoconferencing allows parties to easily and cheaply communicate with one another in real time, while also benefiting from visual and vocal cues. Although in my personal experience of mediating through an online platform there are several disadvantages. Although you are in visual contact this is limited and the subtleties of body language are much reduced when one is communicating with a stationary head, rather than being able to see the tapping foot etc.

Although it can be both cost-effective and convenient, it can have other drawbacks. It may not be suitable for those lacking in computer skills. Accessibility to e-mediation may present difficulties in lesser technologically developed countries, and it must be taken into account that lack of accessibility to technology is often paired with a distrust of online services. The vulnerability to cyber-crime can also be a negative factor making confidential information less secure. With this in mind, for business disputes in which the parties are concerned about protecting their trade secrets e-mediation may not be a suitable option. Skilled mediators need to take into account relevant socioeconomic factors of all the parties that may affect the appropriateness of such techniques and present their clients with alternatives.

In all models of mediation, it is not unusual for a party to find it stressful and to walk out of a mediation session. In a virtual space you cannot follow them out and work to reengage them in the process by rebuilding trust, instead you are faced with a black square in the corner of the screen where the party had previously been visible. If this happens during a joint session the mediator may not know whether the party has merely switched off their camera or has left the room with the intention of returning or has exited the whole mediation process. In that moment the mediator must take care not to discuss anything with the remaining party as the other party may still be in a position to overhear such conversation.

Evaluative Mediation

Evaluative mediation draws on a legal model for resolving disputes and emerged in court-mandated or court-referred mediation. It is modelled on settlement conferences as held by judges. In these conferences, the judge must not seek to impose any duress or pressure on the parties to make an agreement. All parties plus any carers or family must agree to any decisions made in a settlement conference and if no agreement is made the case goes to a final hearing. In using this approach it is usual for lawyers to work with the court to choose the mediator and to be active participants in the mediation.

The evaluative approach aims to help parties to reach resolution by the mediator pointing out the weaknesses of their cases and predicting what a judge or jury would be likely to do if the dispute went to court. This leads to the belief that evaluative mediators are primarily concerned with the legal rights of the parties rather than needs and interests, and make their evaluation based on legal concepts of fairness. Other mediation models require the mediator not to be a judge of any kind and to focus on creating an agreement which addresses the needs of all parties to a degree which is considered to be 'good enough', and so acceptable to all the parties, as determined not by the mediator, but by the parties themselves.

It contrasts significantly with a facilitative approach to mediation, as in the evaluative approach the mediator has a much greater part to play in determining the outcome of the mediation. The primary focus of an evaluative mediator is to reach a quick deal which would be understood and accepted within a legal context, rather than to allow as much space as possible for the party's narrative. Evaluative mediators will usually have little interest in the emotional aspects of the disputant's experience, as they would be of no interest to a court. They may appear to be more directive than a facilitative mediator and may make formal or informal recommendations and suggestions and express their personal opinions about the strength of their 'case' to each party. They will certainly point out what they consider to be the legal merits of their arguments and make fairness determinations. Facilitative mediators will not usually think in terms of a mediation being 'a case'.

In terms of the mediation process, evaluative mediators usually employ a series of separate meetings with the parties and their legal representatives, often referred to as 'shuttle diplomacy' or 'shuttle mediation'. This model is also used by facilitative mediators. In these sessions the mediator enables the parties and any legal representatives to evaluate their legal position and to examine the costs vs. the benefits of pursuing a legal resolution rather than settling in mediation. The parties are present in the mediation, but lawyers play an important part, and the mediator may meet with the lawyers alone as well as with the parties. The evaluative mediator structures the process, and directly influences the outcome of mediation.

Evaluative mediators are often drawn from those with a legal background and there is often an assumption that the mediator will have substantive specialist expertise or legal expertise in the area of the dispute. Often the more specialised the knowledge the mediator has of a particular area the harder it is for the mediator to remain impartial.

Facilitative Mediation

Facilitative mediation is considered by many to be the original mediation approach. It was first formally used in America in the era of volunteer dispute resolution centres. In these centres the volunteer mediators who worked there were not required to have substantive expertise concerning the area of the dispute, and usually no lawyers were present. The volunteer mediators did not necessarily have any legal background or expertise but came from all backgrounds. The main requirement was that they could work with the diversity of people and disputes which came to the centre.

By the 1960s and 1970s, it was the most common type of mediation being taught and practiced in the US. In facilitative mediation, it is not the role of the mediator to make recommendations, suggest or impose a decision, instead it is for the mediator to facilitate a process in which each party's deeper interests are explored, with the aim of assisting the parties to reach their own voluntary and mutually agreeable resolution. The mediator must avoid offering their own views, evaluating cases or giving advice, but focus instead on exploring and helping to validate and normalise the parties' points of view, whist searching for the emotional and other motivations and interests which may lie beneath the fact focused presented positions taken by parties. The mediator then assists the parties in finding and analysing options for resolution. Whilst the mediator oversees the process, the parties remain in charge of the content and the outcome.

Thus, facilitative mediators seek to ensure that parties come to agreements based on shared information and understanding. It is usually the case that in facilitative mediations, joint sessions will be held with all parties present so that the parties can hear each other's points of view, but individual sessions may also take place. If lawyers are present a facilitative mediator will want the parties to have the major influence on decisions made, rather than the legal representatives.

Med-Arb

As with Arb-Med, Med-Arb is a blend of mediation and arbitration features but with the process reversed. Contrary to traditional mediation practice, parties normally agree at the outset of a Med-Arb process that the outcome will be binding. The parties then attempt to negotiate a resolution with the help of a mediator. The usefulness of having such a written agreement is to assure that if the mediation ends in impasse, the process isn't over, and the parties can be confident that their conflict will be resolved.

Should the mediation phase not reach a successful conclusion then the parties will immediately move on to arbitration. At this point, the mediator will shift their role to that of arbitrator, and formulate a binding decision quickly based on their judgements regarding the case as a whole, or on any unresolved issues.

In the case that a mediator is deemed to be unqualified to proceed in the role of arbitrator a qualified practitioner may take over the case after consulting with the mediator.

Narrative Mediation

One of the relatively new styles of mediation, Narrative Mediation was developed in the mid-1980s by Michael White and David Epston in Australia. It had its origins in Narrative Family Therapy and offers a similar philosophy and approach. In doing so, it challenges the problem-solving orientation and its positivist foundation, prevalent in many fields of mediation. It works from the belief that people think in terms of stories and their constituent parts (themes, roles, and plots), working them together to create a system of meaning around particular people and events (Cobb 1994/2013). As everything we experience is an interpretation of events, we have it in our gift to reassess our perspective. The approach aims to enable the parties in conflict to create a new 'story' or 'narrative' to understand and reshape the conflict. It focuses on language as the main tool in constructing who we are, how we engage with conflict and behave with others. Our words do not just only describe our experience, but in a sense, serve to create it. By naming something we give it meaning.

The work of Cobb and her colleague Rifkin (1991) were amongst the first bringing social constructivist orientations to mediation, thus challenging the notion of mediator neutrality. Prior to that, there was very little research into mediator neutrality, mainly relying on the mediator's own assessment. Greatbatch and Dingwall undertook research based on the empirical analysis of discussions in the mediation sessions. Most of this work relies on subjective inference, leaning heavily on the participants' reported perceptions of any mediator bias. Cobb and Rifkin contest that the paucity of research and the lack of interest in the parties' narratives, which contain indicators of the individual's understanding and views of power dynamics and neutrality, make it difficult to effectively assess mediator neutrality. Cobb and Rifkin tried to address these research shortcomings by using videotapes of mediation sessions, with taped interviews with mediators from community mediation programmes. They focused on to what extent mediators showed an awareness of justice, power, and ideology. Clearly the sensitivity to these issues is important in all mediations and evidence of the different cultural understandings and practice of these elements is vital when we are considering the impact of culture on mediation practice. Narrative mediation is one of the earliest forms for mediation which overtly explores power issues.

Cobb and Rifkin contest that neutrality is not the same as impartiality. They are critical of mediation training manuals in which they claim 'impartiality' is equivalent to the absence of feelings, values, or agendas; 'bias is to be avoided – it is a strong opinion, value, feeling' (1991:28). They look to Luban (1987) who sees the goal of the neutral as being to produce what Habermas (1979) called the 'ideal speech situation', i.e. one devoid of ideological processes. In whatever way an external observer might assess the mediator's neutrality, '… neutrality of the mediator finally rests with parties. They must perceive that the intervener is not overtly partial or unneutral in order to accept his or her assistance' (Moore 1997). One can see that when considering cultural aspects, neutrality, the lack of bias, and sensitivity to language (verbal and bodily) are of particular importance. When I later consider how an existential/phenomenological approach may be a particularly good approach to consider aspects of cultural and power hierarchies, I shall look to Husserl's 'horizontalisation' which prompts us to consider everything we see and hear as carrying equal importance, but more of that later.

When using a narrative approach, the mediator seeks to help both parties create distance from themselves and the events that provoked their dispute. It is hoped that the parties will then see the causes of their conflict with greater detachment and a fresher perspective. In the mediation, 'narratives are interactively developed, modified, and contested as disputants elaborate portions of their own and each other's conflict stories' (Cobb 1994:53). There is a tendency for such stories to cast parties in the role of victim and protagonist, existing within the polarities of good/bad, right/wrong, truth/lies, etc., which contrast and emphasise the difference between themselves and the other side. This brings in simplistic and limiting concepts of the victimiser, the antagonist versus the vulnerable victim. Reality is never that simple.

For mediation to effectively use the storytelling metaphor and create a cooperative climate among disputants, it becomes necessary to destabilise and challenge those assumptions and theories. The aim is to move parties from a closed personal interpretation (i.e. their story) and open them to new possibilities and interpretations. It is hoped that this new climate of openness will lead to the creation of a new account and mutually satisfying interpretations and outcomes.

In line with the existential psychological and phenomenological approach, which I use, and on which this book is based, there is a belief as in narrative mediation that conflicts are not about facts, but about perceptions, and the emotional responses such perceptions generate. It starts from the belief that there is no one 'truth' to discover, as what will be presented are merely individual interpretations of what was experienced by each individual. All stories are merely emotional representations of events; therefore, the narrative approach and the existential-phenomenological approach place the substantive issues as secondary after considering the primary, relational, and emotional needs of the conflicting parties; the people are not the problem; the problem is the problem.

Unlike the existential approach Narrative Mediation contains a political aspect stemming from its postmodernist underpinnings which involves recognising that one cannot be completely neutral and that mediators must take a stand on issues stemming from the dominant societal discourses which create and recreate systems of oppression. This emphasis means the approach is considered to be particularly effective in working with marginalised groups. There are pros and cons to this as the mediator by taking a stance is making a value judgement and 'picking a side'. They are working from an assumption that all members of a defined marginalised group each hold the same views. However, if the mediator does not challenge people on what they consider to be unacceptable political views, language, or behaviour they lay themselves open to criticism.

Narrative Mediation is interested in resolutions that go beyond simple settlement to consider the effects of the mediation on the society at large and, like transformative mediation, considers mediation as a means for conflict parties to achieve a higher moral self (Bush and Folger 1994). This again places the mediator as some form of moral arbitrator or champion. Many narrative mediators come from a psychology background.

As this is still a relatively new approach to mediation for those wanting to have more detail, I recommend Winslade and Monk (2000) who provide practical examples.

Restorative Justice

Restorative Justice (RJ) is a process aimed at facilitating meetings between those who have committed crimes and those who are the victims of their crimes. It aims to provide a safe space for the victim to explain the impact of the crime and for the offender to appreciate this and accept responsibility.

I am including Restorative Justice here although it is not strictly mediation although it is often confused with it. Restorative justice stems from an ancient idea in which justice is rooted in human dignity, healing, and interconnectedness. Its origins lie in aboriginal teachings, faith traditions, and straightforward common sense.

As with mediation, restorative justice is a voluntary process. Sometimes perpetrators are encouraged to take part in the hope of a reduced sentence, but they can refuse a request from their victim or the victim's family to participate in a RJ meeting.

It is in the division of parties into perpetrators and victims that the biggest difference between mediation and RJ lies. From the start of the RJ process, it is made clear that the central parties are not considered as equal, but that one is considered a 'victim' and the other a 'perpetrator'. These label the role the party held in the precipitating event (usual a crime), but this does not mean that it isn't acknowledged that both parties may have suffered greatly.

All those concerned in the initial incident are invited to attend. The focus is on the impact of a specific criminal event. As Marshall (1999:5) states 'Restorative Justice is a process whereby parties with a stake in a specific offence collectively resolve how to deal with the aftermath of the offence and its implications for the future.' This means that it explores the harm that was caused by the offence, physical, material, emotional, and psychological, but is still forward focused.

There is specialised training available for restorative justice practitioners whose role is to facilitate restorative justice meetings. It is a very structured process, and often RJ facilitators use scripts to keep the process focused. A common form of restorative justice is a face-to-face meeting, usually referred to as a 'conference', which involves the person responsible for the offence and the person harmed. If the people concerned do not wish to meet, the facilitator acts as a 'go-between', facilitating indirect communication through a 'shuttle dialogue' where messages are passed verbally or in writing between the parties.

Before a restorative process begins, the facilitator must check that everyone wishes to proceed voluntarily, that the person responsible for the offence accepts the basic facts of the case and takes responsibility for their part. Once these details have been agreed it is considered that it is safe to proceed. The process focuses on three aspects – what happened, who was harmed, and what was the nature of the harm, before considering what should happen next.

Morris (2002), describes the aim of RJ as being to restore feelings of security, self-respect, and empowerment to the person harmed. For the person responsible for the harm, it is intended to put them in direct touch with the impact of their behaviour on others, with the aim that they acknowledge their responsibility for the harmful behaviour and its consequences, facilitate opportunities to make amends, and take steps to prevent the reoccurrence of harm. There are some remarkable examples of the success of the RJ process. One high profile case is that of Jo Berry whose father Sir Anthony Berry was killed by the Brighton bomb. Jo met Patrick Magee, the person who had laid the bomb in 1999 for an RJ meeting at the Glencree Centre for Peace and Reconciliation in County Wicklow. In an article in the Guardian on 1st December 2009 she describes that it was not an easy process, 'The meeting wasn't easy because it really took me out of my comfort zone ... I had to listen to things that were difficult to hear but one thing that Pat has taught me is that there is always a human being behind the enemy. I know that if there could have been dialogue or communication all those years ago, Pat would never have used force. If he had had other options, he would have taken them. The word terrorist is a label that dehumanises. We need to appeal to humanity. Pat has taught me the importance of dialogue and how we use language. We can either use language to open someone up or close them down and make them more defensive.' Jo explains that she has not forgiven Pat but has a better understanding about him and that has led to reconciliation. In 1984 she set up the organisation 'Building Bridges for Peace' and now runs workshops in war torn areas, often with Pat Magee.

Transformative Mediation

Transformative mediation is a relatively new approach, and probably the most psychologically focused amongst commonly used models. For this reason, it is

Different Mediation Styles 37

more culturally adaptable, as it is founded on the uniqueness of the individual's narratives which will no doubt be highly informative about cultural factors. As this book is informed by an existential/phenomenologically led psychological approach to mediation I am giving this method a little more space than some of the others.

Transformative mediation is based on the belief that conflict is a crisis in communication and that the two parties' relationship and indeed the individual's understanding of themselves and others may be transformed during the mediation process. It was introduced as the newest of three mediation approaches by Robert A. Baruch Bush and Joseph P. Folger in 1994, an approach which they expanded upon in their 2004 book.

Bush and Folger contrast their proposed model against the more dominant problem-solving models which feature a very active, directive, and dominant mediator who focuses on the immediate, short-term presenting problem. Instead, they propose an approach which holds the potential to effect deeper changes in people's perceptions and interpersonal relationships and challenges. They suggested that a transformative mediation model's greatest value lies in 'its potential not only to find solutions to people's problems but to change people themselves for the better, in the very midst of conflict' (2004: xv). It captures the idea that conflict can be creative and promote deep positive change which has the potential to alter their day-to-day lives thereafter. So, for mediators using a transformative approach achieving long-term change not just in behaviour but in perception and worldview is more important than solving a specific problem between parties.

Following on from this, the emphasis in the approach is placed on two elements within the mediation process: empowerment and recognition. To empower the parties, the mediator must not be dominant or direct, but instead needs to embrace the role of facilitator, encouraging parties to define and explore their own issues. The power does not rest with the mediator but with the parties.

When they speak of the importance of recognition, Bush and Folger are emphasising the mediator's role in enabling the parties to see and understand the perspectives, views, and experience of the other party, whilst not necessarily agreeing with them. Bush and Folger describe this as 'the evocation in individuals of acknowledgment and empathy for the situation and problems of others' (2007:94). In other words the aim is that each party sees the other as a human being with similar hopes and fears.

The approach also seeks to enhance understanding of how each of the parties have defined the problem, and how they have come to identify the solution they seek. Understanding these elements enables the mediator to have a greater understanding of the important underlying elements and motivations which would need to be covered in a successful and sustainable settlement.

When Bush and Folger use the word empowerment, they are not referring to it in the way in which it is used in common usage, as attempting power-balancing or redistribution, but rather, to increasing the skills of *both* sides equally, so they are better able to make decisions for themselves. They define empowerment as restoring 'to individuals a sense of their own value and strength and their own capacity to handle life's problems' (ibid). They believe that through empowerment, disputants can gain 'greater clarity about their goals, resources, options, and preferences' and that they can then use this information to make their own *'clear and deliberate decisions'* (ibid).

To make knowledgeable decisions the mediator aims to facilitate the parties to clarify,

- Goals
  - Parties gain a better understanding of the meaning of want they want and why.
- Resources
  - Parties better understand what is available and what they need to make an informed choice. Parties need to learn that they hold something that is of value to the other party, so they can communicate effectively with the other party.
- Options
  - Parties become aware of the range of options, understand the relative costs and benefits of each option.
- Preferences
  - Parties reflect and deliberate on their own, making a conscious decision about what they want to do, based on the strengths and weaknesses of both sides' arguments and the advantages and disadvantages of each option.

Developing clarity in these areas is sometimes referred to as *skill-based empowerment*, meaning through which the parties are empowered by improving their own conflict-resolution skills, learning how to listen, communicate effectively, analyse issues, evaluate alternatives, and make effective decisions.

Given the focus on the parties, not the mediator holding the power, transformative mediators usually meet with parties together believing that only the parties can give each other 'recognition', and therefore it is more effective to keep them together. This differs from other models who will use individual as well as joint sessions during the mediation process. Having said this, transformative mediators will encourage the parties to structure the process and not be confined by a mediator-led framework. Although transformative mediators will work from a structure if this is needed or requested, they will not rigidly stick to it. In this approach the parties are always the leaders, and the mediator follows in this way making it very different from the evaluative approach.

Bush and Folger in *The Promise of Mediation*, offer a list of ten hallmarks of transformative mediation which they feel distinguish it from other forms of mediation. They believe that transformational mediators,

1. in the opening statement, explain their role, and the objectives of mediation as being focused on empowerment and recognition.
2. leave responsibility for the outcomes with the parties.
3. are not judgmental about the parties' views and decisions.
4. take an optimistic view of the parties' competence and motives.
5. allow and are responsive to parties' expression of emotions.
6. allow for and explore parties' uncertainty.
7. remain focused on what is currently happening in the mediation setting.
8. are responsive to parties' statements about past events.
9. realise that conflict can be a long-term process, and that mediation is one intervention in a longer sequence of conflict interactions.
10. feel (and express) a sense of success when empowerment and recognition occur, even in small degrees. They do not see a lack of settlement as a 'failure'.

Although it doesn't define itself in this way, transformative mediation is essentially a form of psychologically informed mediation.

Psychologically Informed Mediation

This book focuses on a psychologically informed mediation process. Unlike other approaches, psychologically informed mediation is not a separate approach but a philosophical way of working, which could be used in all the styles previously introduced. Before I explain more in part two about how the psychological elements are used in mediation, I wish to give a brief description of what the practical process of mediation looks like.

Chapter 4

The Mediation Process

In describing the process of mediation, I shall refer to mediator in the singular, but it is common practice for there to be two or more mediators, known as co-mediators. I shall discuss later the positives and negatives of working with another mediator.

While there is no formal standardised mediation process that a mediator is required to follow, mediation will usually follow certain steps.

Pre-mediation

The first phase starts with the mediator drawing up a mediation contract covering the ground rules and practical details of the mediation such as confidentiality, who will attend, fees, venue, etc. These are important, as it is essential that all parties agree with what they are signing up to. Details such as the soundproofing of any suggested room for the mediation and ensuring that a venue is considered acceptable to all parties help in establishing trust and creating an open environment. Some mediators, including myself, send a short leaflet to all involved explaining the mediation process and introducing the mediator and any co-mediators.

Once there is agreement to mediate and the pre-mediation contract signed, if the mediator is working from a psychological stance there is still more work to be done. I then embark on the first confidential conversations with each person involved. These may take place by phone, online, or in person. I believe these sessions to be very significant and so may choose to have quite long meetings or calls, and there may be more than one. All of what is said is held in confidence and provides the client and mediator with the opportunity to connect for the first time in a safe and confidential space away from the other party.

I have stressed the importance of relatedness, and this is the first opportunity to bring this aspect into play. This phase of the mediation allows the party to discuss any worries they may have about attending the mediation such as the process, how it may be to be in the same room as someone you may perceive as your enemy or who you fear, or are angry with, how they feel about me as the mediator – style, gender, race, specialist knowledge, etc. At this stage the mediator would check if there were any concerns about cultural and or power differentials between the parties. Through listening respectfully at this stage and holding back on any challenges or requests for clarification the mediator begins to set the tone for the coming mediation and to build the trusting working alliance which is needed for mediating a meaningful and successful mediation.

The Mediation Day

Most mediation cases only last a day or two, although some may only take hours. This is partly because a mediation is quicker and easier to set up and therefore less cumbersome than litigation. It is also the case that people typically take smaller disputes to mediation and save larger claims for litigation. The larger business, divorce/custody, and international mediations may last significantly longer, running into weeks or months, but are still much quicker than traditional litigation.

In some forms of mediation, the parties may never meet, and in others the parties remain together with the mediator throughout the process. I use the Harvard model as a framework. In this model, having spent time in person or by phone separately with each of the parties, the mediator will then facilitate a day in which all parties come together.

On the mediation day, the mediator will invite and welcome the parties into the same room, taking care to address them in the way which has been agreed during the pre-mediation process. There are many books which deal solely with where to seat people during a mediation and the mediator will take care to sensitively seat the parties in what seems to be the most comfortable way for those involved. Some people will not wish to look the other in the face or be uncomfortable without there being considerable physical space between them. When everyone is settled, the mediator will go through the ground rules, stressing the confidential nature of the process, and that everything said is without prejudice and cannot be repeated in court if the mediation proves unsuccessful. Depending on the nature of the dispute, the mediator also needs to check that each party has the authority to settle. All these points should have been covered in the pre-mediation conversations and in the pre-mediation contract but by repeating them it emphasises their importance and allows time for all the parties to settle in, during what can be a very stressful moment when they are coming together in the same room, sometimes for the first time or even after many years.

At this point, the mediator will stress that their role is as a neutral facilitator; they are not there to judge. They will explain how the day will work and that there will be a mixture of joint and individual sessions. Once this is clear for everyone the mediator will invite each party to give a brief opening statement. Sensitivity is required in choosing who will go first. It should not matter to the process which person is chosen, but it will matter to the individuals if they are not given an acceptable reason. This may just be because the mediator always goes alphabetically, or because if the case went to court the claimant would be heard first. Whatever the reason, one needs to be given. It is dangerous to leave the choice to them as it could cause a new dispute.

At this stage some mediators ask for no interruption from the other side. If the mediator does this then they will have to 'police' the situation and risk antagonising one or more of the parties. More experienced mediators may be comfortable in managing any interruptions, and so allow them to happen. This gives the mediator an early opportunity to see how parties react. Having said this, the mediator must be sensitive to any power dynamics in play and not allow any party to intimidate the other. The mediator must check that any discomfort they are feeling belongs to the parties and not just to themselves. It isn't unusual for the parties to be more comfortable than the mediator with robust language and raised voices. Despite the intention being that at this stage each party in turn will give a brief overview of what has brought them to mediation, an experienced mediator may let any mutual discussion which starts between the parties at this session continue if the mediator is confident that both parties are equally comfortable, or indeed equally uncomfortable.

The mediator will try not to get involved in discussion with either party at this stage but merely thank them for their contribution so far and remind them that they will have plenty of opportunity to develop things further in the confidential private individual sessions. One reason for not getting into discussion at this stage is because anything which is said in front of the other party will be listened to carefully in case it shows any bias. Parties will seek to assess whose side the mediator is on by noting the tone of voice, and the amount of time the mediator gives to responding to each of them.

After these opening remarks the parties adjourn to their own rooms and throughout the day the mediator will meet with each party separately and confidentially. Should any party have something which they want the other side to know, the mediator must carefully check the content of the message and confirm that the party is giving the permission for the mediator to take that across to the other side. Confidentially is an important aspect of mediation and any breach is serious and could result in the mediator being sued.

If there seems to be some common ground the mediator will usually bring the parties together and use this as a starting point for discussion. At this stage things can run smoothly, or the differences may become more apparent. If this happens the mediator will go back to individual sessions and this mix of joint and private sessions can continue throughout the mediation.

Once there is agreement this will be drawn up and signed by the parties and witnessed by the mediator. Parties' lawyers, if present, may help in drawing up this agreement, and may also sign as witnesses. The mediator needs to ensure that involving lawyers at this stage does not favour their client over the other party.

The mediator does not require any legal training for drawing up a Heads of Agreement but must draw on their common sense, checking each aspect as to whether it is realistic and deliverable. This includes being alert for anything which could be misinterpreted, or commitments which do not look deliverable within the timescale and finances available. The mediator must continue to facilitate any further necessary discussion to clarify any point, even if it feels this may risk the parties not signing.

It is common for disagreements to arise during this part of the process. This may require further individual meetings with the process being repeated many times before agreement is reached, written up, signed, and witnessed. The process is not linear or chronological and may require the mediator to return to the early stage in which the key aim is to build trust between the mediator and the parties.

It is important to be aware that during the mediation, and especially towards the end of the process, things may appear to get worse before they get better, with parties trying to hold fast to their original stance. This is often referred to as the *diamond of divergence*, the *mediation time warp*, or more emotively as *the diamond of pain*. If an agreement is not reached, the mediator will summarize the progress which has been made, and what if anything, the parties have agreed on.

The above is just a framework and mediators will vary it according to the needs of the parties. For instance, in some mediations the mediator may intend to have individual sessions but they may not be needed. It is also possible to have a successful mediation without the parties ever being in the same room.

Co-mediation

It is now becoming common for two or more mediators to work together as co-mediators. When thinking about mediations which are dealing with cultural differences this can (although not necessarily) be an asset, with Richbell defining co-mediation as, 'the harmonious working of two complementary mediators who offer a diversity of skills, experience and personality' (Newmark & Monaghan 2005:302).

There are different styles or models of co-mediation, which are explained fully in 'Co-Mediation; using a paired psychological approach to resolving conflict' (Hanaway (ed) 1st edition 2012, 2nd edition 2014, Romanian edition 2013). Some mediation partnerships consist of a lead mediator and 'assistant' mediator/s, whereas others may work as equal partners. The level of autonomy given to the assistant may vary even where there is a designated lead. The co-mediator may be invited to contribute whenever they want, whilst other lead mediators may ask the co-mediator to remain silent unless specifically asked for their opinion. In some cases, the assistant is required only to be there to take notes and look after practicalities. The financial split of the fee in this model will be up to the lead mediator and may be half the fee or nothing at all if the assistant is inexperienced.

In the equal partnership model the co-mediators remain together throughout the process, meaning that there may be two or more mediators in a room with one party. This may sound as if it could feel overpowering for the individual, but I have not found this to be the case. Other than in special circumstances, the co-mediators do not split up, as I believe that to do so allows for possible collusion between mediator and party, with the danger that a party sees one of the mediators working with them as their advocate.

Mediators using a psychological approach will show this same awareness of psychological elements being present in their relationship with co-mediators. The fact

Table 4.1 Co-mediation: Consideration of Advantages and Disadvantages

Advantages	Challenges
• Practical	• Need for trust
• Emotional support	• Choosing the wrong person as a co-mediator
• Offers another perspective	
• Can offer diversity	• Danger of manipulation
• Offers a role model	• Communication
• Value for money	• Ego
• Provides opportunity for each co-mediator to supervise the other	• Financial
• Provides CPD	
• Co-mediation as supervision	

that both are mediators does not mean that they will not get into conflict with each other. Just as the parties may see each other as 'alien', co-mediators may at times experience each other in that way too. It is possible for co-mediators, through their facilitation of a dispute, to show how two individuals with differing worldviews can come together, using different perspectives on the dispute to create movement and creative change. Their differences can be used to add richness to the resolution.

There are advantages and disadvantages to co-mediating (Table 4.1).

Practical

It is helpful to have more than one person to cover the administrative aspects of a mediation – contracts to be written up, agreed, and signed. Arrangements agreed for times, venue, fees, etc. A solo mediator may have time for the mediation day itself, but not for all the pre-mediation work.

Another practical consideration is that mediation can be exhausting, both physically and psychologically. Throughout the day, energy levels will peak and drop. If a mediator is working alone there is little recovery time. With more than one mediator the likelihood is that each mediator will have peak energy at different times.

Mediations are emotional so it is not unusual for emotional walkouts to occur. If there is more than one mediator one can remain with the parties left behind whilst the other goes and speaks with the person who has walked out.

In the final stage, the drawing up of the settlement agreement can be conducted and supervised by both mediators. At this stage things can happen very quickly, and it is important that a mediator remains alert to any verbal or non-verbal signs that a person may be feeling unsure or pushed. This is much easier with two mediators. Both co-mediators will sign to witness the agreement.

Emotional Support

Co-mediators can offer each other not just practical but also emotional support, as mediation can be emotionally draining. Working with another mediator can help to maintain good creative energy levels throughout the mediation. Each mediator can support each other by noticing and reacting to any signs of tension, frustration, or exhaustion. Co-mediators can take advantage of the time moving between individual sessions to check how they are both feeling about the progress of the mediation, and to discuss what themes each has identified in the parties' narratives. They can also use the time to check on each other's well-being. Some disputes are very emotionally charged and can be distressing for a mediator, and one mediator may find it very difficult to work with a particular individual party who does not create the same reaction in the co-mediator. By being honest about their individual responses, the co-mediators can plan which of them should take the lead with any party.

Another Perspective

One of the clearest advantages of co-mediation is that the parties get the benefit of two brains and their different perceptions.

Offering Diversity

Some sectors of the mediation community argue that a mediator should share ethnicity, culture, or language with the parties. There are clear advantages and disadvantages to this which I shall explore in more detail throughout this book.

Co-mediation can provide the opportunity to offer a male/female partnership and partner mediators from different cultures, races, and backgrounds. This can be helpful in certain types of mediation, e.g. a divorce case where the male party may assume that a female mediator is more likely to understand and be more sympathetic towards another woman. This is a misguided but quite prominent view.

Modelling

Any competitive or collaborative behaviour between the co-mediators will be visible to the parties. This means that consciously or not co-mediators working together are acting as role models.

Co-mediators can demonstrate that it is possible to hold different perspectives in a way which is creative rather than conflictual. They can model this through positive behaviour and respect for difference in simple ways, such as being punctual, reliable, honest, open, and non-judgmental. They show respect to their co-mediator by respectfully listening to what they have to say. If there is disagreement, they model how to respond to this in a positive way by not trying to take control, putting their co-mediator down, or overtly challenging the other's thinking. They can explore the difference in perceptions in a respectful way clarifying those differences when they are away from the parties, or if the trust between the mediators is sufficiently strong. They may choose to model how to explore such different views and how to make a challenge which validates the other.

Co-mediation provides a model for the parties of how to care for each other's self-esteem while exploring different perspectives. Although the importance of modelling as a technique in effecting behaviour change is well documented in psychology literature (Bandura, 1977, Mischel 1968), it has not been adequately researched in relation to mediation, although briefly discussed regarding co-mediation in Hanaway (2014:75–77).

Financial: Value for Money for the Clients

The client benefits financially from having co-mediators as the fee is likely to be the same whether using one or two mediators. This may not be a selling point for mediators but certainly benefits the clients.

The clients have added value by having two points of contact prior and post the mediation and having access to double the skills, experience, knowledge, energy, and perspective, together with the synergy between the co-mediators which can help to generate more creative thinking.

Supervision and Continuing Professional Development

By mediating with another person, mediators have the opportunity to learn from each other. They can reflect on their work throughout the day and discuss progress, frustrations, blocks, individual prejudices, and ideas. As O'Hehir and O'Kennedy (in Hanaway 2012:78) report, '...we continually learn from one another. We constantly discover and rediscover each other's skills and abilities and are inspired by the insights and energy that both bring to mediation...'

The Tensions and Challenges of Co-mediating

Trust

Working with another opens a mediator to scrutiny which can result in praise or criticism, so co-mediating calls for trust in each other and the ability to accept and learn from feedback.

Choosing the Wrong Co-mediator

There are times when a mediator does not have a choice about fellow mediators as they may be part of a panel who allocates out the work. This means that trust will need to be developed very quickly. A good equal relationship based on trust removes the need for competition, or the need to prove oneself which may be present if there is not a good match with mediators.

There are different mediation training organizations, and they do not all share the same ethos, with some focusing most strongly on the psychological aspects of conflict, whereas others focus more on the process, legal aspects, and structure.

A mismatch in their philosophical approach to mediation can bring about a very uncomfortable situation for the mediators and the parties.

Whenever we work with others, power dynamics comes into play. It is essential that co-mediators are aware of how they individually use their power, both in relation to each other and to themselves. Any competition between the co-mediators will get in the way of collaborative, creative, and successful working.

Ego

Co-mediators work as a collaborative team. If one mediator forms a positive relationship with a party and is making good progress, the other must resist the temptation to say something just in order to justify their presence and boost their ego. If it is going well for one mediator, it is going well for both.

Danger of Manipulation

Some co-mediation models do not have the mediators staying together throughout the process. One of the dangers of a co-mediating model in which the co-mediators separate is the potential for the parties to attempt to engage in manipulative behaviour attempting to set one mediator against the other, with statements like, '*Your colleague agreed with me that...*' '*That's not what your co-mediator has been saying...*' etc. Even in those mediation models where co-mediators intend to stay together, it can be tempting when pushed for time to try to split up, but this increases the danger of things being misinterpreted or manipulated.

Communication

The way the co-mediators communicate together must be thought through and carefully carried out. This is easier if the same co-mediating pair always work together and develop a deep understanding of the way they each communicate. When they are not in agreement, co-mediators need to show respect to the other, knowing when they need to speak and when to leave a silence for their co-mediator.

The Advantages of Sole Mediation

Financially there is a gain for the mediator, as the fee does not have to be split two ways. The need to take into account the dynamics of working with another person may be difficult and so it may seem easier to work alone. For some mediators their ego may make co-mediating less attractive and more complicated than being entirely 'in charge' of the process. A co-mediator risks their mistakes being visible to another professional, which is avoided by mediating alone.

Part Two

Psychologically Informed Mediation Using an Existential-Phenomenological Approach

Chapter 5

Why a Psychologically Informed Approach is Needed in All Mediation but Particularly in Culturally Sensitive Disputes

Introduction

In Part One, I have shown there are many processes for dealing with disputes, including some which are grounded in legal processes and behaviours. Many focus on a futile attempt to 'find the truth', to 'get to and establish the facts'. In this section I am focused on a different approach which is more concerned with the psychological aspects of conflict and finding meaningful (rather than logical) sustainable solutions.

I believe that such an approach is necessary. I consider that it is largely a pointless exercise to go in search of 'the facts' or to focus on historical events, as we cannot change what has happened, and 'facts' and 'truths' are subjective, flowing from an individual's unique experience of an event. This is borne out by research within the legal sector which has shown that the accuracy of 'facts' in a witness statement can be from as high as 79% when it has not been discussed with anyone else, to as low as 34% after discussing it or retelling it to others, especially co-witnesses who will have their own set of 'facts'. It would be extremely rare for disputants in a mediation not to have been over their narrative of the conflict many times with friends, families, Human Resources (HR) professionals, lawyers, trade union officials, or just interested colleagues.

Witnesses will unconsciously bring into their narrative cultural factors from their own upbringing and experiences, and these will include any prejudices and the propensity to stereotype, e.g. if we think young people are naturally aggressive, we are more likely to see and report a young person as an aggressor. This may be due to cultural bias and prejudice but also because all our experiences are always subjective rather than objective and will therefore be influenced by presumptions, what we expected to see, our fragile and malleable memory, the amount to which others have influenced our experience, and stereotypical assumptions. In more than 2,000 studies on eyewitnesses over recent decades, recollections have been shown to be prone to decay, distortion, and suggestion. Although people are attempting to be honest and are well-meaning, they often simply misremember or misreport what they believe they have seen.

Much of the research has centred on the identification of perpetrators of crime. In an experiment conducted in 1974 more than 2,000 people were shown a 13-second video clip of a mugging, and then asked to pick out the perpetrator from a six-man line-up. Only 14 percent did so correctly, a success rate lower than that of random guessing. In a 1999 study, 150 college students watched videos of a shooting and then of a five-man line-up. Every one of them identified a suspect, even though the culprit was not featured in the line-up. Factors such as fear, poor lighting, the presence of a weapon during a crime, and the passage of time have all been shown to cause mistakes in identifications, even when the witness is the victim of the crime. Worryingly, witnesses were found to be particularly inaccurate, when asked to remember the facial features of someone of a different race.

If neutral witnesses' memories can be so badly distorted even when they have nothing to gain, how much more will this be the case for a person fully involved in a dispute and believing they have a lot to lose or gain through the outcome of a mediation. Unfortunately, the need to 'stick to the story' can cause people to become more and more vehement about the truth of their story. Lawyers, juries, and even mediators tend to give too much credence to those who appear confident in their memories and are seen as having little motive to lie. As Gary Wells, a psychology professor at Iowa State University put it, 'The legal system is set up to kind of sort between liars and truth tellers.' When we are in an emotionally aroused state, our perceptions are filtered through the fog of adrenaline. We may believe we are telling the truth, but we are merely reported on our perceptions of an incident, which will subtly change through each retelling.

Cultural bias is not just present in the way a witness may interpret and report an incident, but also in how that report will be received by others, and the level of credence given to it. Frumkin and Stone (2020) explore the extent to which factors such as status, race, accent, gender, perceived educational and professional levels, and age may influence the way a witness is perceived in court. Perhaps, not surprisingly their findings indicated that 'eyewitnesses with higher-status accents were rated more favorably than those with lower-status accents and younger black eyewitnesses were rated higher than older black witnesses. White eyewitnesses were more favorably rated than black witnesses although this was qualified by results suggesting anti-norm deviance.'

Cultural assumptions are also evidenced where no criminal activity has necessarily taken place. If a young person is black and male, then there is a greater likelihood of them being perceived as a potential aggressor, with UK stop and search figures for the year ending March 2022 showing that 47% of such searches were of people categorised as 'black other' (Table 5.1).

The above are quite well-known examples of the ways individuals make assumptions about other people. There have been many studies that explore how quickly we make and form first impressions. Some studies consider we make our minds up very quickly about people, with it only taking milliseconds. Princeton psychologists conclude that it only took a tenth of a second! According to one university

Table 5.1 From Gov UK website, updated 10 April 2024

Ethnicity	Rate of stop and search	Number of stop and searches
All	8.7	516,684
Asian	8.9	48,929
Bangladeshi	11.5	7,417
Chinese	1.1	468
Indian	3.1	5,814
Pakistani	9.5	15,098
Asian Other	20.7	20,132
Black	27.2	65,502
Black African	13.7	20,404
Black Caribbean	23.0	14,339
Black Other	103.3	30,759
Mixed	9.4	16,207
Mixed White and Asian	3.7	1,817
Mixed White and Black African	6.9	1,714
Mixed White and Black Caribbean	10.1	5,176
Mixed Other	16.1	7,500
White	5.6	274,287
White British	5.2	232,287
Gypsy or Irish Traveller	9.1	619
White Irish	7.2	3,674
Roma	N/A	0
White Other	10.3	37,707
Other	6.8	8,538
Arab	1.5	501
Any Other Ethnic Background	8.7	8,037
Unknown	N/A	103,221

study*, people make eleven decisions about us in the first seven seconds of contact. This is known as "The 7/11 Rule". Just looking at a person's appearance and body language, perceptions are formed regarding their:

1. Education Level
2. Economic Level
3. Perceived Credibility, Believability, Competence, and Honesty
4. Trustworthiness
5. Level of Sophistication
6. Sex Role Identification
7. Level of Success
8. Political Background
9. Religious Background
10. Ethnic Background
11. Social/ Professional / Sexual Desirability

(*Source: Michael Solomon, PhD, Psychologist, Chairman, Marketing Department Graduate School of Business, NYU.)

According to this study the rest of the time is spent finding evidence to prove the original impression of that person, whether that impression is true or not.

The above assumptions are based purely on visual clues. Once we hear someone speak then further assumptions are likely to be made. As George Bernard Shaw wrote in the preface to Pygmalion in 1913, 'It is impossible for an Englishman to open his mouth without making some other Englishman despise him.'

Researchers into accent prestige theory, such as Anderson et al. (2007), Fuertes, Potere, and Ramirez (2002), Cantone, Martinez, Willis-Esqueda, and Miller, (2019). Ko, Judd, and Stapel (2009), and Krauss, Freyberg, and Morsella (2002) all found that an individual's accent and voice were used by others to form strong perceptions about the speaker. They see these perceptions as having two dimensions: status and solidarity. Status forms impressions about intelligence, education, and social class, and solidarity is concerned with friendliness, kindness, and trustworthiness.

Even if we only look within the UK, we discover unconscious bias and linguistic discrimination over speech patterns, with the way we speak being inextricably linked to assumptions about race, class, gender, sexual orientation, etc. Foulkes and Docherty (2006) point out that individuals use their linguistic experience to construct their identity to position themselves within the social world. If they are not doing this positioning themselves, then others will do it for them.

Even today, there remains a hierarchy of British accents, with higher class accents – 'received pronunciation' – considered to be the norm or indeed accentless, whilst others are considered as divergent or inferior with some people still told to try to change the way they sound if they wish to progress. Even people who have excelled in their field have been subjected to bias perceptions based on their speech. Digby Jones, an ex-member of the House of Lords recently criticised the pronunciation by BBC presenter Alex Scott (who represented her country at football), during her coverage of the Tokyo Olympics. Lord Jones tweeted, 'Alex Scott spoils a good presentational job on the BBC Olympics Team with her very noticeable inability to pronounce her 'g's at the end of a word.' Ex Home Secretary, Priti Patel, also entered the debate, saying Alex should be given elocution lessons. In response, Alex replied, 'I'm from a working-class family in East London, Poplar, Tower Hamlets & I am PROUD of the young girl who overcame obstacles and proud of my accent! It's me, it's my journey, my grit.' Another example is that of BBC journalist, Steph McGovern, who was told that her Northern accent was a 'terrible affliction'. It is not just that people do not like the sound of certain accents but that they form judgements based on them. We also repeatedly see Angela Rayner, the current deputy prime minister, shamelessly mocked for her Northern accent.

Sweeping assumptions are made about all kinds of personal characteristics and attributes linked to specific accents. I have a rather upsetting example of my own. My psychotherapy practice is in Oxford, and so draws lots of clients from the University from both the student body and the faculty. I had been working for some time with the wife of a university don and on one occasion she was unwell, and her husband phoned to let me know she could not make her scheduled session. At our next session she reported back in a jocular fashion that her husband (who she defined as a 'snob') had asked her if I was qualified as I 'had a Northern accent'! She had found this both funny and embarrassing. For me, the fact that based on hearing me say nothing more than, 'Thank you for letting me know and do pass on my best wishes for a speedy recovery', he had formulated a picture of me which made him question my qualifications and therefore also my professional competence was a shocking reminder that such prejudice exists.

Indeed, the response to the differences between Northern and Southern accents in the UK is well known. A YouGov poll ranked the Birmingham accent as the ugliest, followed by Liverpudlian, with the Southern Irish accent being considered the most attractive. However, it is not just the level of auditory attractiveness of the accent that is judged but assumptions about the character of person may also be made without any additional information. Just hearing a voice, without any visual cues, can lead to some strange assumptions. Collins (2000) asked a group of women to judge whether men were more likely to have a hairy chest by listening to an audio recording of men's spoken vowel sounds. The women considered the more low pitched the male voice the more attractive and hairier a man was. Needless to say, there is no correlation with body size and vocal pitch although this has been contradicted elsewhere (Evans, Neave, & Wakelin, 2006).

I have already mentioned how people may be considered as potential criminals from an external visual assessment of their body and the assumptions made about race and class. Such perceptions are also to be found when considering accents. A study by Dixon, Mahoney, and Cocks (2002) explored how regional accent affects judgments about guilt in a British criminal justice context. In their study, speakers with a Birmingham regional accent were much more likely to be perceived as sounding guilty than speakers with a standard accent. If you are black with a Brummie accent you run the risk of being suspected of a blue-collar crime. These assumptions are not exclusive to the UK. Cantone, Martinez, Willis-Esqueda, and Miller (2019) found comparable results for a US American context where you were more likely to be found guilty by jurors if you were Mexican American, or Black American defendants as compared to White defendants. Where a defendant had what the authors described as a 'stereotypical accent' the likelihood of a guilty verdict increased. Indeed, studies examining the effect of both skin colour and accent repeatedly show accent has having a bigger effect than appearance (Kinzler, Shutts, Dejesus, & Spelke, 2009; Paladino & Mazzurega; 2020). Adults and children are more likely to accept another person as being 'one of us', if they sound the same even if they do not look the same. Where there was a perceived inconsistency between the categories, e.g. 'sounds the same but looks different' or vice versa then it took longer for people to make up their minds and categorise people (Paladino & Mazzurega, 2020).

Derwing & Munro (2009) point out that speech patterns are also used as a way of identifying perceived outsiders, making those with non-native accents feel they don't belong (Gluszek & Dovidio, 2010). Studies (Russo, Islam, & Koyuncu, 2017) showed that this group suffered greater harassment and negative judgements from managers in their workplace, leading to poor mental health and quality of life. An important point for mediators is that there was evidence that native speakers invested less effort in listening to and understanding foreign-accented speech, due to a subconscious assumption that the speaker will be difficult to understand (Derwing & Munro, 2009), resulting in a self-fulfilling prophecy of communicative failure.

None of us are immune to making such assumptions. My first degree was in Fine Art, and I remember my first day on the course very well. Coming straight from a convent grammar school for girls, I was far from being worldly wise and confident. I entered a room of what appeared to me to be a crowd of confident, trendy young people who all seemed to know they had a right to be there, what they were doing, and unlike me were not frozen by first day nerves. I looked around nervously to see if I could spot if there was anyone 'like me' and I identified another tall, slim 'girl' (as we would have called ourselves then), with long straight hair, colourful tee shirt, and flared jeans, and whose name indicated that she had Irish origins, just as my own name did. In fact, our names were the same apart from one letter. In seconds my own insecurity had conjured up a whole back story for her in which her history was so like my own we could have been twins! By doing so I felt less alone, isolated, and scared. However, I quickly discovered how wrong my assumptions were. Yes, she was Irish, but instead of growing up in Manchester with a wonderfully supportive and loving family, she had grown up in rural Ireland, where she had been a bit of a rebel, becoming pregnant at 14 when she was shipped off to Manchester to avoid scandal and had been living alone in bedsits with her 4-year-old son ever since. Our life journey could not have been more different.

Many years later, on yet another 'first day' I once again fell into making assumptions. This time it was the first day of a master's course in psychotherapy. There were sixteen of us in the room with the lecturer. As everyone went round saying what had brought them there and giving a bit of their history, I began to feel quite intimidated. Once the lecture started, this only got worse. One woman was very inspiring as every few minutes she would add information to what the lecturer said, quoting writers and giving relevant dates and background information. I was overwhelmed with feelings of inadequacy and spent the whole day in silence, trying to deal with an awful headache and convinced that I had been offered a place by mistake. As I got to know my colleagues, I became friendly with the woman I had felt intimidated by and was shocked to learn that she too had made wrong assumptions that day. She had interpreted my silence as total confidence, believing that I had no need to try to justify my place by 'shouting out' any relevant thing I could think of, as she had. I came to understand that we had both perceived one another as strong and confident when we were both anxious and fearful that we were not as clever or as good as everyone else. Apart from this being an example of the very common imposter syndrome it shows clearly how we misinterpret people's behaviour, and they misinterpret ours.

Why a Psychologically Informed Approach is Needed in All Mediation 57

Cultural bias is not just seen in relation to physical appearance, accents, or speech and language patterns, which are usually linked to racial stereotyping, but we also see it applied to gender, sexual orientation, and disability.

What is the relevance of this to mediation? I would suggest that this is also true of the way in which parties in mediation are experienced and judged by the other parties, and the mediator. Although it is a requirement that a mediator is neutral and non-judgmental, however much the mediator works hard to remain neutral there is always a danger of unconscious, or indeed conscious bias. I shall address later ways in which a mediator can work to minimise this.

Even in a non-emotionally charged context two people can 'see' different things. Indeed, one person may see something and almost simultaneously see something else. We are all familiar with illusions such as Rubin's Vase or the image in which we can see an old lady and a young lady. These provide examples of how figures or images change depending on a viewpoint, perspective, background, or context (Figure 5.1).

It is almost impossible to see both images at the same time, but we can flit very quickly from one to the other. In a mediation we are hoping to enable participants to see that there may be two (or more) equally compelling and valid views, and we hope for a willingness to engage, at least for a short time, in the possibility that the other's view is understandable from their perspective, even if we do not agree with it, or cannot even see it.

Even when we think we are seeing the same thing, how do we know that we are? As a small child this fascinated me. I must have been a source of irritation to my mother with constant questions such as, 'we both say that object is red, but how do we know that although we are using the same word, we are not describing something we see differently?' In other words, how do we know that our experiences of the world are shared, rather than we are merely using a shared a vocabulary to describe our unique experience of a shared experience or phenomenon? We tend to live life through a veil of assumptions. I am not criticising this here as life would be very complicated if we were not to do so. We seek and need a sense of commonality to feel a sense of belonging and security.

Figure 5.1 Alternative Perceptions

However, when we are in a dispute, disputants, and often the mediator too, are likely to focus on the difference between the disputants. The person we disagree with is seen as alien, as though they do not share the experiences of humanity, vulnerabilities, and life challenges. This makes it difficult to find empathy or even basic connection. We may become invested in the view that they are fundamentally different from us, for to connect with their humanity and vulnerability may mean we need to open up the space to really listen to them, and in doing so risk the possibility of understanding and even agreeing with them. It is hard to stay in conflict if we are focused on the human commonality between us. We cannot allow ourselves to feel the shared pain of being in disagreement, or the frustration of not having our perception shared and understood or our goals and needs acknowledged. Instead of seeking to find commonality, most people's initial response is to prolong the dispute, in the vain hope that the other person will come to see things their way and prove them to have been right all along. To do this they must continue to see the other person as 'alien', indeed, as 'the other' to be feared, overcome, and destroyed. We may not wish to physically destroy or kill them but we certainly seek to kill their argument so we can be proved to be right.

A psychologically informed mediation approach calls for everyone in the mediation to be authentic and in touch with their shared humanity, whilst at the same time acknowledging that we are all unique and have our own ways of seeing the world; what we refer to as our 'worldview'. My own approach to mediation, and to life in general draws on an existential and phenomenological philosophical understanding. These philosophies understand that we live in an 'interpreted world', created by each of us, they honour our uniqueness as individuals whilst exploring those things which we all share, and which are often referred to as 'the existential givens'.

Yalom (1980) identifies four primary givens or 'ultimate concerns' which we all share: death, freedom, isolation, and meaninglessness. We can add to these with other shared concerns such as how we deal with uncertainty, authenticity, and time and temporality (including death) and the existential anxiety of being temporal beings in an uncertain world. These may seem like philosophical concerns far removed from mediating a dispute between neighbours, but we shall find these concerns somewhere within the narrative of the dispute and by identifying what these are we can uncover the deeper motivations and needs which are in play. This allows us to work towards a settlement agreement which carries more meaning than one which is founded entirely on logic.

Different cultures hold different thoughts and events to be 'logical' and normal. What one culture may experience as 'weird' or supernatural will be a daily 'normal' experience for others. In working with a client of Afro-Caribbean descent I was at first surprised when he identified the sound of my bamboo plant, tapping on the window outside my consulting room during a storm, as his grandmother asking to be admitted to the session. He explained that as his grandmother she was responsible for his well-being and so it was 'logical' that she would wish to be present in the therapy room. Many cultures have a much deeper connection to their ancestors than those in the West, they speak of 'blood memory' and have a greater connection with what Jung referred to as 'the collective unconscious'; the idea that a segment of the deepest unconscious is genetically inherited and not shaped by personal experience. If a mediator is working in a culturally sensitive way, they will be working psychologically, so the beliefs an individual party holds are relevant to the dispute and must be respected and worked with, rather than challenged and dismissed by a mediator who does not share those views or ways of interpreting the world.

Although we are unlikely to work with any ancestorial connections overtly in a mediation it is important to remember that there are many people connected with the dispute who will not be present in the mediation room or even in the expressed narratives of those involved. These may be people in the family or at work who the disputant wants to impress by returning with a good settlement, or they may be ancestorial, cultural, or religious conventions which a person may hold consciously or unconsciously but which may influence what they will see as an acceptable solution. It they choose to go against these embedded internal cultural values this may leave them feeling guilty even if the settlement is a good one. It is often an absent person or a silent person who holds the power when it comes to the final agreement.

The success of mediation does not lie in strict adherence to process, although some mediators working in a more translational style act as though it does. The key task of the psychologically informed mediator is to understand the uniqueness of all parties in the dispute; what is important to them, and what might enable them to move on, and what presents a barrier to change and ultimately to settlement. These things are not usually about the 'dispute' but lie within the psychological makeup of those in dispute. The mediator will not discover these underlying meanings and the importance of the dispute to each party by focusing on the perceived 'facts' surrounding the cause of the dispute, but instead needs to seek an understanding of what meaning each party has attached to the event and therefore what needs to be addressed in a successful settlement.

A mediator needs to always start with the understanding that conflict is always inter-relational and psychological. We need something, or someone, to be in conflict with. Even if I am struggling with inner conflict, the conflict will be between two or more opposing wants and aspects within myself, and so is still relational. The understanding that conflicts are primarily emotional and psychological, not rational and logical, is not new. We have known this, but chosen to ignore it, for a long time. Sun Tzu (545 BCE–470 BCE), in The Art of War wisely informed us that, if 'you know the enemy and know yourself, you need not fear the result of a hundred battles' (2009:11). The importance of knowing oneself is often ignored. We must listen carefully to others to understand how we are perceived by them, but we also come to know ourselves by listening to what we say. Hearing ourselves speak out loud and noting the passion with which we do so is an opportunity which mediation offers. Often, we are surprised to hear what elements we emphasise when we speak, and to feel the strength of emotion we attach to certain statements and not others.

The fact that mediation and indeed conflict are always relational means it is essential to know, and understand, all parties in any conflict, 'If you know yourself but not the enemy, for every victory gained you will also suffer a defeat. If you know neither the enemy nor yourself, you will succumb in every battle' (Sun Tzu ibid). People often invite or demand that a party in mediation should try to empathise with the other person. This is a difficult task. When speaking of empathy here, I am not talking about being sympathetic or caring, but about the ability to connect with the emotional experience of another person. This is a very challenging request to make. As this is the last thing a person wants to do when they enter mediation. They often feel that they are there to present and defend their side of the argument as if they were in court, an approach which some mediators from legal backgrounds, or those working in a more evaluative way may consciously or unconsciously encourage. A psychologically informed mediator will be listening out for commonalities of values, beliefs, experiences, and emotions which they can bring into the mediation to weave a thread of understanding and commonality between the parties. They will not push for this but will be alert to it when it arises.

A better term than empathy to describe this would be 'emotional dwelling' which carries a greater sense of dynamism in that it is active and emotionally engaged. The concept of emotional dwelling requires a person to cultivate the capacity to enter another person's reality without importantly losing their own. Atwood and Stolorow (2016:1) describe 'dwelling' as not merely seeking, 'to understand the other's emotional world from the other's perspective. One does that, but much more. In dwelling... and exploring human nature and human existence, one leans into the other's experience and participates in it, with the aid of one's own analogous experiences.' Freud (1909) in the case of Little Hans describes something similar in his call on us to approach another's experiences through a kind of floating, open attentiveness, free from assumptions, or goals. An impossible task, but one to aim for.

A psychologically informed mediator will aim to use an emotional dwelling approach to introduce and model a respectful atmosphere of trust and show an authentic curiosity in the narrative of each individual present. They may use an existential-phenomenological framework to guide them in exploring the worldview of each party and its importance in how the conflict is seen and how resolution may be achieved.

I have already mentioned that my development grew out of existential-phenomenological thinking and so I believe it is important, before taking you through the process involved in psychologically informed mediation, that I share a little of some of the key concepts in these philosophies which have much to offer the mediator.

Chapter 6

Key Existential Concepts for Mediation

Existential thought provides a framework on which a mediator can draw when exploring the worldview of the disputants in any mediation. We have already noted that as human beings we are unique and yet share some universal givens. We can see that mediating with these two key concepts in mind as our baseline we are better fitted to engage with cultural difference.

Let us start with looking at what we all share, regardless of our race, creed, gender, sexual orientation, physical and mental challenges. An understanding of the importance of the commonalities in existence has been an important base for the thinking of existential philosophers like Søren Kierkegaard, Friedrich Nietzsche, Jean-Paul Sartre, and Martin Heidegger, all of whom have explored these givens, whilst each emphasising different aspects. Xuefu Wang (2019:19) put it very simply by identifying the two basic concerns which human beings share, 'People have two basic concerns: One is to survive; one is to exist. The former only asks to go on living; the latter asks for meaning. The former concerns itself with how to live, the latter with why to live, the meaning of living.'

These shared challenges are often referred to as 'existential givens'. We have no choice about what these givens are, but we do have choice about how we interpret and work with them. They provide grounding for our choices, actions, and understanding of the world and our existence within it, both internally, alone, and collectively, with others.

Yalom (1980) is perhaps the person most known for writing about the existential givens, although he was not the first to write about them. As with all those gathered under the existential banner, different existential theorists have taken different approaches to the givens, although they would all include the following in a list of what they would identify as shared existential concerns,

- Freedom, Responsibility, and Agency
- Death, Temporality, and Finiteness
- Relatedness and Isolation
- Meaning and Meaninglessness
- Emotions, Experience, and Embodiment
- Uncertainty

Let's look briefly at each and how they relate to both mediation and culture.

Freedom, Responsibility, and Agency

Existential thinking gives high importance to issues of freedom and responsibility and calls on individuals to acknowledge their agency in all the decisions they make, and the actions they take. One cannot separate freedom from responsibility no matter how hard we may try. If we think we have succeeded in doing so, we are being inauthentic and merely trying to convince ourselves of something which we know at heart is not true and may lead to feelings of guilt and anxiety.

When thinking of these givens in the context of culture, the obvious question which occurs is whether it is true that we all have equal access to freedom. There is no ultimate freedom. Even when we take a decision to end our own life rather than wait for fate to deal its hand, we cannot guarantee we shall be successful, or that we may find the experience more terrifying and painful than we anticipated. Within the freedom we do have there are limitations. Heidegger, one of the most influential philosophers of the 20th century, in 'Being and Time' (1927) refers to these limitations in his concept of 'throwness' (Geworfenheit). By this he means that all human beings find themselves 'thrown' into the world into a context and situation which they did not choose and cannot fully control. We cannot choose from whose womb we enter the world. We may find ourselves thrown into a financially and socially challenging situation or one of relative wealth and ease. We have no choice over the period of history we are born into, the geography of our birth, the familial and community culture of our families. These factors provide the backdrop to our lives against which we use our freedom to decide to what extent we passively accept any inherent limitations or fight against them, always seeking new possibilities. Geworfenheit acknowledges that we enter a pre-existing cultural world of meanings understood by 'our' group/family/community, but we have the freedom to challenge or accept these. If we choose to challenge, then the journey may be a lonely and difficult one, so many people choose to opt for a perceived security by adopting group beliefs and behaviours. However, once we accept the agency of our actions, we must live with our choice of whether to live an inauthentic existence in which we behave as though we believe the majority, or bravely take the responsibility to live a more authentic existence. Jean-Paul Sartre often reminded us that we are condemned to be free and that although we are free to shape our lives, we cannot escape the responsibility of the implications of our actions for our self and others. This paradox can be hard to deal with and so leads to existential anxiety or angst.

Existentialism is often misinterpreted and seen as giving the individual freedom to do whatever they want. This has meant that at times at times it has been portrayed as a type of nihilism. This is far from the truth as there is an acceptance that we do not exist in a vacuum but live in a world with objects and others and we must form relationships with both. We are always living in a 'being-with' state, we live in a relational existence. This belief affirms the essential plurality and relational and social aspects of existence, and so calls on us to not just take responsibility for our actions, but to consider the implication of these actions for other people and our environment.

The existentialist, Simone de Beauvoir, in her book 'The Ethics of Ambiguity' (1947:39) puts equality and freedom and responsibility firmly within the cultural context of self and other, when she writes, 'A freedom which is interested only in denying freedom must be denied. And it is not true that the recognition of the freedom of others limits my own freedom: to be free is not to have the power to do anything you like; it is to be able to surpass the given toward an open future; the existence of others as a freedom defines my situation and is even the condition of my own freedom. I am oppressed if I am thrown into prison, but not if I am kept from throwing my neighbor into prison.'

We cannot, however, assume that a lack of political freedom means that a person does not have freedom. Indeed, a person can avoid embracing their existential freedom despite being offered great political freedoms. Frankl (1984) offers a powerful example of the ways in which we remain existentially free when our material freedom is severely limited. He writes of his experience in the concentration camps where all his political and social freedoms were taken away. Despite these limitations, he credits his survival to his psychological freedom which allowed him to find and embrace meaning in the midst of what appeared to be meaningless suffering.

What is important to existentialists is that we honestly and bravely examine what are real obstacles to our freedom and what are excuses for refusing to accept our agency and 'preventing' us from taking on responsibility for our actions. Otto Rank puts it more forcefully when he states that the degree to which a person is unaware of the forces which influence them, they are controlled by them. If a person chooses not to be aware of these influences, whether passively or unconsciously, they have still made a choice.

When a person comes to mediation, they generally feel powerless, deny any agency, and carry some level of shame that they have not been able to sort the problem without bringing in a third party. Part of the role of a psychologically informed mediator is to enable all those involved to acknowledge that they do have power and choices, and so encourage them to take responsibility for their agency.

Just as Frankl found meaning and a power in his situation in the concentration camps, a mediator can never assume which party in a mediation is the most powerful, nor assume that there will be a victim and a perpetrator. If the mediator does choose to think in terms of victim and perpetrator, the powerless and the powerful, then the mediator needs to consider how they can rely on the belief that they can intuitively know which is which. This may present a challenge when dealing with culture in mediation as we will hold assumptions about power based on our own culturally influences, beliefs, and values. I shall return to this dilemma in part three.

However, it is true that there is always a strong element of 'thrownness'. Nobody can change what happened to cause the dispute, but it happened in the past. This is a past (even if the initial conflict was extremely recent) which is experienced within its own cultural timeframe and culturally referenced assumptions of right and wrong. The time and culture in which the mediation takes place will also be influenced by the current zeitgeist and what is considered to be 'normal', 'acceptable', and 'right'. Added to that, each person involved in the mediation, including the mediator, will bring their own cultural heritage and beliefs to the meeting. The mediator needs to have worked hard to explore, understand, and own their own assumptions, so that they do not cause any bias. Parties are unlikely to have done this, and part of the mediation process is to give them the freedom to explore any such beliefs which may impact on their understanding of the dispute, and to allow a safe place for them to consider using their freedom to see things differently. In that moment we have the freedom to change our understanding and perception about the meaning of what happened.

In a psychologically informed mediation, the process should facilitate a greater self-awareness and an acknowledgment of the freedom the parties need to let go of sedimented beliefs and wants, and to move from seeing the other party as the problem, to seeing the conflict as a shared problem, the resolution of which frees both parties, giving them back the freedom to re-engage with their lives. Changing one's mind and being prepared to engage with different perceptions to your own may be uncomfortable but can also be liberating, allowing the parties to consider more creative and meaningful solutions to their shared dilemma.

Death, Temporality, and Finiteness

Although it may be uncomfortable to contemplate, the primary existential given is the reality that life is finite, we will all die. Just as we are born alone, we will die alone. We may be surrounded by other people, but these are two journeys which we must traverse by ourselves. The experiences of birth and death, although common to us all, will be unique in our experiencing of them. They represent the ultimate examples of thrownness.

Knowing that those we love and indeed ourselves will inevitably die shapes our existence. If we choose to engage with this truth, it brings more meaning into our lives and presents a challenge to live life to the full. Our actions are experienced as more significant, both in the moment of, and also potentially beyond our death. Heidegger, in all his writings, stresses that by authentically engaging with our finitude we develop a more intentional quality to our lives. Tillich (1952), in 'The Courage to Be', goes deeper, stating that if we are to truly embrace being alive, then the reality of non-being must be faced. It is this concept of *nonbeing* which is perhaps even harder to engage with than physical death. We cannot know what, if anything, comes after death, and so we would rather create a belief in some kind of afterlife or form of reincarnation rather than engage with the possibility of non-being.

Unfortunately, many human beings prefer to pretend death does not exist. As Simone de Beauvoir wrote in 1947, 'today, however, we are having a hard time living because we are so bent on outwitting death' (1947:193). Things haven't changed much since she wrote that, with a growing desperation to ward off death and aging. However, as Becker (1973) reminds us, it would be impossible to live in constant conscious awareness of death, as such awareness would prove to be too overwhelming and would drive people to neurosis or psychosis.

In order to deny the reality of death Yalom (1980) suggests that we have developed two ways of attempting to do this. He suggests that we seek to take a role either as 'the ultimate rescuer' or the 'special one'. These roles are often played out within a mediation. If they have become an individual's self-identity, and way of coping a mediator needs to be very careful in exploring this with a party. The cultural background of a party will intensify the need for an individual to see themselves as omnipotent, a protector, a leader, a competitor, or alternatively a follower, more submissive and conflict avoidant. Gender, race, physical ability, and sexual orientation will also create stereotypes for people to embrace or reject.

Most mediators are unlikely to have to mediate in a matter of life or death but there are examples of mediations which do. I was asked to mediate in the case of a seven-year-old girl who had been diagnosed with a terminal illness. The girl had seemed perfectly healthy but over the period of ten days became very ill. Her parents were in the middle of a messy divorce. The doctors told the parents that they were unable to save the girl's life. They could extend it for about six months, through a series of unpleasant and painful treatments. Alternatively, they could make her remaining time very comfortable but believed she would only live for a matter of days. The mother wanted to make her daughter's remaining time as pain-free and comfortable as possible whilst the father wanted to use every treatment possible to extend the child's life, including taking her abroad for specialist treatment. Fortunately, before the mediation happened the grandparents on both sides intervened and both parents decided not to pursue any further treatment, and the child died peacefully two days later.

Medical case mediations are ones in which there are often cultural or religious issues involved and so create challenges for health care providers and systems in trying to meet the cultural, social, and religious needs of patients, families, and communities. The National Library of Medicine (www.ncbi.nlm.nih.gov/books/NBK493216/) offers an overview of some of the underlying religious and spiritual beliefs which impact on health treatment and care. They range from issues around prebirth – contraception, abortion, use of pain relief in labour – through what treatments are deemed acceptable, such as blood transfusion and organ transplants, together with what treatments should be available to the terminally ill, and how the bodies of the deceased should be dealt with. All these concerns can result in a dispute between doctors, patients, and families, which can often be addressed through mediation.

However, as I stated earlier it is not often that mediators are presented with these kinds of life and death issues. Instead, mediations are often about losses (small symbolic 'deaths') such as redundancy, dismissal, ending of a relationship, etc. The meaning and importance of all these losses will have cultural as well as personal implications which a psychologically informed mediator will be alert to. The mediator does not need to explore them in depth but does need to be careful that any resolution offered by one side is not going to be perceived as an attack on the other's beliefs and values.

Relatedness and Isolation

It is another existential given that we must find ways of being alone, and of being with others. We each live our own unique lives but always in relations to the people and things around us. Irvin Yalom (2013) describes this as 'the unbridgeable gap between self and others, a gap that exists even in the presence of deeply gratifying interpersonal relationships.' Friedrich Nietzsche, writing in 1883 puts it more poetically but strongly when he writes, 'In loneliness, the lonely one eats himself; in a crowd, the many eat him. Now choose.'

Being alone is an intrinsic part of being human. We must face our own thrownness and limitations, whilst acknowledging and using our own responsibilities and agency. If we were to be alone in the world we would have no reference point, we would not know what it is to be alive if there were no death, we would not be able to define our gender, race, age etc. if there were not others in the world to help us identify what we are not! Indeed, there would be no culture.

Being alone may present us with a challenge but being with others also presents difficulties. In existential thought there is considerable importance given to the knowledge that we are 'beings-in-the-world-with-others'. Heidegger (1889-1976) noted that we live in a world which is primarily a 'with-world' where we are always in relation to others and therefore inter-subjective. We can never be truly detached or objective about ourselves, our situation, or others. In fact, we co-create our existence, and without others there would be no existence. If we choose to isolate ourselves from others, we can only do so if there are others to isolate from. Bugental (1992) speaks of being 'a-part-of and apart-from' identifying the two ends of the relatedness continuum whilst acknowledging that both polarities hold a need for 'the other' to either be with or be apart from. Others can help us fulfil our dreams or can provide obstacles to that fulfilment. As Sartre famously put it in his 1944 one act play, 'Huis Clos' (No Exit), hell can indeed be other people.

Living authentically is another aim of existentialism which can present a challenge when considering isolation and relatedness. Living authentically, according to Heidegger, means acknowledging and confronting the reality of our limitations. If we are to be authentic, we must aim to stay true to our beliefs and values. In some situations, this may result in us being alone as we are not in agreement with the truths, values, and behaviours of those around us. The struggle for authenticity can often be seen where the culture of the majority is at odds with an individual's culture. The individual may try to acclimatise and take on the majority behaviour patterns and beliefs. Sartre may term this 'bad faith' where we clothe ourselves with the uniform of the group, potentially causing feelings of confusion, guilt, and abandonment. The tension in standing out and remaining true to minority values and beliefs can often result in conflict between individuals, and between individuals and the groups (family, religion, work, etc.) which the person may be part of. A mediator would attempt to create an open and respectful dialogue around such differences rather than try to pretend they are not there.

All conflicts are in some way relational. We are in conflict with others (including organisations), or we are in conflict with ourselves. The latter is the focus for self-reflection or therapy, although it may well play an important role in a mediation. In a dispute the disputants can lose sight of their human connectedness and create a fantasy of the other person as being alien or other, separate and very different from themselves. If we dehumanise a person, it remains easier to be angry with them, to blame them, and to sustain negative feelings about them. Once we can connect with the shared experience of being human, we can see not just our differences but begin to understand that individual perceptions and beliefs do not make us a different species, with different existential anxieties.

Existential thinkers such as Sartre and Beauvoir have explicitly considered the place of the 'Other'. Simone de Beauvoir writes of alterity (Otherness), distinguishing between two forms of otherness: namely, existential alterity and sociopolitical alterity and considers a view of reciprocity. Sartre's '(1960) Critique of Dialectical Reason', anticipates much of the crucial work being undertaken in 'race' critical theories, arguing that race is a social construct, formed by social struggles, informing processes of inclusion and exclusion, racial subjectification and subjection, and so he stresses the necessity to deconstruct the stereotypes. He maintained that discrimination was institutionalised in the structures and rituals of everyday life; and held a vision of broadening an appreciation of how race and racism function within the neocolonial global order.

Despite the commonly held misunderstanding that existentialism is purely focused on the uniqueness and agency of the individual and so is all about self, and not others, this is far from the case, as the emphasis on relatedness and being-in-the-world-with others shows. This makes an existential approach as described by thinkers such as James Bugental, Rollo May, Irvin Yalom, and others who are profoundly relationally focused, an excellent framework for the psychologically informed mediator, particularly when working with issues of diversity. The mediator will work to explore commonalities of experience, values, and beliefs without crude invitations to 'put yourself in the other person's shoes' or ask, 'how do you think it made them feel?'

A psychologically minded mediator will be alert to the power dynamics inherent in feeling alone, or feeling one has the backing of others. They will seek to gain trust early and to develop a strong working alliance with each party aiming at allowing them to let go of the need to alienate the other and to at least meet on the common ground of their shared existential struggles. As Rumi is credited with reminding us, 'Out beyond ideas of wrongdoing and rightdoing, there is a field. I'll meet you there.' It is the mediator's task to gently travel with each party into that field within which connection and resolution can grow.

Meaning and Meaninglessness

As humans we have a need to find meaning. Existentialists would say that it is meaning that can make existence bearable, and that the lack of meaning is one of the greatest existential terrors. Frankl (2000:133) who I explained, spent time in the concentration camps, describes despair as 'suffering without meaning', by which he means that if we can find meaning in something it saves us from falling into despair and being consumed by meaningless suffering. According to Becker (1973:196) finding meaning allows us to exist without being overwhelmed by our place in the cosmos, 'Man cannot endure his own littleness unless he can translate it into meaningfulness on the largest possible level.'

The existentialist position is that there is no true meaning handed down to us by a supreme being, but that it is the duty of the individual to seek out and create meaning. If it is the case that we make our own meaning, influenced by our culture in its broadest sense, then it quickly becomes clear that there is a great potential for disagreement and misunderstanding. Each individual will imbue every action, every word, and every movement which took place during the event or events which started the conflict with symbolic meaning of their own. From this they will form perceptions, often experienced as 'truths' as to what and why things happened as they did.

In line with the existential emphasis on the paradox of our individual uniqueness, and the truth that we only exist in relation to and because of others, culture is shaped by both our personal perceptions and the cultural experiences which we encounter in our interaction with others. We will have been born into and grown up surrounded by a set of meanings belonging to our family, community, close religious or secular groups, and socio-political groups. Through these we develop a sense of 'normal' behaviours, beliefs, values, practices of particular groups, of society. From our early years we witness sets of values formed from the special meaning given them by the culture we are born into, and these become seen as universal givens. If we take the concept of time as an example, we see very different meaning attached to it in different cultures. Putting it crudely, many Western societies see time as linear, and so emphasise punctuality and schedules, while in some Eastern cultures, time is experienced as more fluid, and so those cultures value the natural flow of events over strict adherence to deadlines.

Of course, these are sweeping statements, and individuals and groups within these large cultural and geographical groupings will all have their own understanding of the meaning of time, created by individual experience and environmental factors. The UK, where I was born and raised, and still live, sits within a group of countries generally grouped as Western cultures, and yet we are all aware of the idea of Mediterranean time, manana (the Spanish word, indicating it will get done 'tomorrow', actually meaning 'sometime'), and how this contrasts with the English irritation with people not doing what they say they will, at the time they say they will do it, and a national obsession of clock watching. We cannot attach a national meaning about time to even a country as small as the UK. Although still within the UK, Cornwall seems to embrace the Spanish meaning of time, using the word 'd'rectly' not to mean immediately as it may be supposed, but an indicator that it may get done some time ... or not.

Personally, I experience time as quick moving and very valuable, so I value punctuality. This can mean that I attribute a meaning of being late to showing disrespect for another person's time. This leads to me trying to make the most of each minute and not wasting the moment, finishing what I start, etc. Some of this meaning set comes from my family, education, community, and the geographical areas I have lived in. It is also due to having a parent who died suddenly at a young age and so growing up with a lived experience that life is transitory, and our lifespan can be very short. This may seem like a negative view of life but the main meaning I attach to it is positive, seeing time as a great gift resulting in the need to fill life with meaningful activity and not to put things off. Interestingly, when I visit Italy, one of my favourite countries, I enjoy the different experience of time which seems to have a more leisurely pace. However, I shall still try to make the most of that time, not necessarily through being busy, but by meaningfully and mindfully deciding how to use the time I have, even if that means a leisurely swim, reading a novel, or taking a siesta.

Time, and the meaning given to it by each participant, is an important factor in mediation and a psychological approach requires the mediator to understand what meaning all participants give to time. If being on time represents a show of respect to one side, while the other perceives being tied to specific times as an attack on their individual freedom, there is an immediate additional conflict to the original dispute. The mediator must not ignore this but negotiate a way forward that will work for everyone, helping people to understand the meaning that the other person may attach to time-related behaviour. It is never a good idea in mediation to tell the parties that they shall each be given equal time in the private sessions as some people will need a lot of time and others less. To offer equal opportunity to express themselves is a more authentic offering.

How people use language, and the pace of their speech is also cultural, and laden with meaning. Some individuals with a 'time is money' worldview, who value quick thinking and decisiveness may try to push the mediation along. Their language may be very fast paced, and solution focused, and a mediator who tries to slow this down, using a lot of metaphor and narrative is likely to frustrate the party and lose their trust. Another person may be more reflective, speaking more slowly and using silence to reflect. The psychologically informed mediator will respect and work with these differences, matching the individual's pace and use of time, rather than trying to change them.

In a mediation everyone will be very aware of the body language, gestures, and rituals of everyone concerned and will attach meaning to them. Some cultures attach being first to an acknowledgment of status, whereas other cultures will interpret the need to be put first as evidence of low self-esteem. For this reason, the mediator needs to be aware of everything they do, starting with who they invite to speak first. Where people are seated will also carry cultural meaning, and parties will interpret everything, including how the seating is arranged, who sits nearest the mediator, who is in direct eye contact, etc. How the mediator addresses the parties at the start of the meeting will also carry meaning, the mediator needs to consider how they will address everyone, be it very formally using their title and surname, or just their first name. The best way to approach this is to ask the parties how they would like to be addressed and not to challenge any discrepancy between the sides, such as one party offering their first name and the other asking to be called 'sir', but instead respecting their individual preference.

Most legally based approaches to mediation are unlikely to give much time to trying to uncover the meaning behind how each participant has experienced the dispute and what is needed to form a settlement which is meaningful to both sides. A meaningful resolution may be harder to reach but it stands a greater chance of sustaining than one which has only addressed the more overt transactional aspects of the conflict.

Let me give an example of how legislative procedures, and many mediations, can miss the 'meaningful' aspects of a person's needs. In my work as a psychotherapist, I had a client come to me who had just 'successfully won' a court case over unfair dismissal. She had worked very successfully for an organisation for 14 years but unfortunately made a mistake for which she was dismissed. The organisation had failed to follow correct procedures in dismissing her and after many years of angry communications the case eventually went to court, and my client was awarded a considerable financial settlement. It was only after receiving the money that she entered therapy. She reported that she could not touch the money as it in some way felt dirty. When I asked her about the meaning behind this feeling and what would have been a meaningful outcome to the conflict, she was very clear in her reply. She accepted that she had made a mistake, but that the process of going to court had come to represent for her a meaning that she was in some way a bad employee. Money held no meaning for her and so although she had been awarded a settlement it failed to have any meaning for her. When asked what would have been meaningful, she did not hesitate, 'if someone had said that although I had made one mistake, I had been an excellent employee for fourteen years. The process made me feel that the whole of my professional life had been meaningless.' A psychologically aware mediator would have identified the meaning which needed to be addressed in any settlement. One positive affirmation of her work would have saved years of pain and a considerable amount of money.

Emotions, Experience, and Embodiment

How different cultures treat and express emotions varies greatly. Some cultures encourage emotional expression, whilst others would much prefer that we keep 'a stiff upper lip' and hide our emotions from others. For example, in the United States it is acceptable to express negative emotions like fear, anger, and disgust both alone and in the presence of others, while Japanese individuals only do so while alone (Matsumoto, 1990). Matsumoto, Yoo, and Nakagawa (2008) found that individuals from collectivist cultures were more likely to engage in suppression of emotional reaction so they can evaluate which response is most appropriate in a given context (Matsumoto, Yoo, & Nakagawa, 2008).

Having said this, research indicates that the facial expressions used to express emotion are universal and are similar not just across human beings but shared with non-human primates such as chimpanzees and orangutans (Darwin, 1871, Ekman & Keltner, 1997). They suggested that there are seven universal emotions which are associated with distinct facial expressions – sadness, happiness, fright, disgust surprise, disgust, contempt, and anger.

Despite this, Ekman and Friesen found some cultural differences, with 95% of participants in the United States associating a smile with happiness, whilst only 69% of Sumatran participants made the same association. Similarly, 86% of participants in the United States associated the wrinkling of the nose with disgust, but only 60% of Japanese made the same association (Ekman et al., 1987).

There are cultural differences in the degree to which people focus on the face rather than other parts of the body (Masuda, Ellsworth, Mesquita, Leu, Tanida, & Van de Veerdonk, 2008). The social context will also play a part in this (Malatesta & Haviland, 1982). Even when the face is the focus there are cultural preferences for where on the face the gaze is directed when we are seeking to discover more about the person's emotions. (Yuki, Maddux, & Matsuda, 2007). For example, people from the United States tend to focus on the mouth when interpreting others' emotions, whereas people from Japan tend to focus on the eyes. Cultural differences exist when evaluating and interpreting emotional experiences that underlie facial expressions of emotion but there is a distinct in-group advantage. Individuals from the same culture will recognise the emotions of others of the same culture somewhat better than those from a different culture.

There are also distinct cultural norms which are associated with different genders. These are shaped by a combination of factors – biological, psychological, social, and cultural. Fascinating as it is to discuss which of these factors may be the most influential, it is not the purpose of this book to spend time on this, but to look to focus on how the emotions are expressed and responded to.

We have all heard it said that 'big boys don't cry'. Socio-cultural expectations mean that in many cultures, males are still expected to be rational, assertive, less emotional (unless expressing anger), to take charge, show less emotional intelligence, and so hide vulnerability. This limiting stereotype is beginning to be challenged in some cultures, particularly amongst younger people. In the UK there is a growth of support groups specially aimed at enabling men to recognise, affirm, and express their emotions with the aim of reducing emotional struggles and mental health issues.

There are cultures which do not discourage men from showing emotion. These include Mediterranean and South European. Latin American, Polynesian, and Indigenous cultures. Nordic countries whose cultures embrace gender equality and emotional openness encourage men to take more of a part in child rearing and to express emotion. Even some cultures with more traditional views on masculinity such as Lebanon, Turkey, and other Middle Eastern countries will encourage emotional expression in family and friendship circles.

There are other contextual and cultural factors which can limit or liberate emotional expression. One of the most common places to see men of all cultures expressing emotion is at a football match or other sporting events. As a child I would attend Manchester United home games with my father and noticed how more emotions were in evidence once the club started to sign more European players. Perhaps the most significant signing was that of Eric Cantona. For a time, many fans would attend the match wearing Cantona masks. When wearing these their language was more emotional and accompanied by increased waving of arms and shrugging of shoulders. This may be seen as merely imitating their idol, but the words and gestures were easily accessed from within, which might indicate that they were there all the time but the change in the culture of the club allowed cultural change in the mode of expression. Interestingly, in speaking with several of my male psychotherapy clients who say they never express emotions, they will remember tears of sadness, frustration, or elation in relation to sporting events or their pets! Culturally, somehow, they felt these were places where a man could legitimately cry without losing a sense of their masculinity.

Being in a conflict situation is always an emotional experience. So inevitably mediations will be stages for emotions, expressed or not. Those calling for the mediation may well feel embarrassed that they have been unable to sort the situation themselves; they feel shame and humiliation regarding the process, in addition to the emotions that they hold around the precipitating event and towards those on the other side of the argument. Even if someone is there only to represent a firm or organisation, they will have an emotional reaction to the responsibility. They will have to bring back a settlement which will potentially be deemed a success or a failure, and so influence the way in which they themselves will be seen. This will be expressed in the way they behave during the mediation.

An existential approach to mediation welcomes emotions and so differs from the more solution-focused approaches to conflict resolution, where the first aim is to 'take the emotions out of it'. This is impossible because even if a mediator can remove the expression of emotions, they are not removing the emotions, just burying them. The likelihood of unexplored emotions resurfacing towards the end of a mediation and sabotaging the resolution is a very real one. Even if a resolution is agreed, if it does not address the emotional meaning and emotional needs of the parties it is more likely to unravel.

I wish to emphasise how important it is for a mediator to engage with and explore any emotional expression from a party, instead of feeling afraid of it. Through these emotions a mediator can open a door to greater understanding. As I have stated, emotions are always about something. If we are angry, we are angry about something. If we are sad, we are sad about something. If a skilled mediator can identify what the real cause of an emotion is then they will find that it is often related to the values and beliefs held by the person expressing that emotion. Heidegger (1993) states that emotions, or moods, give us a more essential understanding than any factual statement. To dismiss or ignore an emotion robs us of a deeper understanding. However, a mediator must not try to evoke or suggest emotions where they are not been expressed. Often, being silent is just as strong an emotion as shouting.

As a painter, I think of each expressed emotion as being like a colour added to an artist's palate. Each colour brings greater opportunity for creativity. When encountering emotions the mediator must put aside any cultural expectations they may hold about what are appropriate emotions. The acceptability of the expression of emotions differs considerably between cultures and emotions can be expressed very differently depending on racial, heritage, gender, and other cultural influences.

Assumptions are often made about surface emotions. If a person is shouting or waving their arms about this may be interpreted as an expression of anger. However, it could indicate many different feelings, such gestures may come from passion or excitement, or an attempt to hide vulnerability. The mediator needs to be skilled in exploring the underlying meaning and facilitating the shared understanding of both parties' emotional language.

The embodiment of emotions is healthy as expressed by writers such as Bugental, Heery, and Nietzsche. They do not call for us to be a slave to our emotions and to blindly follow and express them but instead to understand what they are telling us about ourselves, what they are expressing to others and how they can be used positively. The mediator needs to understand the cause of the emotions and its connection to a person's value systems and cultural beliefs. This requires gentle enquiry but stops short of therapeutic analysis. The mediator is only engaged in such exploration when it serves the greater understanding of the dispute, the parties, and what a successful resolution may look like.

Uncertainty

The final existential concept I am introducing is focused on uncertainty. Most of us are very uncomfortable with uncertainty. As a species we long for simplicity, certainty, clear binary boundaries, and distinct definitions between what is right and wrong. These things give us an inauthentic sense of safety, a safe framework for our behaviours, and a sense of having firm ground on which to stand. Existentialists call on us not to cling to such falsehoods, but to hold an awareness of the often uncomfortable truth of the uncertainty of existence. There is very little I can be sure of other than that I was born, and I shall die. Just because I want to conceive does not mean I can; if I am pregnant, it does not mean that I shall give birth to a living child. Should I attempt to take control of my death through suicide, there is no certainty I shall succeed. De Beauvoir (1947:9) reminded us that 'from the beginning, existentialism defined itself as a philosophy of ambiguity.' Ambiguity offers us a playing field of possibilities.

However, tempting, a mediator must not collude with desires for certainty, often shown in requests for advice, often phrased by a party as 'tell me what to do', 'what is the best step now', 'what would you do', 'what is the best resolution for me'? The mediator will no doubt have their own opinions of these questions but by pretending certainty exists, they are laying claim to an untruth which can lead to a desire to move quickly to a 'logical' black and white and not fully considered resolution. The novelist Dennis Lehane called certainty the most gorgeous lie of them all. It is very seductive and would make life less complex should it exist, but at the same time more boring. Indeed, the only thing we can be certain of is uncertainty. The existential phenomenological principle of uncertainty urges us to treat each instance of the unexpected as an invitation to explore previously unforeseen or unconsidered possibilities. It is uncertainty which makes mediation a creative process which frees it from the need to find conventional solutions.

Chapter 7

Existential Dimensions

Having looked at how the knowledge of the existential givens can prove constructive to a psychologically informed mediator, I wish to introduce another existential concept which may be equally useful. We have seen that the 'givens' provide tensions and paradoxes which the individual encounters within their lives. The contexts in which these givens are played out can simplistically be divided into four dimensions of human existence.

I have already stressed that authenticity is an important existential value. People can get very confused about what is meant by this, just as people can take a very simplistic view of the term 'equal opportunities' taking it to mean we must treat everyone exactly the same. As we have already explored, we are all unique, therefore different, and with different needs. I have two daughters, with very different personalities; as small children they had completely different preferences when it came to showing physical affection, one would ask to be hugged until she 'couldn't breathe' whilst the other hated to be hugged tightly, preferring a gentle stroking of her hair to show emotion. I believe I treated them equally, giving them both the same amount of attention, but demonstrating affection in the different ways that they preferred. In both cases I was being authentic in demonstrating my love for them, but an observer might have felt I was not treating both the same.

Returning to the question of authenticity, philosophers, psychologists, social scientists, and others have all debated whether it is possible to be truly authentic. When we speak generally about authenticity, we are referring to being true to oneself, staying with our values and beliefs regardless of pressure from others. Sartre, Heidegger, and others were very interested in exploring the concept of authenticity. Heidegger suggested that authenticity comes from confronting the reality of existence, whilst Sartre focused his thinking on the battle between freedom and responsibility with authenticity requiring an acceptance of our agency, acknowledging that we have choices and must take responsibility for our actions. Like Heidegger he saw authenticity as living in accordance with one's values rather than conforming blindly to societal expectations. Although both emphasise the importance of being true to oneself, they are both placing this within the context that we are beings-in-the-world-with-others and therefore must consider our actions in light of potential implications for others. Of course, this will be interpreted in different ways by different cultures, particularly regarding how collectivist or individualist the culture is. So, social and cultural concepts, with differing ideas as to what constitutes 'the self' and how fluid that self may be across our lives, will influence perceptions of what it is to be authentic, and these may be in conflict with the individual's idea of authentic behaviour.

From the above, we may realise that we can be true to ourselves even in the different contexts in which we find ourselves. Existential psychotherapists and psychologists use a framework termed 'existential dimensions' to help them explore what we may call a person's 'worldview' and how this is evidenced in different areas of their existence. Existentialists do not seek to divide people into types or parts but look to the different levels of experience and existence in which we operate: our ways of 'being-in-the-world', which can be placed on a 'map of human existence' comprising four dimensions.

Binswanger (1881–1966) identified three dimensions: the Umwelt, the Mitwelt, and the Eigenwelt. In 1984 van Deurzen introduced a fourth dimension: the Uberwelt.

The Umwelt is concerned with the physical dimension and the ways in which we relate to our environment and to the givens of the natural world around us. This includes our relationship with our own body and bodily sensations, our own bodily needs, our health, and to our own mortality. It goes beyond our own bodies to those of others and beyond that to the surroundings we find ourselves in, the landscape, climate, and the weather.

Perhaps the dimension most easily observed and experienced by others is the Mitwelt, the dimension of being-in-the-world-with-others; the social dimension in which we relate to and communicate with others in the public world. This includes our response to the culture we live in, including the class, gender, sexual orientation, and race we belong to (and indeed those we do not belong to). This dimension can challenge our authenticity with our need to belong and avoid isolation, meaning we may develop the ability to be an adaptable chameleon. Fluidity and flexibility can be good, but not if the result is that we behave inauthentically, or in bad faith as Sartre would term it.

The Eigenwelt is concerned with the psychological dimension and the ways in which individuals relate to themselves, and so create a personal world. This dimension includes views about past experiences and future possibilities and facilitates the development of a sense of one's own character and identity. It is concerned with our thoughts, memories, self-identity, and the similarities and differences we perceive there to be between ourselves and others. Of course, it is influenced by our culture including collective history, myths, and narratives.

The fourth dimension, the Uberwelt (the over world), is that of the spiritual realm in which individuals relate to the unknown and create a sense of an ideal and meaningful world, an ideology and a philosophical outlook. For some, a belief in a religion provides such a framework, whereas others need to discover and attribute meaning in a more secular and personal way.

I could propose a fifth dimension, the Unterwelt (Hanaway, 2024), the counterpoint to the Uberwelt. This 'under world' can be one which encompasses our

Jungian shadow world or equally those dimensions from which we seek to anesthetise or sedate ourselves. This can be the dimension in which we choose to ignore our values and beliefs or pretend that they do not exist or interact with those values, needs, and wants which we may feel would not be acceptable or understood by others. It is this world which is most private, and which we may never give others access to, or restrict access to the very few who we believe will accept this part of us.

There may be cultural restrictions on how we can express ourselves in certain dimensions, and cultures will differ on the level of importance given to each dimension. More collective cultures may give precedence to the more social dimensions whereas the individualist cultures may prioritise those dimensions which are more focused on self.

An exploration of these dimensions, through simple actions which I shall describe later, will enable mediators to build a picture of the world each individual inhabits, how they interact in their world, and the culture, values, and beliefs which inform those behaviours. If, as a mediator, I can understand the values and motivations of those involved in a dispute, then I can facilitate a settlement which is meaningful to the individuals, even if such a resolution may not appear logical or rational to the outside world.

Chapter 8

Key Relevant Phenomenological Concepts for Mediation

An existential approach often employs a phenomenological method of enquiry. I shall explain further later on how this is used in practice during mediation; I shall start with a brief definition and overview for those new to phenomenology.

Emmy van Deurzen (2012:8), describes the objective of phenomenology as being 'to gather information and understanding carefully. This is always done from multiple perspectives: we do this by going round the houses and investigating different aspects and different interpretations of reality until a true picture emerges. Phenomenology is the science of the way in which things appear to us. It proceeds by systematically describing a phenomenon from different angles until we can intuitively grasp its essence in quite a new way.'

The philosophical tradition of phenomenology was started in the first half of the 20th century by Edmund Husserl, and developed by Martin Heidegger, Maurice Merleau-Ponty, Jean-Paul Sartre, and others. It can be defined as the study of structures of experience, or consciousness. When we talk of phenomenology, we are literally referring to the simple study of 'phenomena', that is the appearances of things as they appear in our experience, and the meanings which we then give things in our own experience. It is concerned with how things are experienced in the first-person perspective.

More recently, the philosophy of mind uses the term 'phenomenology' in a more restricted way, mainly using it to relate to the characterization of sensory qualities such as seeing and hearing. It is useful to give importance to these sensory aspects, however, our experience is much richer in content than mere sensation. In the phenomenological tradition, phenomenology is given a much wider range, and addresses the meaning things hold in our experience, the significance of objects, events, tools, the flow of time, the self, and others. These are all explored as they arrive as phenomena and are experienced in our 'life-world', a term used by Husserl to describe the pre-theoretical, lived experience that forms the foundation of all knowledge and science; the world as experienced in everyday life, before any scientific or philosophical abstraction.

Despite this, phenomenology does contain some key beliefs. A central concept is that of 'intentionality', initially developed by Franz Bretano and taken up by Husserl, which refers to the idea that we are always in relation to something. This includes our thoughts, perceptions, and feelings: they are always about something. This is very important in mediation when encountering strong emotions as by attending to what the emotions are about, we will discover important aspects of a person's worldview, particularly their values and beliefs.

An equally important lesson for mediators is that of 'Epoché'. This is a term used by phenomenologists to describe the act of consciously suspending judgement and setting aside assumptions and prejudices. This includes any projections we may have of how a certain culture (used in the broadest sense) will experience and perceive things and assumptions about how this will influence behaviours. This act of setting aside is often referred to as 'bracketing'.

If we are not busy listening to our inner voice with its all its assumptions, then we can listen more deeply to others. Husserl points out that our experiences of things are always set within a context, with an implicit framework of other possibilities, which he calls 'horizons'. Everything we see, hear, and sense is important and will at some level be related. For this reason, we have to treat everything as having equal importance. If in a mediation someone talks about something which does not seem to link directly with the dispute, more transactional mediators may call them to task, asking them to focus on 'the matter in hand'. More psychologically minded mediators will understand that everything which is said enhances their understanding of the individual's worldview, and therefore the meaning the dispute has for them, and consequently what will be needed to reach a settlement which fits with their values and beliefs making it more likely they will stick to the agreement.

When we are listening carefully and in a non-judgemental way, we will notice that most of what is said has two components, there will be the factual component and the emotional component. A person will usually describe what they saw or heard along with how that impacted on them. Husserl uses the terms the noema and the noesis. Noema is directional, '...the object (the what) that we direct our attention towards and focus upon' (Spinelli, 1989:13) and noesis is referential, the '*how*' through which we define an object. There is no universal truth in any experience, just an interpreted one; things only exist through the meaning we give them.

As I have suggested earlier, engaging with the emotional aspect is more fruitful and creative than focusing on the so-called factual elements. As I have shown, witness statements cannot be always relied on, and what they are talking about is a past event, which cannot in itself be changed. What can be changed is how we reflect on, and *then* perceive that experience, potentially also leading to changing how we feel about it, and so what we want to do about it.

Phenomenology calls on us to study various types of experience through attending to perception, thought, memory, imagination, emotion, desire, and volition to bodily awareness, embodied action, and social activity, including linguistic activity. We can see how this can enable us to work in a more culturally aware and sensitive way acknowledging that all these modes of experience are influenced by personal and collective cultural 'norms'.

Having offered a very broad overview of some existential and phenomenological thinking and how these serve a mediator who wishes to work in a psychological and culturally sensitive way, I shall move on to show how these are integrated into the practical stages of mediation.

Chapter 9

The Process of Psychologically Informed Mediation

The psychological approach can be used in all types of mediation. For those of you new to mediation, I shall take you through a commonly used framework based on what is known as the Harvard Model and which is sometimes referred to as 'Shuttle Mediation'. In the previous chapters I have referred to reasons why using a psychological approach, based on existential and phenomenological concepts helps the mediator and the parties to more thoroughly explore the meaning of the dispute and the hoped for outcome and so increases the likelihood of reaching a more sustainable and culturally meaningful resolution.

Pre-mediation Phase

Meeting With the First Party to the Dispute

Not all mediation models have a phase which happens before the mediation day itself, and amongst those that do there are often different aims, and so the meetings cover different grounds. Some mediators will use pre-mediation communication solely to cover transactional issues such as setting out the contract, agreeing the fee, and the time, date, and venue for the mediation. However, it also provides an opportunity to make sure that those attending have the authority to settle the dispute. All these details, plus information about confidentiality will then be written up and signed by everyone concerned, including the mediator or mediators, in a pre-mediation contract.

In all approaches, the pre-mediation stage provides a space in which a mediator will speak with the parties separately, in confidence, and 'without prejudice' (I am using this in the legal sense, meaning nothing which is said can be referred to in court if the mediation does not result in a settlement and the dispute moves into litigation). This initial contact may be in-person face-to-face, through an online platform such as Zoom or Teams, or over the phone

A psychologically informed mediator will use these sessions to clarify the same practical points as any other mediator and to draw up the pre-mediation agreement but will also use the opportunity to begin to build trust and understanding through getting to know each party, exploring their worldview, and beginning to explore how they see the dispute which has brought them to mediation. These sessions can be quite long but can prove very valuable. In some cases which I have mediated these sessions have resulted in there being no need for a mediation day. The sessions in themselves have brought new insights resulting in the opposing sides getting together and sorting out their differences first.

An example of this was a case of two professional men, one of whom worked with the other within a high-status context. They were finding it difficult to get along professionally and causing each other considerable anxiety and stress. One, I shall call him James, was a charismatic leader who was used to inspiring others and having people quickly and unquestioningly follow up on his ideas. He could not understand why Simon, the person working to him, did not react as others had, be inspired by his suggestions, and run with them. For practical reasons due to the busyness of both men the mediation was planned to take place over two weeks. The first pre-mediation meeting with James took place over two hours during which I invited him to share his thoughts about the conflict, his relationship with Simon, but also his values, beliefs, and motivations.

I was interested in his use of language. He would often make quite assertive statements and then quietly add, almost in a whisper, 'that must make me sound arrogant'. The third time he did this I reflected back to him that this seemed to be a question he was constantly asking himself, or perhaps asking of me. He shared that he was worried that I might consider him to be arrogant, and I asked if he also felt that other people, including Simon, might think that of him. His whole mood softened, and he moved from appearing to be a super confident individual, yet quite defended, to someone who had merely taken on the robe of the super confident, to mask some vulnerabilities, expressing that he did not like the thought of being arrogant but suspected that was how a lot of people saw him. I also noted that when speaking he had referred a few times to his work as providing him with the opportunity to be a hero and used superhero metaphors in his narrative. He stressed that he was prepared to share his status with others, so that together they could become a legion of superheroes, and that he had used that analogy when speaking to Simon.

A week later I had my two-hour session with Simon. I could see quickly that he and James had very different cultures, with very differing ideas of what a good leader was. Although many of their overall values were shared, some were significantly at odds. Simon was not drawn to the charismatic transactional leadership style but favoured a quieter servant leader model in which he remained in the background and supported his staff to be in the limelight. James' use of the superhero narrative, instead of inspiring Simon had alienated him. However, he was very aware of the skills and knowledge that James had and wanted to learn from him, but not in a way where he was just expected to agree with everything James said. He was able to share how James could help him in some practical ways, which would mean James and he working more closely and effectively together.

The mediation day was planned for the following week, but two days before I was contacted by James to say it needed to be rescheduled because of an urgent business meeting involving Simon. He then asked if he could use the time set aside to speak with me again.

In that second individual session James expressed how much he had taken from the first session, realising that he and Simon were 'basically speaking different languages'. He had subsequently put time into thinking how to reframe his own language to fit better with Simon's values. He and Simon had met up during the week and Simon had expressed his admiration for James and how he felt James could help him develop. This was a revelation to James who had felt that Simon just saw him as 'an interfering, arrogant bastard' who he didn't want anything to do with. To hear that Simon wanted to spend more time with him allowed him to drop the all-knowing superman cape, and for the two of them to relate to each other person to person. This had led to a complete change in how they were able to relate to one another and for them to agree that they did not need a further mediated joint session but would schedule regular meetings with each other where they could have an honest and respectful dialogue.

Most pre-mediation sessions do not result in the parties sorting things out for themselves before the mediation day but can be an extremely important factor in the success of the mediation. Some time ago, I was asked to mediate between Maria, a headteacher, and Farah, a learning support assistant (LSA) in an urban primary school. The dispute touched on cultural issues of race, class, and power.

Maria, the headteacher was a white woman who would commonly be perceived as a white, educated, middle class, and confident woman. She had worked for five years as a teacher before becoming a headteacher four years ago. Her first years as a head in a more suburban and predominantly white school were deemed a great success. Two years ago, she moved to her current bigger school, in a more diverse community with many Muslim families. Her Board of Governors had asked her to go into mediation with Farah who had worked in the school for five years, and who was currently on sick leave due to stress, which she claimed was due to her treatment at the hands of the headteacher.

In the pre-mediation meeting with Maria it became clear that she was very reluctant to go to mediation, believing that the staff member was not ill but just 'lazy, insubordinate, and difficult' and had chosen to stay away from work because the two of them had been involved in a major disagreement during which the LSA had criticised the Maria's management style, general attitude, and health and safety policy.

Maria had been shocked to receive Farah's criticism as she had not experienced any difficulties in her previous school and believed that all her staff should do what she instructed them to do without question. When joining her current school, Maria had been surprised to find that there was a very active union membership amongst her staff and she had already had some difficult meetings with them about several issues. She felt very let down by her governors who she believed had not backed her but instead had pushed her to mediate. She was feeling isolated, unsupported and very angry. She understood that Farah was planning to bring a trade union official with her to the mediation day, and although she did not object to this, it added to her feelings of abandonment. She saw the mediation as a way of 'proving I am right'.

Maria also shared with me that she was concerned that she may be branded a racist, or a person who was using her power and privilege against the LSA, who was a Muslim woman, whereas she was a white, middle-class woman with several qualifications to her name. She was keen to explain that she did not come from a privileged background, but had grown up on a council estate, and been the only member of her family to attend university. She described her struggle to finance her studies, working throughout her course in the local library. She showed insight into how she may be seen by others, and expressed how she had adopted what Sartre would term a 'false self', that is, learning to speak and dress differently to fit in with others holding similar positions of status to her own. She was proud of how hard she had worked and how much she had achieved and was terrified that this may all be taken from her if the mediation 'found her at fault in any way'. I explained that my role was not to judge anyone but to look forward not backward, with the hope of both parties finding a way forward which worked for them both.

Meeting With the Second Party to the Dispute

Farah was reluctant to meet me face to face and so the pre-mediation session was by phone from her home. In the session she explained that she was very afraid of Maria who she believed to be a bully. Farah had been signed off work by her doctor having experienced a panic attack on her way home after a confrontation with Maria. The focus of their disagreement was on health and safety procedures.

Farah explained how she had been instructed to take a class of thirty children to a swimming lesson. The fifteen minute walk to the pool meant crossing several main roads. When she heard that the two other staff members who were due to be doing this with her were off sick, she considered it unsafe to take such a large group on her own and refused to do so. She told me that when she had expressed her concerns to Maria she had been shouted at, and told she must do what she was told and take the group to their swimming lesson. As she described this encounter, I noticed a change in her breathing, and I recognised that she was about to have a panic attack. I talked her through her breathing and managed to prevent her experiencing a full attack. In her upset state, she said she did not wish to proceed with the mediation, as she feared that she may experience an attack on the day and be unable to cope. I explained that she could go through the same breathing and calming exercises that we had just done together. We then discussed whether it may be good for the headteacher to see and understand the level of stress she was experiencing. With this understanding she agreed to attend a day of mediation.

At no point in this pre-mediation phase did Farah make any mention of there being a perceived racial element to the conflict. I did ask how she felt about me as the mediator, being a white woman like Maria. Farah did not see this as a problem and volunteered that she had never thought of Maria as racist as she 'had seen her treat other *white* LSAs with the same disdain'. She did, however, feel that Maria was 'arrogant, didn't listen and tried to put everyone down, especially those she saw as being of a lower class and less educated than herself.' She had heard from other members of staff that Maria believed that she was faking illness and was very upset by this as honesty and truthfulness were important values for her.

In the pre-mediation meetings with both parties, I learnt a lot about the ways each party saw the world and what was important to them, particularly regarding their self-concept and the values which informed that. Most non-psychologically informed mediators would not have unearthed such rich and useful material, as they would have focused on gaining agreement from both parties to the material requirements to set up the mediation day. These aspects were discussed and agreed but were not the focus of the discussions.

When listening to each party it is hard for a mediator not to be drawn into each narrative, and we may be more drawn to one character than the other. A mediator must work hard to recognise and then put to one side (bracket) any such feelings or any assumptions as to who the 'injured party' is. In most mediations all parties are suffering.

This case did proceed to the mediation day, where Farah did indeed suffer a panic attack in front of Maria. On seeing this Maria changed her stance, realising that Farah was genuinely stressed and unable to work and a programme of phased return was agreed.

The Mediation Day

Throughout the mediation a mediator needs to be both a follower and a leader. In the early stages the mediator is the leader, giving clear information about how the day will proceed, and what can be expected. In the latter private sessions, the mediator follows, slowly unwrapping the meaning of what is being presented.

The Opening Joint Session

The mediation day starts with all parties being invited into the same room. The mediator must give thought to the sitting of everyone in the room, taking any cultural needs and other sensitivities into consideration. It is possible that in some mediations the parties may find it impossible to start in the same room and the mediator needs to respect this.

The mediator reminds everyone of the process of mediation which will include private individual sessions and joint sessions, as well as some essential points which will already have been covered in the pre-mediation contract and sessions. This includes explaining the facilitative nature of the role of the mediator, who is there as a neutral third party who will remain nonjudgemental; that the process is confidential (apart from the usual limitations regarding potential harm to self or others, child abuse or exploitation, proceeds of crime, etc.), and that the content of the mediation is without prejudice and so cannot be referred to in court or other litigation. The mediator will also make a final check that those in the room have authority to sign off any agreement. Even though the participants will have heard this before it gives people a chance to settle and direct their attention to the mediator instead of to the 'enemy' whose presence they may well have avoided for some time prior to the mediation.

The mediator will then invite each party to make a brief statement explaining their position. The mediator listens without comment. To get into any discussion at this stage, with everyone present, runs the risk of a participant analysing the mediator's comments looking for bias towards one side or the other.

Individual Sessions

The mediator will then invite the parties to retire to their individual rooms, letting them know who they will speak to first. This is obviously very sensitive, and it is important the mediator stresses that there is no advantage to going first or last. The mediator will explain that they will offer everyone an equal opportunity to speak with them, but as some people speak more slowly than others this may not amount to the same amount of time.

The mediation then moves on to individual sessions, which take place in the rooms allocated to the different parties with the mediator moving between them. There may be cultural requirements which challenge the mediator, for example a female participant may not be comfortable with sitting alone in a closed room with a male mediator. A request to keep the door open slightly may challenge the mediator's usual way of ensuring confidentiality and so the mediator must discuss this with the party and agree a way of addressing this.

At the start of each of these private sessions the mediator will remind the parties that everything remains confidential, unless they give the mediator specific permission to take something across to the other side. In these early meetings, the mediator remains open to listening to everything the party wishes to tell them, even if it does not seem directly relevant to the dispute. If one listens well, it is likely that there will be themes running throughout even a disjointed narrative which will indicate what is important to the person. This intense active listening enables the party to experience being fully heard without any initial judgement or censorship being imposed. This allows the mediator to build a rich picture of each person's worldview, values, beliefs, hopes, and coping strategies by following where the party leads, trying not to interrupt unless for clarification, and reflecting back what they believe they have heard so that the party can either agree that they are understanding them, or put right any misunderstandings. As the party realises it is safe to speak openly to the mediator, trust will be developed, allowing the mediator to move on to the next stage.

What happens within each of the private sessions could be seen as being divided into two main non-linear and non-chronological components, consisting of 'tuning in' and 'tuning out'. The 'tuning in' process (through active listening) is the central element in building a trusting working alliance between the mediator and all parties. This is the core aim of the early part of the process. It is achieved by entering uncritically into the party's worldview, and so understanding something of their value sets, coping strategies, and emotional reactions. At this stage the mediator does not try to control or influence the direction or content of the narrative.

Once a trusting working alliance is established between the party and the mediator, and the mediator has developed a 'good enough' understanding of the other's worldview, then the mediator can move to the 'tuning out' phase. This does not mean that they stop listening but that they begin to tune out of the wider aspects of the party's existence and focus more on the world of the dispute, beginning to explore how what they have learnt relates to the person's perceptions and understanding of the conflict and their hopes for what needs to be included in the settlement.

The mediator repeats the same process with all parties. This may take many private individual sessions.

Joint Session

The mediator will only invite the parties to enter a joint session when there is a reason to do so. This usually happens when the mediator notices a shift of perception and identifies potential areas of commonality, often concerned with shared values and hopes. This commonality allows the parties to stop seeing each other as aliens, moving to a position of shared humanity if not of agreement. This move allows the mediator to explore solutions for a potential agreement which is 'good enough' for both parties.

Flexibility

The above is a framework for a mediation but unfortunately every mediation is different, and the mediation process is neither chronological nor linear. The trusting working alliance may be built and lost several times throughout the process. When this happens, the mediator needs to acknowledge that trust has been damaged or lost and turn their attention back to rebuilding it rather than trying to rush ahead. This can mean that some mediations never have individual sessions, whilst others never come together for a joint session.

The Skills Needed in a Psychologically Informed Mediation

Tuning In

I have already mentioned that the process can be divided into two processes – 'tuning in' and 'tuning out'. Both call on slightly different skill sets, although the core skill is listening.

Listening

In 'tuning in' the emphasis lies in consciously listening for descriptors of the inner world of each party, showing their emotions, values, beliefs, and coping and behaviour patterns. It is important to take everything which is said as being of equal importance and significance in line with the already mentioned Husserl's rule of horizontalisation. Husserl considered intuition to be the most reliable source of evidence as it is permanently engaged with reality. This echoes Heraclitus' statement that every 'unapparent' connection is stronger than an 'apparent' one. Although we may not immediately see the relevance of what is said it is important not to dismiss it as irrelevant or disconnected. This openness to all that is said was used by Freud and other psychoanalysts who taught us to accept that all that is presented contains unconscious communications as well as conscious ones. Although the mediator is not a therapist, and is not digging for emotions or unconscious communications, they do need to remain alert to the possibility that everything which is said will carry information about the person's worldview, and therefore will help the mediator to connect with the party and understand what is most important to them.

The party may find it hard to tell the mediator things which make them feel vulnerable, stupid, or guilty, or where they feel the mediator may disagree with them. They may find it difficult to admit and to describe how they experience paradoxical responses to the dispute and/or the people involved. Such communication may be given subtly rather than in overt statements. This reticence can be intensified when a party may feel there is a cultural chasm between themselves and the mediator. They may fear being misunderstood or even ridiculed.

The mediator is likely to pick up several themes. Each theme will have a level of relevance and so the mediator may decide to follow any theme, even if it seems very far removed from the actual dispute. The mediator will then go on to deconstruct or unpack it. At this stage, the mediator needs to work to control their own ego needs to find or offer a solution or to make 'inspirational' links. Instead, the mediator needs to continue in the role of follower, slowly unwrapping the meaning of what is being presented by paraphrasing, reflecting back, and summarising what is heard, without any judgement. This intense listening is a lot harder than we may think.

There are a few simple skills which can help to improve the quality of listening of the mediator. Some of these are particularly culturally challenging. To 'listen' effectively we need to take note not just of what is said, but also what is felt, and seen. The mediator needs to be sensitive to body language. There are lots of books and articles which offer stereotypical ways of reading body language, unfortunately many give very monocultural interpretations – folded arms mean someone is being defensive etc. If we are employing a psychological and culturally sensitive approach, we will not make assumptions about what is being expressed, but instead will choose to note and explore non-verbal communications if the culture of the individual would welcome such exploration.

The use of silence is another important tool. It may be hard not to interrupt, try to call a party back to the 'issue', or make suggestions. These interruptions may mean we shut down something important that the party was going to tell the mediator or rob the parties of essential reflective time. It is important to remember that different cultures have different reactions to silence, some being very comfortable with it, whilst others find it oppressive. There is not a simple East-West spilt here. In some Western cultures such as the United States silence can generally be experienced as awkward and uncomfortable and in professional settings silence may be interpreted as showing ignorance, not knowing what to say, failing to have a ready answer, or showing a lack in interest or engagement. In other parts of the Western world, it is seen as a natural part of communication, an indicator of thoughtfulness and a willingness to thoroughly engage and reflect, flowing from a respect for what the other person has said. In Japan silence is highly valued and deemed to be a way of showing respect and politeness and used as a tool to avoid expressed conflict, whereas in China a silence may be used to indicate a disagreement and be used strategically. In countries where overt emotional expression is valued, such as in many Mediterranean cultures, silence in conversation is unusual, uncomfortable, and confusing. Many African and indigenous cultures experience silence as a show of wisdom, contemplation, and self-control. The mediator needs to show an understanding of these cultural nuances regarding silence. This understanding cannot come from reading lots of texts but must flow from the connection they develop with each party, allowing the mediator to give an intuitive but informed response stemming from their lived experience of being with and listening to that person.

The art of questioning is another area which needs careful consideration. It is generally considered that if we are to get the best and fullest information from a person, we should use open not closed questions. If we ask closed questions, that is those which can be answered either yes or no, we usually get short answers which are unlikely to improve our understanding very much. If we phrase our enquiries not as questions, but as invitations, inviting a person to tell us more about something, we are more likely to elicit greater information and build deeper rapport. Having said that, there are people who welcome very short, direct, closed questions and feel unsafe and confused when approached in a more invitational way. A sensitive mediator will quickly pick up and respect any such discomfort.

During this part of the mediation, once the trust has been built, the mediator will feedback any contradictions they hear between values and actions, between body language and verbal content, or any other shifts in approach or outlook. They will explore the assumptions which are being expressed and their emotional context, whilst working to set aside (bracket) their own assumptions or judgmental thoughts.

The mediator will try to identify any coping strategies which a person uses. People are often afraid of experiencing powerful emotions, being confronted by different ways of thinking, or being challenged and so will develop coping strategies in response to life's challenges. We often develop such strategies early in life and continue to use them as an automatic or default response even when they are no longer serving us. In mediation, a person can identify and develop different ways of coping without losing self-esteem by acknowledging that they have agency and are in charge of their own behaviours, meaning that they can choose to abandon them if they have ceased to be suitable for purpose and may in fact, in some incidences, be working against them.

Once the mediator has clarified a party's worldview and priorities and so feels they have a good sense of everyone in the mediation and what is important to them, they can move on to the 'tuning out' stage.

Tuning Out

From focusing on understanding each party, the mediator then moves on to focus on how what they have learnt impacts on the dispute, and the mediator begins to facilitate each party's increased understanding and sensitivity to the perceptions of the other. The aim is to enable them to start to engage, preferably together, with all possible solutions which could lead to a settlement which is acceptable to everyone.

The mediator shifts from tuning in to the individual worldviews and draws on the trust which has been created, to challenge assumptions, ambivalences, and ambiguities. They will remind the parties of what time is left within the mediation and may choose to invite the parties to consider the implications, psychologically, emotionally, and financially of settling, or not settling in the mediation.

Joint Session

Once there has been some movement in the parties' understanding and perceptions, the mediator can invite the parties to come together and begin to draw up a settlement.

When parties start discussing what they can each agree to being in a written agreement, the disagreement may reappear, and the mediator must work with this and not try to brush it aside. The mediator must ensure that what is agreed is workable and will write up the agreement and sign as a witness to the signatures of all parties.

The above simply takes you through the process but mediations do vary. In some the parties never come together, in others they remain together throughout. Not all mediations require signed written agreements and in workplace mediations the agreement can to be in the form of an ABC: Acceptable Behaviour Contract.

In this section of the book, I have aimed to introduce the psychological approach to mediation which I believe is more culturally sensitive than other models. In Part Three I shall focus more on what I understand by culture and what this means for the practice of mediation as the practice develops and grows.

Part Three

Bringing Together Thoughts on Culture and Mediation, Exploring the Issues for Mediators and the Need for Change

Chapter 10

What is 'Culture'

Introduction

In the first two parts of this book, I have focused on introducing readers to different kinds of mediation, with a focus on using a psychologically informed approach which I consider the most suitable of all the models in working with cultural difference.

In this section I aim to explore what we mean by culture and how this needs to be acknowledged and worked with in mediation. In this I include the cultural history of mediation, the current cultural responses to mediation, the skills and consideration for practicing mediators, but also the implications for the profession of mediation itself, with the need to explore cultural issues further, and to develop future training, and cultural competency requirements for current and future mediators.

I shall start by looking at what people are meaning when they allude to 'culture'.

Culture is a notoriously hard term to define, with some writers differentiating between what they term 'real' culture and 'ideal' culture. The term 'ideal' culture refers to the cultural guidelines which are publicly embraced and aspired to by society, whilst 'actual' culture refers to the behaviours, norms, values, and beliefs we see evidenced in people's ways of being. Often there is conflict between the two.

The anthropologist Kuper (1999:245) warned that, 'to understand culture, we must first deconstruct it. Religious beliefs, rituals, knowledge, moral values, the arts, rhetorical genres, and so on should be separated out from each other rather than bound together into a single bundle labelled culture, or collective consciousness, or superstructure, or discourse. Separating these elements, one is led on to explore the changing configurations in which language, knowledge, techniques, political ideologies, rituals, commodities, and so on are related to each other.' So, Kuper concluded that we all have multiple identities and even if we choose to identify ourselves through a primary identity, we may not conform to it, and that it is not necessarily constant. This fits well with my own view on culture. He believed that culture theory may draw attention away from what we have in common instead of encouraging us to communicate across ethnic, national, and religious boundaries. Finding the balance between a respectful and informed understanding for cultural heritage and identification whilst working with human commonalities is a challenge for us all.

DOI: 10.4324/9781003528890-13

Despite the fluidity of views like Kuper's, others have sought to compile lists of definitions. Kroeber and Kluckman (1952) listed 52 definitions, but these failed to result in a universally agreed definition of culture. Definitions depend on the context and discipline from which they originate. The disciplines which have given most time to the consideration of culture include anthropology, sociology, psychology, and the field of communication studies.

It is not unusual for people to confuse identity and culture. Hofstede (2001) differentiates between the two describing that people's identities flow from the answer to the question: where do I belong? 'They are based on mutual images and stereotypes and on emotions linked to the outer layers of the onion, but not to values' (2001:1).

However, most definitions of culture do include shared beliefs and values, language, ideas, customs, symbols, and accepted norms as evidenced in social behaviours, institutions, laws, and art. As early as 1871 Edward Taylor, often referred to as the father of cultural anthropology, offered a definition of culture which provided the foundation for subsequent sociological and anthropological ideas about culture when he described culture as being that complex whole which includes knowledge, belief, art, morals, law, custom, and any other capabilities, and habits acquired by man as a member of society. Cultural anthropologists take a holistic approach considering the full range of human experience and interconnectedness, whilst focusing on cultural variation among humans, and ways in which culture impacts on how individuals understand and interact with the world. Anthropologists will often seek to learn about and understand culture by living among the people whose culture they are studying and by looking to compare cultures seeking to identify universal patterns and cultural diversity.

The anthropologist Clifford Geertz (1973) reminds us that we are faced with enormous variations of human behaviour, even within identifiable cultural groups. He suggested that culture is best not seen as 'complexes of concrete behaviour patterns' but as a set of 'control mechanisms – plans, rules, instructions – for the governing of behaviour'. To step outside those rules risks cultural rejection and abandonment and therefore has strong pulls on the way we behave and interact with others. Geertz states (1973:44), 'Our ideas, our values, our acts, even our emotions, are like our nervous systems itself, cultural products – products manufactured, indeed, out of tendencies, capacities, and dispositions with which we are born, but manufactured nonetheless.' This calls for those working interpersonally to address emotions and values, which I have stressed is an important part of developing an understanding of a person's worldview. Indeed, Geertz specifically uses the term 'worldview' in his definition of culture, a concept which is so important in an existential/phenomenological exploratory approach. He writes, 'The moral aspects of a given culture, the evaluative elements, have commonly been summed up in the term "ethos," while the cognitive, existential aspects have been designated by the term "world view." A people's ethos is the tone, character, and quality of their life, its moral and aesthetic style and mood; it is the underlying attitude toward themselves and their world that life reflects. Their world view is their picture of the way things in sheer actuality are, their concept of nature, of self, of society. It contains their most comprehensive ideas of order' (1973:126).

Perhaps one of the most comprehensive views of culture as worldview is offered by Mark Davidheiser, Chair of the multi-institutional Africa Peace and Conflict Network, who specifically addressed its relevance in mediation, writing, '"Culture" is often glossed as the values, norms, and habituated patterns of behavior shared among members of a given social group. There is a widespread tendency in conflict resolution and other fields to equate culture with national, racial, and ethnic identities.' He believes this conventional approach 'fails to capture its significance or profound impact on conflict styles. Cultural orientations impact more than communication styles or goal hierarchies. Sociocultural influences extend to the deepest level, fundamentally influencing cognition and behavior by shaping one's view of life and how one perceives, interprets, and responds to particular events and phenomena. Due to the complexity of these influences, the term "worldview" may be preferable to "culture," since the former is less suggestive of a single, homogenous cognitive–interpretive mazeway shared among all members of a given group' (2008:72).

We exist not only within the sphere of our own existence but also within that of the communities and organisations in which we find ourselves through birth or choice. Arnold (1993:41) draws attention to the need to consider individual and collective cultural meanings ascribed to behaviours and experiences, speaking of a 'particular way of life which expresses certain meanings and values not only in art and learning but also in institutions and ordinary behavior. The analysis of culture, from such a definition, is the clarification of the meanings and values implicit and explicit in a particular way of life, a particular culture.'

The binary nature of attributing cultural identity is questioned by anthropologists such as Avruch (2004) who draws our attention to the multiplicity of cultures to which an individual belongs, stating 'that culture is a quality of social groups and perhaps communities, and that members may belong to multiple such groups. Therefore, an individual may "carry" several cultures, for example, ethnic or national, religious, and occupational affiliations' (2004:393). This point is emphasised by Savage (1997:273) who suggests, 'it is of limited helpfulness to conflate "culture" with "ethnicity" because that ignores the impact of other sources of diversity which contribute to cultural identity and perpetuates false dichotomies.' This view is further reinforced by Gold (2005) who considers culture to be learned, not inherited, but reinforced by interactions within the family, friendship and peer groups, faith communities, the media, and a variety of other sources. He does not consider culture to be static, seeing it changing as we experience the world, because 'by observing the behavior of others around us we learn about details such as the use of eye contact, the uses of space and silence and the treatment of children and elders' (2005:298).

When sociologists look at culture, they are working from a rich and nuanced approach to understanding society through highlighting the complex interplay between societal structures and emerging cultural elements. They are concerned with tensions between material (physical objects, resources, and spaces) and non-material culture (practices, beliefs, values, norms, aesthetics, etc.). They seek to identify elements which are common to all cultures, yet which manifest differently in diverse cultures, and are interested in cultures developed within subcultures, where groups share a specific identity apart from the majority, and countercultures which reject and oppose significant elements of the majority culture. How cultures are expressed, including the use of myths and metaphors, is another area of interest and one which a mediator needs to be aware of, paying attention to the use of symbolic language by participants in a mediation. Geertz, who I mentioned earlier, was a leading symbolic anthropologist (1973:89) and as such described culture as a 'system of inherited conceptions expressed in symbolic forms by which men communicate, perpetuate, and develop their knowledge about, and attitudes toward life.' whilst Pierre Bourdieu (1972) introduced the concepts of 'habitus' and 'cultural capital' and focused his interest on those habits acquired through socialisation. It is through cultural capital (i.e. the perceived non-financial social assets of a person such as education, speech, intellect, style of dress) that social mobility is enabled in a layered society.

Psychologists also share an interest in the symbols and meanings which are created through social interaction and psychological processes, with cultural psychologists differing from many more general psychologists who tend to assume that their findings are universal, as cultural psychologists, not surprisingly, consider their findings to be culturally variable. Ci-Yue Chui, a social psychologist at the University of Illinois described people as active cultural agents, rather than passive recipients of cultural influences, offering a more dynamic model of culture than some others.

In Communication Theory, Geert Hofstede (1991:5) is known for his work in cross-cultural communication, defining culture as 'the collective programming of the mind that distinguishes the members of one group or category of people from others.' He emphasises the belief that culture shapes how people feel, think, and act. He developed a Cultural Dimensions Theory to be used as a framework for understanding cultural differences across countries and examining their impact on contextual behaviour and how people from different cultures approach conflict resolution and mediation. In the table below I have shown what I believe to be the links between Hofstede's theory and existential themes, and its overall relevance to mediation practice.

Hofstede believed that culture is more often a source of conflict, than of synergy, and saw cultural differences as often a nuisance at best and quite often a disaster. I would not see culture in that negative way, as it may seem to imply that in order to resolve conflict, or indeed do the impossible and eliminate conflict, we would need to deny our complex individual culture and behave inauthentically. However, I do embrace his thought that the ways in which conflicts are resolved, and harmony restored, are influenced by the same values that determine the way in which power is distributed, goals pursued, uncertainty tolerated, time perceived, and life enjoyed. This touches on some of the key existential themes, such as uncertainty, freedom and responsibility, time and temporality, and meaningfulness which I have shown earlier are always part of a conflict dialogue and which psychologically trained mediators will tune in to.

Some theories of culture consider that there needs to be an element of legacy, with cultural elements passed down from generation to generation. This would

Table 10.1 The Relevance of Hofstede's Framework to Mediation and the Psychological Approach

Hofstede cultural dimensions	Relevance to mediation	Link to psychological and existential themes
PDI Power Distance Index Concerned with the extent to which the least powerful members of society able to accept the power imbalance	High PDI cultures might prefer hierarchical approaches to mediation, where a respected authority figure plays a key role in resolving disputes. Low PDI cultures are more likely to favour egalitarian mediation approaches, where all parties have an equal voice.	Freedom and Responsibility
IDV Individualism vs. Collectivism Concerned with the degree to which individuals are integrated into groups	Individualistic cultures may prefer mediation that emphasises individual rights and personal interests. Collectivist cultures might focus on group harmony and community well-being in mediation processes, often valuing consensus over individual preferences.	Authenticity Relatedness Identity
MAS Masculinity vs. Femininity Concerned with the accepted interpretation distribution of emotional and value role differences between the genders	Masculine cultures might approach mediation with a competitive mindset, aiming for clear winners and losers. Feminine cultures are likely to seek solutions that ensure mutual satisfaction and maintain relationships, emphasising collaboration and compromise.	Authenticity Identity
UAI Uncertainty Avoidance Index Concerned with societal tolerance of uncertainty and ambiguity	High UAI cultures and individuals might prefer structured and formal mediation processes, with clear rules and procedures to reduce uncertainty. Low UAI cultures may be more open to flexible and informal mediation approaches.	Uncertainty

(Continued)

98 Exploring the Role of Culture in Mediation

Table 10.1 (Continued)

Hofstede cultural dimensions	Relevance to mediation	Link to psychological and existential themes
LTO Long-Term Orientation vs. Short-Term Normative Orientation Concerned with the focus on future rewards or short-term benefits	Long-term oriented cultures might focus on mediation outcomes that ensure long-term harmony and future benefits. Short-term oriented cultures may prioritise quick and immediate solutions to conflicts.	Time and Temporality
IVR Indulgence vs. Restraint Concerned with the degree of focus on and freedom to fulfil human desires	Indulgent cultures might favour mediation strategies that allow for open expression and consideration of individual desires. Restrained cultures might approach mediation with a more reserved and controlled manner, emphasising duty and adherence to social norms.	Freedom and Responsibility Authenticity

seem to set aside the possibility of new cultures emerging as new groupings of people establish themselves, thus begging the question as to whether new sub-groupings of society have a distinct 'culture' which separates them from other groups. It could be said that cults have their own culture and even small informal social groups such as those formed primarily around artistic preferences flowing from music and fashion, such as punks, mods, rockers, emos, rappers, etc. could be said to develop a distinct shared culture. The idea that culture does not need a long history to embed itself, fits with Scott's (2014) definition in which he offers a wider view of culture, describing it as all that in human society is socially rather than biologically transmitted. Our understanding of culture and our attempts to define it will continue to develop. As globalisation and access to more information through electronic means continues to grow, it could be argued that culture becomes less bound to a geographical area, race, or religion. This may also mean that culture takes on a more time-limited and fluid nature rather than hereditary and long standing as humans begin to move more fluidly between groups. We can see aspects of this, particularly in pop culture, whilst at the same time, particularly in the political arena, we see groups with very little in common forming together to oppose other groups.

People with identifiers which they consider they have in common are now more likely not just to form a group, but to develop it and identify it as a culture and to use the collective power that brings. One example of this can be seen in the increased visibility of people with disabilities, or as some would prefer it termed, those who are differently abled. Davis (1995) pointed out that, 'People with disabilities, Deaf people, and others who might not even consider themselves as having a disability have been relegated to the margins by the very people who have celebrated and championed the emergence of multiculturalism, class consciousness, feminism and queer studies, from the margins' (xi). Members of this group, who have many individual differences and worldviews, through becoming an identifiable group (with many subgroups within it) have gained visibility and strength. With the Paralympics in both London 2012 and Paris 2024 drawing huge crowds and television audiences the public had more exposure to this group of people, to their achievements and their challenges. Despite a growing awareness of Disability Culture, and the celebration of achievements at events like the Paralympics and the Invictus Games, there is still a long way to go. Even as I write, I am reading of Baroness Tanni Grey-Thompson, an 11-time Paralympic gold medallist, having to crawl off a train in London, when after 25 minutes no assistance was given to enable her to disembark.

However, we have seen some positive shifts in how those with disability are portrayed. We see more use of actors with disabilities in film and TV and in marketing campaigns. Fashion is playing more attention to the physical needs of people who do not fit the stereotypical fashion model looks, we are beginning to see people who use wheelchairs or walking sticks on the catwalk, companies such as Able2Wear, or Dressability focus exclusively on clothing for people who find much of the available clothing difficult to get on or take off. Most high-level designers are also considering the needs of this group, with Christina Mallon, the Chief Brand Officer at Open Style Lab stating, 'Fashion is giving people a warped view of what the world looks like...Fashion and beauty and the runway create culture, and we need to create a culture that is truly inclusive' (Vogue 27th August 2021). Some equipment needed to help with specific disabilities is no longer produced only as merely functional and often ugly items but is becoming stylish. We can now access specially designed attractive transport such as the Wizzybug for kids with limited or no mobility. More attention is being given to the creation of prosthetics which look more like pieces of sculpture produced by companies such as Limb-art and Creative Boom. These limbs are not trying to mimic flesh but to celebrate the uniqueness of the individual. We can see this approach celebrated in the art of the artist and sculptor, Sophie de Oliveira Barata, who started the Alternative Limb Project in 2011 and whose aim is for amputees to embrace their difference and send out a message without speaking, to say how they feel about their bodies.

Some people within the community of those with disability are more interested in taking a political approach to disability culture. Brown (2002:34–50) writes of the difficulty of defining disability culture (a challenge shared with all attempts to define cultures), pointing out that the words, '"disability" and "culture" are each value-laden, charged with emotion in every culture I have encountered'. In 1994, he contributed to the Final report, entitled 'Investigating a Culture of Disability', which researched disability culture, 'The existence of a disability culture is a relatively new and contested idea. Not surprising, perhaps, for a group that has long been described with terms like "in-valid," "impaired," "limited," "crippled," and so forth.'

We can begin to see change, with Ben Ngubane, the South African Minister of Arts, Culture, Science and Technology at the Celebration of Disability, 25th November 2000, in Durban, offering an optimistic view on the development of disability culture, 'The struggle for inclusion is going to be a long one as the evolution of "disability culture" is still in an infant stage in our country. A key function of "disability culture" is the celebration of the uniqueness of disability. It is my belief however that it will blossom as people with disabilities increasingly identify with each other and begin to express themselves more artistically and participate in the cultural life of society as a whole.' By identifying as a visible culture, a stronger, empowered individual and collective identity is created, which may be used to counterbalance differing views in society. Belonging to a cultural group is about visibility and self-value, it provides a platform to challenge myths and misperceptions and to lobby for what is needed.

One group who have taken a particular stance on cultural identity are members of the Deaf Community, within which cultural differences, values, and beliefs can easily be seen. The terms 'Cultural model of Deafness' and 'Deaf Culture' have been embraced by those people within the community who wish to give prominence to the use of sign language as opposed to anything which they perceive as a wish to be other than deaf/part of the majority, such as the use of lip reading, hearing aids, cochlear implants, etc. The most radical members might even refer to these as a betrayal of their cultural identity, rejecting the medical definition of deafness as either a loss or an impairment. Instead, they see themselves as a community and a culture and campaign for those using British Sign Language to be recognised as such with its own language. Indeed, writers such as Paddy Ladd, refer to the Deaf Liberation Struggle. He invites us to look beyond the medicalisation of deafness and invites us to look at the arts and cultural expression of not a 'sad' community, lonely and isolated but instead to recognise what he terms as 'Deaf Resurgence', a group who have 'found the psychocultural space to begin to ask what a Deaf person could, and a Deaf community become?' (2003:3), answering his own question with the vision of a community portraying a clear sense of ingenuity, determination, and humour by which they struggle to resist oppression. As with all communities, some deaf people are drawn to the idea of a deaf culture, rejecting 'oralism' whilst others will seek to be more integrated within the hearing community and associated culture. I have a cousin who has been deaf since the age of two, and many years ago, when I was about ten years old, I was a bridesmaid at her wedding which was conducted entirely in British Sign Language. I remember my own feeling of isolation and disability as I couldn't understand the ceremony or share jokes with her lively group of attractive friends who only communicated through sign language. It was clear that they had their own culture, and I was not part of it.

Those with disabilities or those who chose to live in non-normative social and cultural groups, also inhabit more dimensions where these are not their immediate identifiers. We belong to several cultural groups, many of them are through personal choice and present a way in which we can be seen and categorised by self and others. Other culturally influential groups we may belong to give a less personal picture of who we are. These are mainly institutional or organisational cultures such as our work context. People will assume, often wrongly, a lot about us purely through knowing our profession or the name of the company we work for. When we join a company there will be a company culture whether this is made explicit through mission statements, posters of company values and aspirations posted on walls, or may be more subtle and only discovered over time. I have referred to these organisational cultural aspects in describing the Hofstede framework earlier, but others have also sought to understand organisational cultures and I shall give an overview of some of the best known. All have many shared aspects and some differences.

Schein (2017) developed a model to illustrate the three levels at which we find organisational culture. He termed these Artifacts, Espoused Values, and Basic Underlying Assumptions. Included in Artifacts are those signifiers which are visible and tangible, such as dress codes (whether laid down as rules or developed apparently informally over time), the office layout, rituals, and symbols. He suggests that although these are the most accessible, they can be difficult to interpret. Espoused Values include those beliefs, values, and norms which an organisation claims to follow, and which may be made public on websites, mission statements, codes of conduct, or listings of corporate values. The third category includes the unconscious, taken-for-granted beliefs that truly drive the organisation and which are deeply ingrained and hard to shift. Schein emphasises the need to look below the surface-level artifacts and seek to uncover the deeper underlying cultural assumptions.

Schneider (1993) offered a model made up of three processes, Attraction, Selection, and Attrition, which suggests that people within organisations reinforce its culture, so as to create a homogenous environment. He saw individuals as being attracted to organisations that they perceived as having similar values to their own, with organisations seeking to select individuals who were aligned with their values and cultures. This reduces the likelihood of challenge. The majority of those who did not fit within the organisational culture were more likely to leave than attempt to change it. Some of my own strongest internal conflicts have come when I have joined an organisation because of their values and found that with a change of leadership or economic necessity those values changed. Sitting in a meeting where someone is saying 'we believe...' when one knows their statement goes against your own values is deeply disturbing, or at least I have found it so.

Cameron and Quinn (2021) developed a two-dimension model known as the Competing Values Framework which posed two questions about the organisation's culture. Firstly, does the organisation prioritise adaptability or consistency, and secondly, is the focus on internal development or external relationships. From this they identified four cultural types, Clan Culture, Adhocracy Culture, Market Culture, and Hierarchy Culture. In the first, the organisation has a family-like atmosphere prioritising mentoring and teamwork. An adhocracy cure is innovative and entrepreneurial favouring flexibility and risk-taking. Market Culture values competition and is results driven, with focus on external achievement. Within Hierarchy Culture we see a more structured and formal environment with the emphasis on efficiency and stability.

Deal and Kennedy (2000) also present a two dimensions model, based on the nature of work undertaken by an organisation. It consists of Feedback/Rewards Systems and Risk Orientation from which they identify four types of organisational culture. The first is Work Hard, Play Hard which is used to describe organisations in which feedback is rapid and low risk. This is followed by Tough-Guy, Macho Culture, which also has fast feedback but is high risk. Slow feedback and low risk are termed Process and Culture, and the final type is Bet-the-Company Culture which has slow feedback and high risk.

Johnson and Scholes (2001) offer us a 'Cultural Web' view which identifies six interconnected elements of an organisation's culture: Stories, Rituals and Routines, Symbols, Organisational Structure, Control Systems, and Power Structures, which shape the dominant paradigm of the organisation. The Stories refer to those narratives which are internally shared about company successes, failures, and people. The daily habits and procedures expected of those within the organisation make up the Rituals and Routines. Symbols include office design, dress codes, logos, and branding. When referring to the Organisation Structure Johnson and Scholes' focus is on the structural distribution of power and responsibilities, whilst the individual sources of power and influence are placed under the Power Structure heading. Finally, they use the term Control Systems to group all those ways in which performance is monitored and rewarded or punished.

Martin (1992) offered three perspectives on how organisational culture can be understood: Integration Perspective, Differentiation Perspective, and Fragmentation Perspective. In the first culture remains consistent with a unified and cohesive view of culture and values which are shared across the organisation. The second highlights the subcultures which exist within the organisation where different groups have shared values and goals which may differ from those of the organisation. Finally, the fragmentation view is that of an organisation whose culture is fluid and fragmented where ambiguity is prevalent, and which is lacking in a clear consensus.

Handy (1978) proposed four cultural categories of organisational culture. These were Power Culture, Role, Culture, Task Culture, and Person Culture. Where the focus is on power, we see centralised control with power residing in a small number of individuals and where decisions are made swiftly. In Role Culture he places bureaucratic organisations with clearly defined roles and authority based on structural hierarchical positioning. Task Culture is team-orientated and project driven with the focus on getting the job done. In Person Culture the organisation exists to serve the individuals within it.

Each of these models provides us with a different lens through which to consider an organisation's culture and its impact on behaviour.

Personally, as I believe will have been clear, I have difficulty in identifying with *one* culture and prefer to be seen as a unique collection of cultural influences. I was born with a disability which for most of my life I did not need to draw attention to and certainly did not wish to be identified by. As I have grown older and the disability has more impact on my life and what I can do, I am more willing to tell some people about it, so they are not left to imagine why I am tired, needing time alone, or not taking part in every social offering available. I need to ask myself whether that means I prefer to be identified as someone with a disability or someone who is anti-social or perhaps even worse – lazy!! It points to a dilemma for us all about the degree to which we seek individual or collective identities and the meaning we place on our choices.

Placing oneself in a cultural group gives a sense of belonging and community, whilst at the same time, potentially setting one aside from other cultural groups. Each of us will inherit many cultural influences which may seem to determine which cultural groups we have admittance to; the extent to which we identify with those cultures will be a personal and perhaps political choice.

In this very short section, I have tried to draw attention to the complexity of 'culture' and to the extent to which we embrace or reject cultural labels. We have seen how difficult it is to define culture. Before moving on to clarify how I am using the word in this book I looked for definitions which related specifically to conflict resolution work. LeBaron and Zumeta (2003:464) in exploring the connection between culture and disputes offered us an interesting definition, 'Culture is what everyone in a group knows that those outside the group do not know. Culture relates to symbolic aspects of our lives, those places where we are constantly making meaning and composing our identities. All of us have multicultural identities in the sense that we belong to various groups connected to generation, socioeconomic class, race, sexual orientation, ability and disability, political and religious affiliation, language, gender, and disciple at work.' He considers disputes to be cultural acts, as the ways in which we frame and respond to them are culturally determined. This should make the consideration of the role of culture and what constitutes culture competency a central concern to all mediators.

How I Am Using the Word 'Culture' in this Book

In this book I am taking all the definitions briefly outlined above and taking a very broad view of what I am referring to when I speak of 'culture'. Although much of

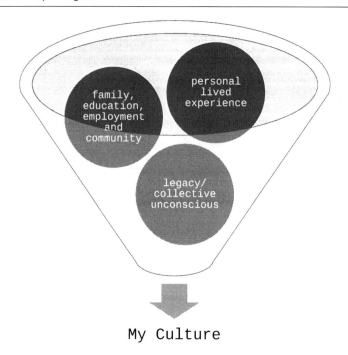

Figure 10.1 Aspects Making Up Our Individual Cultural Identity

our cultural identity is generational and richly influenced by our familial, community, educational, and other contexts, I believe we also develop a unique personal culture which is a synthesis of all of these, but also includes our own understanding of our racial, gender, sexual orientation, and class, and which has the capacity to be fluid, whilst always referencing 'where we came from'.

For each of us our primary cultural identifier will be different and may change at different times in our lives as we experience different contexts and communities. If I am considered to have achieved well and moved out of my family's social class, then class may be the most important aspect of my culture. However, as an outsider I cannot assume what that might mean for such a person. They may feel that they are now authentically in the 'right place/class' for them, they may feel that they have 'betrayed' their family history or 'escaped' it, or indeed may feel both of those things. For others, class may feel insignificant, and their gender may be the most important identifier for them. A person who feels that they have been born into the wrong gendered body may grow up in a struggle with the cultural expectations for that gender which may conflict with their own internal culture. Both these examples are ones in which the change is external and open to being seen by others. This is not always the case. People may feel that the physical characteristics of their racial heritage do not mirror their own self-concept. Here we enter the difficult area of misunderstanding of the term cultural appropriation. People may adopt cultural references from outside their own lived experience because they admire and are attracted to aspects of other cultures, this is most easily seen in the arts and is more correctly termed cultural appreciation. It moves to being cultural appropriation when a majority group adopts cultural elements of a minority group in an exploitative, stereotypical, or disrespectful manner.

It can seem very clear how our families play an important role in developing our cultural identity. Heidegger speaks of 'thrownness' meaning that there are some things we are thrown into and have no choice over. This includes the families we are born into, the geography and circumstances of our birth. Our cultural identity will start to be formed at birth, and to some extent even before that, when cultural familial and community expectations about how one should give birth, gender expectations, racial characteristics, position within the family (i.e. youngest or oldest child), may even precede and influence the birth. Even the naming of the child will have cultural references. My parents felt limited in their choice of names for me and my brother to names that were acceptable to the Catholic Church and to expectations of the extended family. Our names had to be saints' names recognised by the Church, but there was also an expectation that they would be names which already were in use within the family and given as a sign of respect and love to those family members already holding those names. Hence, I have the same name as my mother's sister, and my brother has the same name as our father, and his father. We each have only the one name as culturally within our class and community it was felt unnecessary and a bit 'posh' to have a middle name.

The fact that I was born in Manchester to two very intelligent, supportive, and lovely parents, neither of whom could afford to stay on at school beyond sixteen, as it was necessary for them to find work and earn money, has no doubt had an impact on who I am today, and will also have significancy for my two daughters. The fact that my mother suffered many miscarriages before having me after ten years of trying, meant I was welcomed into the family as a much loved and longed for child. It was assumed that I would be an only child and so I was not limited by my gender, if I wanted to play and support football, I did, if I wanted to wear outlandish fashion and make up I did. Probably most of my friends were boys, but some of my closest were girls. My favourite music was of African and Caribbean origin which at times meant I mixed socially with an almost totally black group of friends. At the age of four, I chose to become vegetarian, having seen someone on the local allotment chop the head off a live chicken, which continued to flap around my feet. On my father's side we came from a long line of butchers, with my grandfather still running the family butcher's shop at that time, so this dietary choice was very much outside the family culture. My immediate family were happy with my choices, apart from my mother's fears that not eating meat would make me physically weak, but for other family members, such as uncles and aunts, some of my choices were outside their zone of cultural comfort and they tried hard to push me back into beliefs and behaviours more in line with their own.

Families are made up of many diverse cultures, or interpretations of cultures, evidenced by their choices and behaviours. Although my own immediate family would be classified as white, Caucasian, northern working class, it is clear from analysis of blood, inherited health issues, and personal research, that this is a far from the case and that despite being blonde and blue eyed, I have a cultural and genetic heritage which is more often found in the Southern Mediterranean, and Northern Africa, places which when I have spent time there have felt very comfortable and strangely familiar to me.

Families will often make choices about education and religion which follow from their own cultural heritage, rather than necessarily their individually formed beliefs and values. Our religious upbringing and membership of church communities is full of cultural references and value sets, which we may over time embrace or reject. Catholicism offered me some of the theatricality of the Mediterranean culture, including the use of the Latin language. Although no longer believing in, or being a member of the Catholic Church, or indeed of any church, I will still visit churches in Italy and enjoy the sensuality of the place, the candles, the incense, the relics, the art, etc.

Being brought up in the Catholic Church, by parents who believed and held to those religious beliefs, meant that I attended Catholic schools, including a direct grant convent grammar school for girls. These schools were steeped in cultural references and expectations. Some of these might be expected and in line with the Catholic catechism and beliefs, whereas others may be different from what might be expected. My grammar school was full of petty rules and injunctions, including the exact shade of tights we could wear, and the length of our skirts and fringes! There were value led expectations about approaches to discipline, behaviour to others, and a strong work ethic, as well as an expectation that we would follow the rules of the church and the fear of what would happen to our souls if we did not. This was a particularly troubling area as it meant that my non-Catholic friends were doomed to hellfire!

However, in addition to this, as an all-female environment we were exposed to powerful female role models (for good or bad, often very bad), we were not taught to rely on men, and were encouraged to prepare for careers, rather than aspire to a role as a housewife or mother (the nuns being neither of these). This expectation was different from those experienced by my cousins who attended the local secondary modern school and wanted to get married early and find a safe non-taxing secure job until they had children.

Despite these aspirations, the fact that the school was situated in a poor part of Manchester, and most pupils were there as a result of passing the 11 plus and an entrance exam, expectations were limited by class and geographical cultural expectations. Any thought of entering pupils for Oxbridge admission never entered the thinking of the staff of the school. The height of ambition was to get into a teaching training college or university. I deviated from these expectations by going off to art college to pursue a degree in Fine Art, leading to prayers being said for my moral well-being!

Outside school I was surrounded by subcultures, I have already mentioned music and fashion as examples. Perhaps the most powerful was the division along football royalties. Manchester is divided into red and blue cultural groups based on which football team one supports. From birth you knew where your loyalty was meant to sit. Different areas of the city were predominantly blue (Manchester City) whilst other areas were mainly red (Manchester United). When I was growing up the teams still had religious links, with Manchester United being seen as the Catholic club. When I started bringing boyfriends home the first question my father would ask is, 'Are you red or blue?' If the answer was 'red' it was safe to continue with the conversation as there was an assumption of shared cultural references. Should the answer be 'blue' then the conversation tended to end there. If we feel we can find a shared cultural reference, we assume an understanding of the other which can make us feel safe.

These family and community cultural influences are added to more generational and heritage cultural expectations. Carl Jung's concept of the collective unconscious places emphasis on the structures of the unconscious mind which are shared among beings of the same species. Jung saw the collective unconscious as different from the personal unconscious, which is composed of an individual's repressed memories and experiences and as something which is inherited and universal with certain content and structures being the same for all individuals. He points to the universality of some symbols, stereotypes, and themes which we find in myths, dreams, and religious practices across different cultures.

Our individual culture is based on all these influences, and our reaction to them. I rejected a Catholic belief system having experienced what I perceived as hypocrisies between beliefs and behaviours. I chose to have a career **and** a marriage and family, which was in line with the feminist cultural aspirations of the time. We gave our daughters names which were considered strange by some family members as they were not saints' names, nor had they previously been used by family members. My experiences at art college extended my knowledge and experience of other cultures. I moved from the North of England, took more degree courses, and worked in areas which were not familiar to my family. However, I continued to value my northern upbringing and for good or bad, have continued to have a strong work ethic, and not always responded well to what I perceived as entitlement behaviour. Like all humans I am a complex mix of cultures.

Not surprisingly, the understanding and development of mediation over time is set within cultural contexts which I intend to briefly note.

Chapter 11

The Cultural History of Mediation

Introduction

Having looked at how 'culture' is defined generally, and how I am using it for the purpose of writing this book, I am moving on to look briefly at the geo-cultural history of mediation. It is impossible within the confines of this book to cover its development in all countries, but I hope to give a flavour through drawing on the development in a few key geographical areas.

Mediation has a diverse and long history spanning cultures, religions, and communities throughout the world. It has developed in line with social, economic, ethical, and political changes which have varied from community to community. We can see evidence of the approach through 'the Kalahari Bushmen, who emphasize group harmony over discord to the ancient Athenians, who appointed all men during their sixtieth year as "arbitrators"…to the "win-win" negotiators of today' (J.T. Barrett & J.P. Barrett, 2004:xiii). Mediation is alluded to in the philosophies of Tao Te Ching, and Confucius, and is considered to be deeply embedded in the Quran and in the bible. In the New Testament, there appears to be a strong endorsement of alternative forms of dispute resolution, 'Come to terms with your opponent in good time while you are still on the way to court with him, or he may hand you over to the judge and the judge to the guard and you will be thrown into prison' (Matthew 5:25). The Quran also calls for 'sunna' which is built around reconciliation and harmony.

Mediation has its roots in ancient civilisations, with evidence of its use in ancient Egypt, Greece, China, and Mesopotamia amongst others. In these early examples mediators were usually drawn from respected members of the community who would be asked to resolve family, land, and commercial disputes. In tribal communities the leader or medicine man may also take on the role of mediator.

As early as 1754 BCE we find the Mesopotamian Code of Hammurabi formally recognising mediation as a process to settle disputes through focusing on restitution and reconciliation, rather than retribution. Whilst in China we can find early examples of Confucian principles aimed at resolving conflict and promoting social order and community harmony through the use of mediation, without resorting to violence or legal processes. Trading through the Silk Road route helped to spread

DOI: 10.4324/9781003528890-14

these principles and the mediation approach into Asia, including Japan and India, where we find religious and community leaders and elders taking on the role of mediators.

Within Europe and the Islamic world mediation processes, usually set within religious and legal frameworks, were developed during the Middle Ages. In Europe the Church would look to canon law principles to provide a framework for mediation models which aimed at reconciliation and forgiveness. Many 'mediation' meetings would use the monasteries or other religious buildings as neutral venues. Mediation was used by all social classes.

Having given this overview, I intend to look a bit more deeply into the development in some geographical areas. For ease, I have put them in alphabetical order starting with Africa.

Africa

Mediation has a long history in Africa as its principles are deeply rooted in traditional African practices based on the concept of 'Umuntu Ngumuntu Ngabantu', which emphasises community building, respect, sharing, empathy, tolerance, the common good, acts of kindness and communication, consultation, compromise, cooperation, camaraderie, conscientiousness, and compassion.

Historically, African societies have sought to resolve conflict through the verbal intervention of elders, community leaders, and tribal chiefs. We see strong examples of the use of councils of elders in several communities, including the Akan in Ghana, and the Yoruba in Nigeria. These councils acted as neutral parties who aimed to facilitate dialogue in order to reach a consensus. Rituals were sometimes called upon to reconcile, and to restore social balance. Such an example would be the Maasai's 'Enkai' reconciliation ceremonies in Kenya which aimed at restoring harmony, resolving conflict, and reinforcing and preserving the cultural heritage of the community. The ceremony started with the invocation of Enkai (God) to observe and bless the process, the elders would then act as mediators and facilitators with conflicting parties presenting their grievances to them and the wider community. The elders would then elicit the views of both parties and the community before making a deliberation. The announcement of the resolution would be followed by rituals and symbolic acts signifying reconciliation. Such rituals included the slaughtering of animals or offerings of blood or milk to Enkai, with the ceremony concluding with celebratory feasting.

When African countries were colonialised, European countries imposed Western legal systems, moving away from the older mediation models. Koopman (1993:48) sees this as evidencing the cultural differences between European and African culture. Writing in Christie et al. (eds) 'African Management', Koopman states, '[W]hites, by and large, are individualistic exclusivists. When managing conflict, therefore, we prefer to apply win/lose tactics, clear-cut and defined structures and procedures. Mostly we alienate ourselves within conflict situations leading us to enter into negotiations in order to control an outcome of "rightness" and "wrongness". Africans by and large, are communal inclusivists. Managing conflict becomes an open sum process involving immediate family, supervisors, elders, etc. within the framework of morals. This necessitates entering into a dialogue from which a sense of fairness and unfairness towards other members in society can emerge.'

Despite the move towards increased use of the court system, these traditional mediation practices continued in more rural areas. As a result, some colonial administrations integrated indigenous conflict resolution methods into their systems, thus creating a hybrid mediation model.

Following post-colonial independence, there was a resurgence in the traditional mediation approaches, and they were increasingly recognised and integrated into the new legal frameworks, and judicial systems. By 1984, we see the establishment of the Mediation Service of South Africa (IMSSA), which was established by a group of trade unionists, employers, academics, and lawyers to offer mediation services particularly in employment disputes. By the end of the 1980s IMSSA had extended its work into community disputes.

In 1993 when South Africa was going through the process of dismantling the Apartheid system, the people called upon their respective leaders to find an alternative way to settle South Africa's problems, outside of the context of war and civil insurrection. At the time, there was a serious danger that the country would tear itself apart and descend into one of the most dangerous bloodbaths in the history of human conflict.

To tackle this, Nelson Mandela looked to a central feature of African culture's worldview – the concept of Ubuntu, which means 'humanity to others' and which emphasises the interconnectedness of all individuals and our shared responsibility towards each other, and the environment, summarised in the Nuguni phrase, 'I am because you are, you are because we are'. In this, it shares many of the fundamental underpinnings of existential philosophy, with its belief that we are beings-in-the-world-with-others and that it is the presence of others which allows us to identify what and who we are, by recognising in others who and what we aren't.

I had the privilege to meet and work closely with Kofi Annan, and Desmond Tutu, Arch to his friends, on projects in South Africa and Europe, mediating gender-based violence in the townships, training young people in mediation skills, and working with conflict within para-military groups. In speaking about Ubuntu, Tutu in his book 'No Future Without Forgiveness' wrote about the essence of being human, saying 'It also means my humanity is caught up, is inextricably bound up, in theirs. We belong in a bundle of life. We say, "a person is a person through other people". It is not "I think therefore I am". It says rather: "I am human because I belong, I participate, I share". A person with ubuntu is open and available to others... For he or she has a proper self-assurance that comes from knowing that he or she belongs in a greater whole and is diminished when others are humiliated or diminished, when others are tortured or oppressed, or treated as if they were less than who they are' (Bujo 2000:31). Benezet Bujo also asserted that 'for Black Africa, it is not the Cartesian *cogito ergo sum* ("I think therefore I am") but an *existential cognatus sum, ergo sum* ("I am known, therefore we are") that is decisive' (2001:4).

By the end of the 1990s, following the National Peace Accord, mediation became popular in resolving family, divorce, and environmental disputes in addition to the original employment issues and has increasingly received statutory support. Despite this, in South Africa, disputants in the commercial arena have been slow to recognise and adopt mediation, unlike in other African countries such as Ghana, Ethiopia, and Uganda where it is established as mainstream practice in commercial disputes, acting as a catalyst to set up initiatives such as the Lagos Multi-Door Courthouse (LMDC) in Nigeria as a public-private partnership between the Lagos State High Court of Justice and a private dispute resolution consultancy, with the overarching objective being to facilitate dispute resolution within the Nigerian Justice System creating the first court-connected alternative dispute resolution (ADR) centre in Africa.

United States

If we look to America we find the roots of mediation in the early colonial period, with Quakers and other religious groups advocating its use within their communities. However, the development of ADR was predominantly led by commercial and political, rather than cultural elements. By the 19th century we see the concept of arbitration take hold, particularly in commercial and labour disputes, with the establishment of permanent arbitration boards in some industries and the provision of a legal framework for arbitration.

By 1941, with the fear of labour disputes potentially hindering wartime production, the National Defence Mediation Board was established to handle employment disputes. This was followed in 1947 with the founding of the Federal Mediation and Conciliation Service which also focused on labour issues.

The growth of the civil rights movement, with its philosophy of non-violent conflict resolution, saw the rise of the community mediation movement for divorce, child custody, and commercial disputes. This was backed by government who saw it as a way to reduce the courts' waiting lists.

The Judicial Arbitration and Mediation Services (JAMS) was established in 1979 and became a significant provider of ADR services. By 1990 the Government had also introduced The Administrative Dispute Resolution Act and the Civil Justice Reform Act to encourage the use of ADR in federal agencies and sought to establish some consistency of practice through the Uniform Mediation Act of 2001.

Prior to this we had seen the establishment of the Pound Conference series in 1976 which aimed to develop the future of dispute resolution and improve access to justice. This increased the popularity of mediation in the USA. The series continued, and by 2016 it became a global movement under the title Global Pound Conferences and then the Global Pound Conversation, bringing together users, providers and advisors and setting up a research series covering changes and developments in mediation throughout the world.

Within the USA, ADR practices became more integrated into the legal system and the use of online dispute resolution (ODR) emerged. ADR use extended into international, environmental, healthcare, and more complex commercial disputes.

China

As with many other countries, China has a rich and deep history of alternative dispute resolution, rooted in its cultural, social, and legal traditions. This can be traced back to Confucianism with its emphasis on harmony, community, and the resolution of disputes through compromise based on moral persuasion. Confucius sought to resolve conflicts peacefully without resorting to legal adjudication, advocating the concept of Li, broadly translated as 'rite' which favoured the use of a system of ritual with the focus on manners, proper conduct, and propriety, whilst addressing the spiritual need for human participation in the larger order of the universe. Early use of mediation was through community leaders and elders with the emphasis being on restoring harmony rather than assessing right and wrong. Even during the imperial period, when the formal use of the Tag and Qing Codes were used, there remained a strong preference for using mediation, with local magistrates acting as mediators and the legal system encouraging out-of-court settlements.

In the early 20th century attempts were made to modernise the Chinese legal system by incorporating Western legal principles and practice. However, despite these reforms, mediation remained popular, especially in more rural areas. With the establishment of the People's Republic in China in 1949 and the introduction of the Maoist Period, the communist government actively promoted mediation as part of its judicial policy. People's Mediation Committees composed of ordinary citizens were established to mediate grassroots disputes, reflecting the government's focus on social harmony and collectivism.

The Cultural Revolution of 1966–76 saw major disruption in the formal legal institutions, and people's mediation initiatives played a crucial role in maintaining order. From 1978 the Reform Era of Deng Xiaoping brought a renewed emphasis on the development of more formal legal systems, although mediation remained a key component of the system, with the People's Mediation Law of 1989 formalising the role of the mediation committees.

Despite actions which may appear to contradict this, in its policies China remains committed to the promotion of mediation and ADR. It has established mediation centres as part of the integration of mediation and the court system, with courts required to encourage mediation with the aim of lessening their burden of work and promoting more speedy, efficient, and amicable resolutions. China has also shown some commitment to the use of international mediation to resolve cross-border disputes having launched the Belt and Road Initiative (BRI) to facilitate policy coordination, infrastructure connectivity, unimpeded trade, financial integration, and closer people-to-people ties to reduce the need for court-based responses to disputes. In the same spirit, they have also established institutions such as the China

International Commercial Court (CICC) and the China Council for the Promotion of International Trade Mediation centre (CCPIT).

Europe

If we look at the development of mediation in Europe, we find a history of the use of respected community members to mediate disputes to maintain social harmony. Early philosophers such as Aristotle wrote about the importance of mediation and conciliation in resolving conflicts without resorting to violence. Aristotle understood the inevitability of conflict and that it could be a good and necessary part of a flourishing state. He taught that justice was the main foundation of the order of the world, to which all virtues were subject. Aristotle's notion of justice envisaged the involvement of a third person responsible for deciding conflicts in interpersonal relationships, e.g. a possible breach of an agreement or contract. Essentially, this person, the judge (dikastés), was the mediator of the whole dispute resolution process and held the responsibility for monitoring and implementing the legal process for the benefit of society as a whole. It was not unusual in ancient Greece for free citizens to deploy educated slaves (therapes) to assist them in negotiations by conveying offers and counteroffers between them, as we currently see in modern shuttle mediation practice.

In the Middle Ages we see the Church promoting mediation to avoid bloodshed and maintain social order and playing an active role in dispute resolution, with clergy acting as mediators in disputes among nobility, merchants, and peasants. We still today see religious and community leaders used as intermediaries and quasi-mediators.

During the Renaissance and Early Modern Period Europe saw the emergence of modern legal systems based on Roman Law and the use of secular courts. Mediation continued to be used particularly in family and commercial matters and was the first port of call for guilds and merchant associations wishing to maintain trade relations.

In the same period, with the rise of nation states, mediation became more established as a tool in maintaining or developing democracy, with European monarchs and diplomats using mediation to resolve inter-state disputes. A good example of this would be The Treaty of Westphalia (1648), which ended the Thirty Years' War. The writings of Hugo Grotius and Samuel Pufendorf show that mediation was beginning to establish a code of procedures and rules.

In the Enlightenment, thinkers such as Emmanuel Kant and Jean-Jacques Rousseau believed that reason and negotiation could resolve conflicts. It has been suggested that their ideas laid the groundwork for modern mediation practices by promoting dialogue and mutual understanding. What was missing in that approach, and what continues to be missed in many current mediation practices, is the acknowledgement that logic and reason alone will never resolve conflict. If they could, there would be no conflict and therefore no need for mediation. Indeed, if a rational solution existed it would be clear and obvious to all parties. It is people's emotional attachment to their personal perspective and narrative which often gets in the way of agreeing a 'logical and rational' solution.

By the 19th century we see mediation being used to resolve major conflicts. An example is its use at the Congress of Vienna (1814–15) when following the Napoleonic Wars European powers used mediation and negotiation to re-establish order and balance of power, thus achieving a peaceful settlement and preventing future conflicts. The Industrial Revolution brought profound social and economic changes, meaning that new ways were needed to address industrial practices, deal with work-related accidents, and consumer protection issues. As a result, there was an increased use of mediation to resolve industrial and workplace disputes with the aim of preventing strikes and reducing the number of working hours lost to poor morale, stress, and absenteeism. Mediation became a more formalised process, with the introduction of professional mediators and the establishment of neutral centres in which mediations could take place.

By the 20th century mediation gained further popularity as an alternative dispute resolution process and became well established at a global level with the League of Nations being established at the end of the First World War, to promote international cooperation and resolve conflicts through mediation and arbitration. Although it had limited success, it set a precedent for international mediation, paving the way for the creation of the United Nations, which was established with a strong emphasis on finding peaceful ways to resolve conflict. It embedded in its Charter the aim that mediation should be the primary method for resolving international disputes, leading to the use of mediation during the Cold War period where it played a crucial role in diffusing tensions between the Eastern and Western bloc countries, during which European states often acted as neutral mediators.

India

India has an early history of using village councils, or Panchayats, which drew on traditional local customs and norms, and the religious values of the Hindu, Buddhist, and Jain philosophies of non-violence and reconciliation to resolve disputes through a mediation process. As with other countries which came under British rule in the colonial period, the British legal system was introduced but local mediation practices continued. After independence 'people's courts', Lok Adalats, recognised by the formal legal system, were introduced, providing informal settings for dispute resolution. Today, mediation centres have been established as settings for ADR processes.

Islamic Countries

Similarly to Western countries the Islamic world 'mediators' looked to Sharia law to provide a framework for mediation. From the earliest days of Islam, Muhammad (570–632) encouraged and practiced *tahkim,* or arbitration, to resolve a variety of disputes. For some people the Prophet Muhammad himself is seen as an early mediator because as a young man he was chosen by feuding tribes to resolve a dispute around the reconstruction of the Ka'ba. He found a solution which benefited both parties. Another famous case of *Tahkim* in action, illustrating how minor disputes can spiral into war, is seen in one of the most famous wars of the pre-Islamic period, that of al-Basus, which began with the death of a camel that had been allowed to graze on another man's land. The dispute escalated into a long-running cycle of revenge and counter-revenge and was settled only through the process of *tahkim* and payment of blood money. The Islamic tradition and culture focus more on the group or community than on the individual, with Islamic law encouraging the concept of an independent mediator using *Al Wasata*, the practice of one or more persons intervening in a dispute, either at the request of one or both parties or on their own initiative.

The independent mediator attempts to resolve the dispute by a more active evaluative approach which includes proposing solutions to the parties, who are then free to determine if they want to accept the proposed solutions or not. The concept of *sulh* (settlement) and *musalaha* (reconciliation) are integral to Islamic tradition across the Middle East, North Africa, and beyond, with early mediators being drawn from the Quadis, Islamic judges, who would not just mediate disputes between Muslims, but also disputes between Muslims and non-Muslims using the Quran and Hadith for guidance. Interest in the development of mediation continues in Islamic countries, although at a 1994 conference entitled 'Acknowledgment, Forgiveness, and Reconciliation: Alternative Approaches to Conflict Resolution in Post-War Lebanon', Irani, a Muslim academic and social activist, declared that a better concept would be 'conflict management' rather than mediation, because 'it is impossible completely to solve conflicts; the existence of conflicts goes together with human existence' (Irani: forthcoming). This is a very existential observation supporting the more philosophical and psychological approach I have outlined earlier. He raised the related point that conflicts were interrelated, the resolution of one conflict was contingent upon the resolution of other conflicts. 'The crisis of Lebanon and the Middle East are the best proof of what I am saying,' he concluded (ibid).

Mediation continues to be the preferred method in most Islamic countries, with parties encouraged by judges to take civil disputes to mediation with the aim of finding an amicable settlement to the dispute. The concept of mediation does differ from the current wider Western model in which the mediator is not seen as an expert but as a facilitator, as within the Arab/Islamic approach to mediation, the status and reputation of the mediator and the parties' respect for the mediator are considered crucial to reaching amicable compromise settlements. The mediator is perceived as someone with all the answers and solutions, and so plays an active role, including that of a fact finder, taking an evaluative stance.

Japan

The traditional Japanese Bushido code which was followed by the Samurai influenced their approach to mediation, with its focus on honour and rectitude. As in many other cultures village heads and elders were used to mediate disputes within their own communities. With the Meiji Restoration we see the introduction of more Western legal concepts although traditional mediation practices continued alongside these. Contemporary Japan has now integrated mediation into its legal system and uses both court-annexed and private mediation services.

Russia

The history of mediation in Russia is a complex and evolving one. Its development has been influenced by its cultural norms, legal traditions, and political changes. Prior to the Revolution, informal mediation played a significant part in resolving conflicts, particularly in rural areas, with elders and community leaders taking the role as mediator. The Russian Orthodox Church was also prominent in mediating disputes which were considered to have a moral or ethical focus.

After 1917, in what is termed the Soviet era, the state-controlled dispute resolution mechanisms mainly used the centralised legal system and formal mediation was largely absent. Collective bodies such as trade unions would use mediation for workplace disputes, reflecting the collectivist culture of the time.

With the dissolution of the Soviet Union there were significant changes in the Russian legal system. These included the introduction of alternative dispute resolution mechanisms and the recognition and promotion of mediation through the establishment of the Federal institute of Mediation and the Russian Union of Mediators. In 2010 the Russian Foundation introduced a federal law, rather grandly entitled, 'On Alternative Dispute Resolution Procedure with the Participation of an Intermediary Mediation Procedure', which outlined the principles and practice of mediation. This was followed by attempts to integrate mediation into the federal system with court-connected mediations used to alleviate the burden on courts. However, despite institutional support and encouragement, the acceptance of mediation faced cultural and practical challenges and there remained a preference for more authoritative practices with more informal methods such as mediation being regarded with a level of scepticism.

There continues to be an increasing awareness of mediation and the need to develop the training and accreditation for mediators to increase professionalism and credibility. Despite this recognised need, mediation is promoted in various sectors including family, employment, and community issues. Specialised mediation centres and programmes have been developed, whilst cultural acceptance and practical implementation issues remain as challenges.

In this brief overview of the cultural history of mediation we can see that despite different approaches and structures, in most countries mediation started as a community initiative, using local respected individuals to take the role of mediator. Mediation is still in its development stage in most countries and there are now differences in the degree to which it remains community or legislative led.

Chapter 12

Current Responses to the Use of Mediation

The previous section gave a very brief overview of the history of mediation. It shows that there are a lot of similarities and some differences in the understanding and use of mediation over time. Today mediation practice continues to be practiced in diverse cultural, legal, and social contexts across the globe. Globalization has led to the sharing of ideas about mediation, and to the establishment of cross-country conferences and forums for discussion. Work on the adoption of international standards and guidelines for ADR practice are being established. Global organisations such as the United Nations now promote mediation as the first means to try to resolve most disputes. In 2008 we saw the introduction of the EU Mediation Directive which aimed to raise the profile of mediation, to promote mediation in civil and commercial contexts, facilitate access to mediation, and ensure quality of practice. It also created a standby team of senior mediation advisers. Increasingly, mediation is now used in peace-making initiatives through organisations such as OSCE (Organisation for the Security and Co-operation in Europe) and the increasing use of NGOs in mediation and conflict resolution work, so a lot of progress has been made.

However, there is still considerable difference in mediation practice. Debate continues over whether mediation should be compulsory in some instances, with strong advocates for both sides of the argument. Mediation training programmes differ in the number of hours involved and the focus of the training. Most cover aspects of communication skills, processes such as shuttle diplomacy, use of individual and joint sessions, problem-solving, and the writing up of settlements. I have already mentioned that some training programmes also include some psychological aspects and at least one focuses on that, while covering all other aspects.

There is considerable variation across nations as to how closely the use of mediation is linked to the legal system or operates as a standalone service. In the twenty years I have been teaching mediation in various countries I have seen a move from the belief that to be a mediator one has to come from a legal background. The profession now draws recruits from more diverse backgrounds, including human resource professionals, educationalists, community workers, psychologists, etc. This could perhaps be seen as a return to the more community-based roots of mediation where mediators were mainly people who had some community status and respect.

The degree with which mediation is known about and used also differs greatly from country to country. In the UK, where I am based, mediation has been slow to be taken onboard and used consistently as a first port of call in a dispute. Unfortunately, parties are still waiting for a crisis point to occur before turning to mediation. There is also still a tendency in the corporate world to commission a mediation, not because they expect it to succeed, but as an attempt to show that they 'have tried everything' before going to tribunal. Some compulsory court-directed mediations have also been used as a tick box exercise so parties can say that they considered mediation before litigation, when they may have only signed a form to say they had been told about it. The UK still has a very long way to go in increasing the awareness of mediation, the rate of take up, and the training of mediators.

Younger countries, many coming out of Soviet domination, have been quicker to integrate mediation into common practice. I have had the opportunity to teach mediation in the Baltic States and in Romania where mediation systems are more developed, and training and continuous professional development programmes for mediators are in place. This reduced reliance on more traditional legalistic approaches may be down to the youth of the population in general, with many more senior posts, particularly lawyers and judges, being held by people in their thirties and forties.

My first invitation to speak to judges in Bucharest challenged my assumptions of what I would find. When I walked into a room full of judges, I discovered that the majority were female and under fifty, a very different demographic than I would find here in England. The commitment to publicise the benefits of mediation and increase take up is helped by groups of mediators regularly touring towns and villages holding mediation fairs where they can explain how mediation works and encourage its use. Mediation journals are regularly published, keeping mediators updated with developments in the field and containing articles which stimulate interest and debate. Mediation is an established profession and there is regular access to continuing professional development opportunities, in terms of workshops, advanced training programmes and regular professional updates.

I have also had the privilege of working at the Riga University, School of Law, in Latvia and have been impressed with the dedication of many to extend the use of mediation. Latvian judges are trained in mediation in the Training Centre for Judges and are trained and encouraged to offer parties the opportunity to firstly try to resolve their disputes through mediation. The country hosts annual organised Days of Mediators to support and develop mediators and their work. The Latvian Government shows its commitment through covering the expense of five free mediation sessions with an accredited mediator in family disputes. However, should the parties fail to reach an agreement by the end of their free sessions they are required to pay for the work of the mediator themselves. So, both the carrot and stick approaches are in place.

It is interesting to note that, before the current war, Ukraine had a very well-established mediation profession and mediation was one of the most popular ways of consensual dispute resolution, despite the fact that for many years it had no legislative regulation. This changed with the introduction of the Law of Ukraine 'On Mediation' Law, in November 2021 which regulated not only the mediation of disputes and writing of settlements but also introduced a so-called preventive mediation, i.e. mediation of disputes which can only appear in the future, for example, mediation of the conclusion of a contract or premarital agreement. It introduced provision for mediation to become integrated into litigation at different stages. Training of mediators was well developed, and The Faculty of Law in the Yuriy Fedkovych Chernivsti National University had established a Master's degree educational and professional programme in mediation, supported by a grant from the Mediation Training and Society Transformation Programme (MEDIATS). MEDIATS aimed to expand the range of professional mediators and to promote the development of mediation throughout the Ukraine.

Amongst the countries where I have been invited to run training some still have mediation very firmly placed within the legal sector. I was surprised and delighted when I was part of a small team to be invited to Singapore, where this is the case, as they were interested to know more about using a psychological approach to mediation. Although no doubt quite new to the approach, the participants entered fully into the programme, unexpectedly enjoying the role plays and thoroughly embracing the approach and so commissioning further training.

Overall, the understanding and use of mediation is growing. We have seen the establishment of peer mediation programmes in some schools, which should mean that coming generations will be better informed about the merits of mediation and may already have been taught some of the key skills. These initiatives are aimed at empowering young people and increasing their understanding of the psychology of conflict, increasing communication skills and listening skills, and in a practical way helping to reduce incidents of bullying and school violence and so promoting a more inclusive environment based on understanding and reconciliation rather than punishment.

In the United States such peer mediation programmes are well established and often integrated with restorative justice practices. Programmes have been developed to train students as mediators working mainly with disputes between peers.

Canada uses mediation for disputes between students, but also between students and teachers and in some cases between parents and the school, with local mediation services providing training and support. In Canada mediation is increasingly viewed as an important proactive aspect of their mental health and well-being programme.

Australia too places mediation within the well-being context. Their training programmes focus on active listening and developing skills in empathy, with the government providing support for the implementation of mediation programmes which create safe and supportive school environments.

In the United Kingdom, in those schools which have such projects, they are often part of a broader conflict resolution curriculum, and they use both adult and peer-led approaches, with The National Mediation Council involved in training staff and students. Some schools have actively embraced RJ (restorative justice) practices and tried to create a RJ ethos throughout all school activities, in addition to offering RJ interventions, particularly around issues of bullying and harassment. This broad use of mediation principles in schools is increasingly being used globally as a way not just of resolving conflicts but of introducing a philosophical approach which enhances early insight into difficult situations and improves communication aimed at fostering a safe and positive school environment. It also aims to empower students, teachers, and all members of a school community and to reduce the need for punitive practices.

Across Europe we can find examples of various initiatives aimed at promoting mediation as an integrated part of the school curriculum, often with the support of government policies or EU-funded programmes. Several, such as France and Belgium, have focused on the development of peer mediation networks which share resources and training programmes and facilitate exchange programmes through which students and teachers can share learning and best practice.

In countries with high incidences of violence in schools, such as South Africa, school mediation projects focus on involving the whole community in building a culture of peace and non-violence, drawing impetus from the Peace and Reconciliation Movement. Personally, I have been involved in work in the townships where there was evidence of disempowered young males trying to regain a sense of power through turning their frustration on the even more disempowered young women.

In many countries, such as India, the development of school mediation projects has been led by non-governmental organisations (NGOs) and educational reformers whose focus has been on reducing the traditional punitive disciplinary ethos and methods which were in place. A series of pilot programmes are underway and if successful the plan would be to incorporate mediation approaches in wider ranging educational reforms.

Whilst not as established as in some Western countries we do find mediation in schools in Japan. Such programmes are closely aligned with the cultural emphasis on harmony and group cohesion, and training in mediation techniques is available to teachers and students with the aim of addressing bullying and other conflicts. The country has also started to incorporate some elements of restorative justice practice as part of the process to rebuild relationships and community balance.

This link with the community is also found in countries such as Brazil and Argentina where schools collaborate and work with community leaders and local organisations to address conflicts which arise in or outside school but impact on families and communities. These initiatives, often found in those areas with significant social and economic inequalities are focused on improving social justice and on addressing the underlying causes of discrimination and violence and the conflicts which flow from them.

In conflict-affected areas of the Middle East, initiatives have been established to introduce mediation into school as part of wide-ranging peace-building efforts. They are often led by NGOs and international organisations who provide the staff to work in schools providing training and support aimed at reducing tensions between different ethnic and religious groups.

Those involved in, and committed to the development of mediation are heartened by programmes which aim to embed a mediation approach in the minds of young people. They report positive outcomes, including reduced incidents of violence, improved student behaviour, and stronger relationships within the school and local community. A by-product of mediation training is the development of life skills: empathy, communication, and problem-solving. However, these programmes are not without their challenges including lack of funding, resistance from traditional disciplinary frameworks, and the need for ongoing training and support. In some regions, cultural attitudes towards conflict resolution and authority may also hinder the widespread adoption of mediation practices.

I champion the introduction of mediation and restorative philosophies to young people in schools, colleges, and universities, believing that to have these skills embedded at an early age may not just help resolve conflict but also reduce it. However, I have been concerned by some examples of practice I have encountered. When we train people to listen it encourages speakers to trust them, and therefore to open up and tell the listener more than they would say to other people. In some projects I have found that young people have not had sufficient training, support, or supervision to equip them to deal with some of the things they heard. Some young mediators have not fully understood the boundaries of confidentiality and have carried disturbing information disclosed by disputants.

The Future

The use of mediation continues to grow worldwide, with increasing acknowledgment of its effectiveness, leading to recognition as an approach which is a legitimate form of dispute resolution. Its future development will depend on how mediators address the remaining cultural, legal, and institutional challenges and those barriers which still abound, particularly in societies where adversarial legal systems and hierarchical structures remain, and where leaders may fear that any delegation of legislative power is a threat to their authority.

The mediation community must actively work to expand the use of mediation in diverse contexts and communities, looking to identify ways of integrating its use into common practice, so that it becomes the first port of call in any dispute. This requires a programme of promoting public awareness so that more people understand the benefits it offers in supporting justice, encouraging reconciliation, and promoting peace, as well as increasing communication skills and building greater insight into how each individual makes sense of the world, and therefore how they interpret any dispute. An increased understanding of the psychological causes of conflict and the approaches which may best address them can help to promote a more understanding and accepting world, with greater acceptance of difference.

In the next section I shall focus on what needs to happen to develop a mediation system which is more welcoming and effective across all cultures.

Chapter 13

Key Considerations and Skills for Working with Cultural Difference

Language

I have emphasised listening as a key skill for mediators. Implicit in this is the importance of verbal language, as this is mainly what the mediator is listening to, whilst also learning from the body language of the parties involved. Before looking at body language and the mediator's understanding of non-verbal cues, I shall focus on language as it represents a symbolic system through which cultural sensitivities, beliefs, and values are transmitted.

Different cultures will give different meaning to words and symbols, and different languages contain within them different norms regarding pace of speech, order of words, use of silences, etc. Some languages are rich in metaphors and use storytelling to express meaning, whilst others will focus more on language as a means of transaction, heavy on fact, and discouraging of anything which isn't considered to be relevant or on point.

Earlier in this book, I emphasised the need for the mediator to seek to understand and enter into the worldview of all the parties. There may be very significant differences in the ways in which not just different cultures, but also each individual uses language to express their worldview. The mediator needs to listen out for the degree with which the individual uses linguistical devises. In addition to being sensitive to these, consideration also needs to be afforded to the tone used, and the pace with which a person speaks, and their use of silences.

The mediator will demonstrate their skills through reflecting back, paraphrasing, deconstructing, and summarising as mentioned earlier, but must also try to match the language style of the person they are speaking with. I do not intend to imply that this should be done in a practised, systematic way, as with Neuro Linguistic Programming for example. If we are fully present and tuned in to the other person, bracketing our own assumptions, ego needs, and prejudices, we will intuitively and authentically match the other, through the deep connection we have established. One only needs to look to friends and lovers who are deep in conversation to see this happening. Their body language is likely to naturally mirror that of the other.

Having already looked at these skills in Part One, let us focus a little on exploring the ways in which different cultures tend to use metaphor, myths, and storytelling, remembering that we are all individuals, and as such are unique, and within every culture there will be marked individual differences. Vorontsova Iulia (2021:5) reminds us of the very existential belief that the 'Embodied nature of human thinking means that the source domains for its metaphors come from our embodied experience'. But warns that, 'this does not mean that conceptual metaphors would necessarily be identical in any culture on the basis that we as humans share the same bodily structure and live in the same world'. Indeed, culture plays an important role in shaping the metaphors. According to Kövecses (2004), the main variations of metaphor lie both in cross-cultural and within-culture dimensions.

Metaphors reflect, shape, and express cultural perceptions. Indeed, Lakoff and Johnson (2003) argue that metaphors structure our understanding and experience of the world, and their use reflects cultural values. We can see examples of this in the use of phrases such as 'time is money', 'wasting time', or 'spending time', which not surprisingly are used mainly in more capitalist Western cultures which value productivity, efficiency, and making money, and hold a linear understanding of time. This is contrasted in many Eastern cultures where time is viewed in a more holistic, cyclical way, influenced by Buddhist and Hindu philosophy in which time is seen more as a continuous cycle. We can also see these cultural differences between East and West in the use of metaphors related to self. In Western culture the self is seen as an independent entity leading to the use of expressions highlighting autonomy and self-reliance. In more collectivist cultures the self is considered in relation to the community and so we find the use of metaphors which reflect a belief in interdependence and social harmony, an example being the Chinese concept of 'Guanxi' which is often the basis for business relationships, as it represents an understanding of relationships as networks based on reciprocity and mutual obligation.

Given these differences in culture and value sets, some cultures are rich in their use of metaphor whereas others are not. Chinese culture values indirect communication and relies heavily on using metaphor to express deeper more emotional meaning. We see this evidenced in Mandarin Chinese with its use of idiomatic expression and conceptual metaphor. Japan tends to encourage context-driven communication whilst also favouring indirect communication using metaphor, idiomatic expression, and proverbs. Hindi and many Indian regional languages are rich in metaphor and idioms, using them to add layers of meaning and emotional expression. Many Mediterranean countries, Italy being a good example, draw on an expressive and artistic cultural base and so use emotional and poetic language rich in metaphor. The same is true in several Middle Eastern countries where we find metaphorical and poetic language such as Persian and Arabic in which metaphor is used to convey emotions, deep meanings, and respect. In contrast, in the more Northern Western countries, e.g. Germany, Holland, and Sweden, we find much less use of metaphor and a desire for language to be direct, literal, straightforward, clear, and precise. In my work as a coach, I have coached several high achieving individuals from these countries who were struggling to gain posts in other countries as the directness of their manner and use of language was experienced as blunt and rude, and so what they had been valued for in their own cultures proved a disadvantage. If a mediator is a careful observer and listener, then language will tell them a lot about the underlying values and beliefs which the dispute challenges and they will unearth what is meaningful for all parties and therefore what needs to be in a settlement agreement for it to be both meaningful and sustainable.

As well as differences in the use of metaphor, we find distinct differences in the use of myths, narratives, and storytelling which also give the mediator greater insight into the internal worldviews of all involved in a dispute. Fanon (1986:46) reminded us that 'when a story survives in folklore it expresses in some way a region of the "local soul" and so provides entry into the storyteller's cultural references.' It is important that when a mediator is offered that open door, they do not ignore it, thinking it has no relevance to the 'business of the day'.

Through understanding the role of myth in various cultures we gain insight into the external factors in forming the worldview – how societies perceive the world and maintain their cultural heritage. We may think of myths as ancient stories, but they are living narratives which shift and change over time and so help shape cultural identities and collective and individual worldviews. As with dreams, myths can be important in understanding human psychology. They are important elements in humankind's ability to weave meaningful narratives that go beyond the level of ordinary reality, by providing access to spiritual and unconscious truths which speak of moral beliefs and lessons, the way we interact with others, human and animal, as well as with the environment.

Just as with the use of metaphor, the predominance of myths varies across cultures. Countries like Greece are rich in a mythological heritage, with tales of gods and heroes, which have gone on to influence art, poetry, philosophy, and literature across the world. Japanese culture is also full of myths, following mainly from Shinto traditions, which continue to be celebrated in rituals and festivals. Hinduism, Buddhism, and Jainism have contributed to the strong mythology we find in India best known through epic tales such as the Mahabharata and Ramayana and which are often translated into modern themes in cinema and theatre productions. Many indigenous cultures such as the Native American people of North America, Australia's Aborigine people, and the Māori of New Zealand have strong mythological traditions which are integral to their cultural heritage, community practices, and identity.

Although many Western cultures do have a history of myths (e.g. Roman, Greek, Celtic) they are often seen as less relevant to daily life and seen more as the province of literature, academic study, theatre, film, and other forms of entertainment. They may not be prized in the same way as scientific study and rationality. This is a great shame, as Rollo May warned, 'There can be no stronger proof of the impoverishment of our contemporary culture than the popular – though profoundly mistaken – definition of myth as falsehood' (1991:23). We have the opportunity to learn about a person's values and beliefs by listening to their interpretation and use of myths. 'Myths open a door to a world that cannot be predicted and controlled, where truth is more amorphous, multifaceted, relative pluralistic' (Elkins,

1998:193). These will influence how disputants see their current conflict and how they respond to it. Some truths are hard to vocalise and more easily expressed through a seemingly unrelated narrative. A psychologically informed mediator respects everything they hear in a mediation and will be alert to themes and expressions of values and beliefs.

Even if a culture uses metaphor as a means of expression it does not necessarily follow that it will have a rich mythological heritage which has been valued and built on.

For example, although low on the use of metaphor, Scandinavia offers us a strong history of Norse mythology, with tales of Odin, Thor, and Loki which have heavily influenced current popular culture.

Returning to the existential, a mediator needs to understand that, as Rollo May (1991:15) pointed out, 'A myth is a way of making sense in a senseless world. Myths are narrative patterns that give significance to our existence. Whether the meaning of existence is only what we put into life by our own individual fortitude, as Sartre would hold, or whether there is a meaning we need to discover, as Kierkegaard would state, the result is the same: myths are our way of finding this meaning and significance.'

I want to return to a recent mediation, that of Simon and James, which I introduced earlier, to explore how personal mythology influences behaviour and language and can act as a barrier between people. To remind you, Simon and James were very successful white, middle-aged, and middle-class English men, who shared many cultural similarities, values, and beliefs. James' use of mythological language was evidenced when speaking of his pride in being able to 'fly' in and 'rescue' teams who could be 'doing better' even though they were operating successfully. He invited Simon to 'soar' with him so they could be superheroes together. James seemed inspired by modern Marvel comic mythology and Greek heroes such as Hercules. He could not understand why his colleague had not 'jumped at the chance' to don a cape and join his band of superheroes.

In contrast, Simon's leaning towards Servant Leadership with its values of personal authenticity, strong but collaborative communication, and the empowerment of others, indicated a different mythological inner world in which he did not want to take centre stage but to see this team shine and get credit for their work. He repeatedly used the word 'serve' and spoke of his commitment to 'developing his team and each individual in it' whilst he 'stood in the wings' waiting to support if necessary. This narrative was more akin to some Old Norse myths, such as that of Skirnir, whose name means 'bright one' who felt no need to prove his brightness but was a valued servant of the god Freyr. In the Edda poem 'Skirismal' he woos the beautiful goddess Geror, not for himself, but at the request of Freyr who was in love with her. Skirnir uses his magical powers to encourage her to accept Freyr's proposal. As well as working for the benefit of others, Skirnir is good at seeing the strengths and skills of others and using them effectively, and in one mission he enlists the skills in mining and smithing of the mountain dwarves to capture the fierce wolf Fenrir for the god Odin. Like Skirnir, the party to the mediation took satisfaction and pride through seeing his team's work praised by others and took care to give regular positive feedback. He recognised that in some instances this made it hard for him to offer even constructive criticism but he was more interested in the well-being of the team than going 'above and beyond'.

Through the mediation they came to see that they were using mythological language which was not immediately attractive or meaningful to the other, but instead was alienating, and therefore making it hard for them to work together effectively. Through recognising this and understanding the influencing mythology of the other they were both able to change the mythological biases in their own narratives, and to use different archetypes and words and so find a way to speak more clearly to their shared values and goals.

The above example shows how our conscious or even unconscious usage of symbolism and archetypes can have a profound effect on our ability to connect with others. If we pay close attention to people's myths, storytelling, and dreams they can open doors into a greater understanding of their worldview as they are rich in complex meaning. The symbolic language used will come from a cultural heritage which may be geographical, communal, or, as in the examples above, from a family culture which valued certain ways of seeing and being in the world. If we listen carefully, they will also tell us something of the inner conflicts of the individuals in the dispute, including ambiguities and challenges to their value system, in addition to the specific dispute which brought the person to mediation.

The use of archetypes in dreams and mythology may also be played out in a mediation, the use of a superhero identification in the party described above is a good example. Carl Jung wrote of the collective unconscious, and saw archetypes as universal rather than belonging to different cultures, demonstrating our shared human experience and psychological patterns. Many cultures have their own versions of the most common archetypes, that of the Hero, Shadow, Wise Old Person, and the Mother. So, the use of metaphors, myths, and stories are not a distraction for the mediator, but a gift. They are fundamental to cultural and personal identity and help provide a framework for the cultural identity and the world the disputant inhabits. If we develop curiosity and learn patience, not trying to impose a linear flow, we can gain deeper insights which will be important in forming a meaningful settlement of a dispute.

We may also be called upon to be sensitive to and patient with different cultural language patterns. Such variations of syntax, semantics, and pragmatics are heavily influenced by the cultural context and values which have shaped their development. Across cultures, the manner of speaking can differ greatly with sentences being structured differently, and distinct differences in the meaning given to silence and how it is used, and either encouraged or avoided. How people relate to silence can differ at a micro-cultural level, such as across working contexts, for example lawyers will try to avoid silences as they fear it looks as though they are at a loss for words and therefore ignorant, whilst philosophers and therapists for example will welcome silences as a sign that things are being taken seriously and reflected on.

There are significant differences across geographical cultures too, with many Indigenous people and Eastern cultures valuing silence and pauses which they experience as signs of respect, self-restraint, and thoughtfulness. A mediator also needs to be aware that in these cultures silence can indicate agreement or understanding, and it may not be deemed necessary to back this up verbally. However, it would be wrong to assume that silence always indicated agreement, as a cultural avoidance of conflict can lead to a person not speaking out when they disagree with or disapprove of what has been said. China is an example of a country which often uses silence strategically seeking to avoid confrontation and save face, whilst appearing strong, or as a way of prompting the other party to reveal information. This is very effective when working with Westerners who have greater difficulty maintaining silence. For in Western culture, such as America, silence is more often experienced as uncomfortable and considered to show a lack of communication skills. This leads to more direct and shorter transactional conversations. Northern Europe, however, has a more neutral relationship with silence. They tend not to engage in a great deal of small talk and appreciate silence as showing presence and reflection. In many African cultures silence is used as non-verbal communication showing communal understanding and respect for elders. In Middle Eastern cultures silence is often associated with honour, respect, and modesty and a way of avoiding shame. In Indian culture, particularly Hindu and Buddhist traditions, silence is seen as holding spiritual significance. However, there are significant hierarchical differences in these cultures and those of lower status would be expected to give precedence to others, using silence to show respect.

As well as differences in how people communicate with those they consider to be of a different class, there are cultural differences in the extent to which gendered language is used. For example, in Japan and many Arabic-speaking countries the language has different forms of vocabulary depending on the speaker's gender, whereas in other cultures there will be a desire to emphasise gender equality through the avoidance of gendered language.

Although there are differences in language patterns, there are also differences in how different cultures speak. Some cultures, including American, African, Latino, and Arab countries favour loud, expressive speech whilst others prefer more muted softer, tentative tones. The main cultural differences are in the use of direct communication (favoured by United States, Germany, Holland, Israel, etc.) versus indirect communication (favoured by China, Japan, and many Arab countries). In addition, there are noticeable differences in the importance given to context. Cultures such as East Asian, Middle East, and Latin America rely on high-context communication in which much of the meaning is derived from the context, relationships, and non-verbal cues and so the spoken word is only one part of the overall communication method. In other cultures, e.g. North America and Northern Europe, communication is more explicit with greater emphasis placed on the words used.

There are also distinct cultural differences in the level of formality expected in verbal communication. Some cultures, such as Korean, Japanese, and Russian emphasise formality, and expect the use of titles and honorifics to be observed, whereas other cultures such as Australian or American generally prefer a more informal way of speaking to convey equality and approachability. Other cultures will observe clear distinctions between contexts with very informal language used in social settings and very formal language in professional contexts. Cultures are responding differently with regards to the use of non-gendered pronouns, titles, and more gender-neutral language. Resistance to this movement is not just limited to certain countries but to different cultural, political, and religious groups within countries. Indeed, I was involved in mediating a dispute in the UK between a transgender individual and their work colleagues who they felt constantly and maliciously misgendered them.

Body Language

Body language can tell us many things about a person, some of it personal and some cultural, but it is also an area of communication where great sensitivity may be needed.

To begin with, the level of proximity and the need for personal space differs between individuals and countries, with Latin American, Middle Eastern, and some European countries like Italy, having a cultural preference for less personal space and more intimacy. In contrast, Northern European and Northern American cultures are happier with greater personal space, preferring to stand apart during conversations.

Even the way we hold ourselves differs across cultures. Western cultures tend to associate standing up straight and maintaining good posture with confidence, truthfulness, and professionalism. In some Asian cultures slouching or bowing is experienced as a sign of respect, especially when interacting with elders or those in authority. In Latin American cultures there is a preference for more relaxed informal postures.

Some mediators will welcome parties to mediation with a handshake. This may be experienced by many as confident and authoritative and therefore reassuring, but in some cultures body contact of any kind on first meeting would be considered inappropriate and a slight nod of the head or bow would be more acceptable. Even the firmness of a handshake will have cultural significance, with America and Northern Europe generally expecting a firm handshake, whereas in other cultures this would be perceived as aggressive or challenging.

A main area of cultural difference is in how comfortable people are with direct eye contact. On the whole Western culture will interpret direct eye contact as a sign of confidence, sincerity, and attention. However, for some Asian and Middle Eastern cultures prolonged eye contact is perceived as aggressive, disrespectful, and confrontational. In Middle Eastern countries, although intense eye contact can be seen to indicate sincerity and trust it is more acceptable only in same-gender interactions.

Other facial gestures are also significant. There are gestures, like smiling which are used and understood across cultures, but may differ in intensity and meaning.

A genuine smile in most Western cultures often involves the showing of teeth, whereas most Asian cultures would avoid the exposure of teeth.

Commonly used gestures can have differing meaning in different cultures. In Western cultures thumbs up, a sign considered to be positive and indicating agreement, and so generally believed to be so understandable that it has become an emoji, is an offensive gesture in Middle Eastern cultures. One also needs to be careful about nodding. In Western cultures a nod usually indicates a 'yes', but in Bulgaria and Greece, for example, nodding can mean 'no', whereas shaking one's head from side-to-side means 'yes'.

It is impossible here to consider all the cultural differences in verbal and nonverbal communication styles across cultures and important to remember that there will be big differences between individuals from shared cultures. In a mediation, it is important for a mediator to note and respect the different ways parties in a dispute might communicate. One does not have to have an encyclopaedic knowledge of all cultures. If one is alert one can pick up very quickly on the style of communication. In working with each individual, it is important to remain authentic to who you are, whilst at the same time respecting the other's different language preference, and remain as truthful as possible, whilst adapting one's own style accordingly. This may well mean that a mediator is quite different with each party in the private caucus sessions whilst maintaining a neutral more formal style, not aligned with either party, in the joint sessions. It is important to remember that equal opportunity does not mean treating everyone alike but treating everyone with equal respect.

Use of Interpreters

With increased globalization and mediators working cross-country, it is not unusual for interpreters to be used in mediations. They may offer simultaneous interpretation via headphones, or consecutive interpretation in which the interpreter translates sections of dialogue during the sessions just after an interchange has ended. This requires every speaker to add unnatural pauses which can interfere with their train of thought and narrative flow.

Many mediations could not take place without interpreters, for example, when the mediation contains people who speak different languages, when one person is using their second language rather than their mother tongue, or where one of the parties has a hearing impediment. Without an interpreter there is the danger of inequality in hearing, and the understanding and fluidity of language. In many jurisdictions it is a legal requirement to provide an interpreter if required. However, the use of interpreters does not come without challenges. Adding an additional person into the mediation process creates practical challenges but also adds greater complexity to the group and interpersonal dynamics which are at play in any mediation. For some parties the use of an interpreter by the other side leads them to feel that person has an advantage as they have an extra person to discuss things with during the times when they are away from the mediator. They may also consider that there is a greater risk of confidentiality being breached. The mediator may need to remind parties that anyone can bring a lawyer, trade union official, friend, or someone else to accompany them in the mediation if the other party is in agreement. Although use of interpreters is recommended, currently there has been very little consideration given to these aspects.

If we accept that language, how we use it, how we hear it, and what we understand and interpret from it, are extremely important skills within a psychologically informed approach to mediation, then we need to consider the pros and cons of introducing another 'listener'. Ileana Dominguez-Urban, an experienced mediation interpreter writes, 'Only in science fiction stories do people from vastly different cultures, and sometimes different species, appear able to communicate faultlessly with each other immediately upon their first meeting. From the "preposterous" Universal Language Translator of the Star Trek series to the parody fish-in-the-ear translator of Douglas Adams' Hitchhiker's series, these devices represent the unattainable goal of seamless communication in cross-cultural interactions. In real life, we, as ordinary mortals, must make do with the awkward process of using another individual to serve as the conduit and translator of our words' (1997:3).

Despite its failings, amongst the many benefits of using an interpreter is the potential to bridge the language gap and provide clarity, hopefully reducing the possibility of misunderstandings. If the person is from the same culture as a party, rather than someone who is just fluent in the language, they are likely to have a better understanding of the non-verbal communication which is also taking place. The use of an interpreter can allow parties to express their emotions more easily and fully through using their own primary language. It may also increase a party's trust in the process to have someone who they believe has a better understanding of their cultural context and language than the mediator. This can allow them to more freely express both positive or negative emotions, raising their voices, openly crying or laughing, to wave their arms around or remain rigid in their bodily position, if this is what they would comfortably do in their own cultural context.

When writing up any settlement an interpreter can also help ensure that any record keeping is accurate and the resolution written up in multiple languages if necessary.

However, the mediator must rely on the accuracy of the interpreter in clarifying exactly what the party wants written in the agreement. A skilled interpreter can help to avoid the situation where parties sign up to something which is not entirely clear to them and come to regret it later. A mediator, particularly where they have no knowledge of the party's first language, needs to be aware that an interpreter has the potential to highly influence the party, intentionally or unintentionally, and so potentially change through subtle means, the intention of the party in wording the settlement agreement. Unlike the mediator, who should be trained in identifying and bracketing any of their own biases (although this is not included in many mediation training programmes), some interpreters are unlikely to have had the benefit of such training and such insight.

If interpreters are to be used, the mediator should use the pre-mediation sessions to clarify the role of the interpreter and address any concerns. Both mediators and interpreters may benefit from training in the psychological approach, cultural competence, and effective triadic communication. Currently there is no requirement for supervision and the use of debriefing models, which may be helpful both to the mediator and the interpreter. Everyone should be prepared for the mediation to take longer given the importance of checking understanding and accuracy of what is being conveyed.

Some of the perceived risks involved in using an interpreter may tempt a bilingual mediator to act as an interpreter in the mediation they are facilitating. Even when a mediator is skilled and qualified to act as both a mediator and interpreter, being in both roles divides the mediator's time and focus.

I once worked with a client who was fluent in five languages. She was fluent in English, which was the primary language used for our conversations, however, she did not feel able to fully express her emotions in English, and so we agreed that instead of using interpreters, or struggling with only using English, she could move between languages as she needed to, even though my own knowledge of her other languages was almost non-existent. Perhaps stereotypically she would choose to speak in Italian when feeling light-hearted, romantic, and happy, in German when she was depressed or very serious, and in English when she was somewhat bored! Although I could not translate the words, careful attention to her body language, the tone and pace of her speech etc. gave me more information than I would have obtained by her struggling to find an English word which inadequately expressed the depth of her feeling. I think this helps to support my belief that whilst being sensitive to cultural needs through focusing on the individual, and respecting their way of presenting in the world, verbally and non-verbally, we will form a greater connection, and therefore a deeper understanding of their worldview, than any intense study of languages or cultural differences will allow us.

Listening and Language Skills

Whatever the cultural background of those in the mediation there are some basic skills which a mediator needs to use. I introduced these in Part Two, in the section on the skills needed in a Psychologically Informed Mediation. They are very simple skills which we tend not to use intuitively and consist of reflecting back, paraphrasing, deconstructing, theme finding, using silence, and summarising. These skills are often grouped together under the label 'active listening'.

When reflecting back, we use the same words as the speaker, giving the words back to them and so indirectly inviting them to say more. In paraphrasing we use our own words with the intention that we will receive confirmation that we have understood correctly, or if we have misunderstood that the person will clarify what they want us to understand. From what we have learnt so far in this chapter this may work well with some cultures who prefer indirect communication but may be met with bemused silence from those preferring direct communication who would probably expect the mediator to ask direct questions.

In trying to go deeper into the meaning of communication by deconstructing what is said we are seeking reoccurring themes which will enable us to identify important values and meaning sets. This is where the mediator should listen carefully for what the person's use of myths and stories tells us. Many legally trained mediators may want to quickly move on when a person seems to have strayed from the factual aspects of the dispute and may have little time for what may seem inconsequential narratives. However, as I hope I have indicated there is much to learn from metaphors and myths. By carefully listening to reoccurring themes in a disputant's narrative we will discover their core values, what is important to them and the meaning they attach to things. These are key pieces of knowledge which will enable the mediator to facilitate the writing of a settlement which reflects these values and beliefs. They may also show that the disputants, however different they seem, have shared values which are only discovered within their themed narratives. The mediator may discover that both parties share a value such as loyalty, particularly to family. Finding any commonality of this kind increases the potential for success when bringing the parties together in a joint session, moving them from seeing the other as an 'alien' to both parties experiencing some aspect of their shared humanity.

I have written in the previous section about the importance of silence and the role it plays in different culture, but it always needs to be used with sensitivity. A mediator working psychologically would normally use silence to allow space for reflection and would work hard not to fill silences with suggestions. However, every mediator needs to be aware of the party's cultural response to silence, as well as any personal comfort or discomfort they exhibit with it and adjust their more regular use of silence accordingly. To give time for reflection is welcomed in some cultures but can feel oppressive in others.

It is not just silence which has cultural interpretations, the volume, pace, and vocal nuance of the voice will be heard differently, and different meaning attributed to it by different cultures and individuals. Some mediators, particularly those from a psychology background may tend to speak in a soft slow tone and use what are often thought of as 'psychotherapy-type' phrases, such as 'I hear what you say', 'How do you feel?', etc. As a psychotherapist as well as a mediator I must say these are phrases which I hope I never use. The use of such phrases when working with disputants who come from a hard business culture will only serve to alienate them. Wherever possible the pace and tone used by a disputant should be sensitively and intuitively matched by the mediator, this will happen naturally if the mediator is really listening and therefore authentically connected with the party. Mediators who are afraid of emotions may try to lessen the volume of emotional expression by speaking very quietly or even asking a person to lower their voice. This is likely to annoy the person and for them to feel the mediator does not understand the level of emotion they are trying to express. Of course, care must be taken if different parties are very different in the level of emotion they express and the way they express it. The mediator must be sensitive to any discomfort or power inequality and try to address this without leaving anyone feeling they have been told off or put down.

Whilst stressing the importance of the need for any summary to include the party's perceptions of the facts and the emotions and meanings which the party gave directly or indirectly in that narrative, the mediator needs to be sensitive that some cultures may expect a simple retelling of the 'facts'. The mediator may need to explain that in order to reach a meaningful settlement it is important to discover not just what the party *wants* from the mediation but what they *need* in terms of both financial or material settlement, and also what they require emotionally and psychologically to move on from the dispute and reclaim their life.

Presence, Proximity, and Mediator Body Language

If we are to accept the above, then the importance of the quality of presence and 'being-with' is clear. When we briefly looked earlier at some aspects of existential thinking, we noted that, although we are all unique, we share common existential givens. Amongst these are the need to be heard and to be respected. This may be within the world in general or within our chosen groups – those in criminal gangs want to be listened to and respected by their fellows just as a teacher may look for this from their students, or an executive from their leadership team.

Even before a mediation begins, the mediator always needs to be sensitive to how they set up the room regardless of the cultural background of the parties. As we know, people can attach great importance to seating arrangements. People often choose the same seats whenever they visit a cinema or a restaurant, and when I run training courses, I am struck by how people often seem to occupy the same seats each day throughout the course, although there is no set seating arrangement. Those who don't consistently choose the same seat usually call attention to this, and in doing so stress how unusual it is, 'I thought I would sit somewhere else today' or 'I thought I would mix things up a little', 'I am being brave and sitting next to someone I don't know well'.

In a mediation when the disputants enter the room for the first joint opening session, it may be the first time that the parties have ever seen one another in person, or be the first time since an emotional outburst, or since the presenting dispute itself. It can be a very challenging and emotional time for everyone in the mediation. It certainly presents a challenge to the mediator who will aim to position chairs in a way in which the parties feel connected, yet which is non-intrusive into personal space, at the same time seating themselves in a way which reinforces their neutrality.

It is vital that the mediator picks up on any non-verbal clues as to how comfortable or otherwise a person is with the seating. They must make any necessary changes needed for a party to feel comfortable, unless these changes conflict with the other party's needs. If this happens the mediator is in danger of setting up a power struggle. If the mediator sits the parties next to each other it reduces the basic line of sight, direct interaction, and face to face communication. Although clearly this can be a hindrance, in some cases not being able to see the other person's face can be less intimidating and help the parties feel more secure. In some cultures, it is not acceptable to have direct eye contact, particularly between a man and a woman. Many mediators will favour the corner position where the mediator sits at the corner of the table, and the table itself sets up a distance and a barrier between the parties who sit either side and so have the choice of facing one another at an angle or facing the mediator. It is also a positioning which emphasises equality of everyone, including the mediator. In most of my own mediations I work without a table or other barrier between the parties but will alter this if there is a cultural or contextual reason to do so, such as one party fearing the other or parties needing a more formal arrangement. Often the mediator will be limited in how they can arrange seating and may find they are asked to mediate between two people around a large, fixed boardroom table.

When the parties enter the first joint session at the very beginning of the mediation the mediator needs to clarify how the parties wish to be addressed during the meeting. I have already mentioned that some cultures prefer the use of titles whilst others are more likely to prefer the use of their first names. As a mediator one must respect these differences, even if it means calling one party Sir Frederick Armstrong-Smythe throughout the day, and the other Fred. This may feel odd and seem to indicate a hierarchical inequality, but the equality lies in giving equal respect to what the parties need, not trying to use the same level of informality with both.

It may seem polite to invite the parties into the room for the joint session saying' please take a seat' but even this can lead to problems if they both head for the same seat and an argument ensues. In the opening phase of the mediation the mediator needs to demonstrate that they are in charge of the process, although not of the content. It is at this stage that the mediator needs to be a leader whereas for the rest of the mediation they should be a follower, led by the parties' narratives. It is always better to escort a party to a seat than invite them to choose where they want to sit.

As we can see, this is a sensitive area in all mediations but especially so in mediations where there are cultural issues at play. In one mediation in which I was involved I found it very challenging to be asked by an Asian woman, who appeared very Westernised in her dress and manner, to keep the door open when my male co-mediator or the other party who was a man was in the room. This seemed to challenge every idea of confidentiality, especially as her husband insisted on sitting in the corridor outside the room. Although she had originally agreed to have a male and female co-mediator, and the other party to the dispute was a male work colleague, after discussions with her, her husband, and the other party, we all agreed that I should mediate alone, and the door could be closed. The lesson to be learnt was to always expect the unexpected when it comes to mediating and be prepared to be flexible.

If we move on from the joint first session into the more intimate private one to one sessions, these issues can be even more acute. In a mediation with two parties both of whom are from more western cultures, a mediator may choose to emphasise the confidentiality of the session and to build trust by moving their seat nearer to the party, now that the other disputant is absent. Clearly, this would not be acceptable in some cultures where the need to maintain a physical instance is culturally determined. Careful observation by the mediator will pick up when a person is unhappy with the physical distance and will move accordingly. Although culture places a large part in determining what is an acceptable distance for comfort, it is important to remember that there are big individual differences in the amount of personal space an individual requires, and so the mediator needs to remain alert to this no matter the cultural issues involved. Difficulties can be minimised if the mediator asks permission to move nearer or alter the seating. However, no matter how hard the mediator has tried to establish that they are not there in a hierarchical or authoritative position some parties will always choose to see the mediator as a judge of some kind. They will be keen to be seen in a good light by the mediator and may agree to things they are not entirely comfortable with. Cultures where respect for seniority and power are valued will find it more difficult to be honest with the mediator and tell them if they are not happy with aspects of the mediator's behaviour, even when invited to do so.

Moving on from consideration of proximity, the mediator needs to think carefully as to the best way to convey their attention and presence. For many Westerners maintaining eye contact indicates respect and interest. However, the mediator needs to be aware of the acceptability or otherwise of direct eye contact and consider this in how they position themselves. It is important not to assume anything from the amount of direct eye contact a party gives the mediator, the mediator needs to accept it and work with it.

It is very rare for a mediator to touch any of the parties during a mediation, although they may be tempted to do so if a party is very emotional and tearful, or if a disputant looks as though they are about to stand up or move forward in an aggressive way. In all cases it is best not to do so. However, the different cultural backgrounds of parties may mean that they use touch to express themselves during the mediation, touching the mediator's arm, wanting to hug the mediator at the end of a difficult but successful mediation. A mediator must be prepared to handle this.

How the mediator moves and sits during the mediation is also worth consideration.

Through these movements we send information to others about our attitude, our emotional state, and our level of comfort regarding relaxation and control. Many of those from Western cultures will be more relaxed if the mediator adopts a more informal way of sitting, although when training mediators I have been surprised at how relaxed a position some have taken, e.g. sitting with their feet up under them. This can work in some mediations but must be matched with other body language which shows the mediator is attentive, alert, and interested and not about to fall asleep. In Middle Eastern countries it should be remembered that showing the soles of the feet to others is considered disrespectful and for the mediator to cross their legs is often seen as offensive in Ghana and Turkey for example. These differences are often acceptable if everything else about the attitude of the mediator conveys genuine respect.

Key Considerations and Skills for Working with Cultural Difference 137

Those in a mediation will be acutely aware of the mediator's movements and will look for any indication that the mediator agrees or disagrees with them or shows what they perceive as a bias to the other party. This is true no matter the culture of the people in the dispute, so the mediator needs to be aware that every slight nod of the head or movement of the hand or even a finger will be open to interpretation. To bow to another person may be the height of respect in Japan but be criticised or considered affected in the US.

A mediator may choose to show they are listening by leaning forward and using open hands as an invitation for the other person to speak. This would be considered unprofessional in cultures where a more still, upright position would be considered appropriate in a serious situation such as a mediation. I know that I am quite an expressive person and naturally use my hands and arms a lot when talking, particularly when I am very engaged with the discussion, so I must be conscious of how this will come across to the listener and pick up on their bodily cues. If I am sufficiently in tune with them then my own gestures will be less pronounced and will be closer to theirs. This happens naturally. If I am busy thinking about matching my gestures, I cannot be present to the person I am with, I am not with them, I am in my own head.

I hope in this section I have indicated that although it is useful and respectful to know something of the cultures of the people you are working with, the most important thing is to remain alert, authentic, respectful, and open to picking up on any atmosphere or gesture which might indicate discomfort on anyone's part. If there is something which makes you think a person is uncomfortable or you think you have made a mistake, it is vital not to ignore it, one gains trust and respect if one addresses it, and if necessary, apologizes. We all make mistakes, and it can be a comfort to others if they are acknowledged, and indeed can gain increased trust and respect. To not acknowledge this risks parties sitting with unexpressed anger or resentment which will make any genuine progress toward settlement difficult if not impossible

Having considered what an individual mediator may need to think about when dealing with cultural issues in a mediation, I want to move on to look at how this collectively impacts on the mediation profession.

Chapter 14

Considerations and Implications for the Mediation Profession

Introduction

If we are to move cultural awareness to the forefront of mediation practice, there needs to be a mindset change as well as organisational change. Most people will still think of heading for the legal processes to sort out a dispute. The law is considered to be neutral and logical, and yet conflict is neither of these things. The legal process is competitive and combative, whilst the mediation process aims to be collaborative. Lawyers are taught not to ask questions they do not know the answers to, and to use closed questions whenever possible, keeping dialogue closed, and 'relevant' to the 'facts' of the case. Mediators, certainly in the early 'tuning in' phase of the process will seek to have very open interchange with each party, not making any attempt to filter out what an outsider may consider to be irrelevant. They see their first task as building trust and forming a working alliance with each person involved in the dispute. This trust then allows the mediator to explore more fully what the meaning of the dispute is and how a resolution can be found which fits a person's values, and takes into account meaning led and cultural needs, rather than wants. The challenge for mediators interested in this more psychological approach is to not get stuck in exploring, but to know when they have understood enough so that they can move on to the next stage in which the work does become more focused on the particular dispute. Even at this more focused and less emotional stage, it is important that the mediator does not forget or set aside everything they have learnt, particularly the parties' emotional and psychological needs which must be addressed as an integral part of any agreement.

Despite an increase in those from non-legal backgrounds entering the mediation profession, mediation work is still often filtered through legal organisations such as solicitors' offices and courts, where preference is often given to mediators who are also lawyers. When I first began training mediators, the courses were filled with lawyers who were fearful that any increase in the use of mediation would mean less work for them and were following the 'if you can't beat them, join them' path. Others approaching retirement were looking for a more flexible part-time income stream which they could continue with after retirement. Those lawyers coming to my courses now tend to be lawyers whose personal worldview may be somewhat at odds with the legal sector's mode of practice and are seeking a more collaborative approach. I cannot say that this is a reflection of what is happening throughout the legal profession as the courses I am involved in are clearly based on a psychological approach and for that reason will appeal to some lawyers whilst be very unattractive to others.

Structural Considerations

Cultural Representation in the Mediation Profession

Given the continued strong influence of legal professions on the development of mediation practice, before exploring the position of cultural representation within mediation let's start by looking at the situation within the legal sector overall.

Alice Halsted, a senior early talent adviser at Taylor Wessing, noted that 'the legal sector does not accurately reflect the society it serves', and that although it was working towards change, it takes time. She noted that there has been some improvement but that while women make up over half (52%) of lawyers in law firms, the underrepresentation of women becomes more apparent at senior levels, with female partnerships standing at 21%. In terms of differences in representation across ethnicity she claimed that black lawyers make up 3%, a rise of 1% since 2014, Asian lawyers in law firms make up 14%, 3% come from mixed or multiple ethnicities, and 1% from 'other'. The figures for disability representation show 5% of all lawyers declaring a disability (physical or mental) which is a 1% rise since 2019.

The legal profession is often seen as elitist, and the Solicitors Regulation Authority (SRA) figures show 22% of lawyers attended a fee-paying school compared to 7.5% of the general population. While a greater proportion of lawyers (58%) come from a professional background, compared to 37% nationally, only 17% of lawyers come from a lower socio-economic background compared to 39% of the general population. Interestingly, the SRA reports that a greater proportion (3.5%) of lawyers identify as gay, lesbian, or bi-sexual than the UK workforce as a whole.

Mediation is a relatively new profession and not fully regulated and so similar figures are not available. However, The Centre for Effective Dispute Resolution (CEDR) in their 10th Audit of mediators mainly from legal backgrounds, reported that female involvement in the mediation field improved significantly since the 2018 level of 24%, reaching 41% in 2020, and so is close to comparators such as the Law Society, where 51% of solicitors in private practice (or 33% of private practice partners) are women. In the area of ethnicity, it was found that the profession was still falling short with only 8% of those responding coming from ethnic minority groups compared to 17% of solicitors. Some 6% of mediators reported having a disability and 5% defined themselves as being either lesbian, gay, or bisexual.

Over the twenty years I have been working in the mediation field representation has changed radically, there are now more women attending mediation training, and there is greater diversity in ethnicity and age. The range of professional and non-professional backgrounds from which the participants come is now very varied.

Clearly, if we only have a limited number of trained mediators from different cultures this limits the choice for those seeking to commission a mediation.

Culture Matching

This is a sensitive area with strong opinions both for and against. In all the areas in which I work, mediation, coaching, and psychotherapy, there are groups advocating for the cultural matching of clients to the professionals they commission. Amongst the many arguments for cultural matching within these professions one is the belief that it can enhance understanding and trust with shared cultural backgrounds helping to build rapport and give an enhanced sense of comfort. There is a belief that the same cultural background and language will enable more effective communication and reduce the risk of misunderstanding. Within mediation it is also thought by some that understanding the different cultural approaches to conflict resolution is helpful and cultural matching may enhance the mediator's ability to find a culturally appropriate resolution. This presupposes that both parties to the mediation share the same cultural background and level of language ability, which is often not the case.

The case against cultural matching stems from the role of the mediator which universally works from a skill set focused on active listening, empathy, confidentiality, and neutral enquiry. The need to be neutral and impartial may be compromised through matching, with the danger that the mediator may be tempted to align more closely with one party's understanding and interpretation of their cultural heritage and cultural norms within their current context. The different social background of a mediator and party may be more pronounced than any racial or gender differences. It may also be argued that a mediator from a different culture may bring a fresh perspective and creativity.

People tend to first think of matching in terms of racial heritage, but it is worth also considering it in relation to gender difference and sexual orientation. It is important to remember that gender is not binary, and people may identify themselves in a different way to how they visually present themselves. So, as with everything in the mediation process it is important to make no assumptions.

In 2009, Dr Lorig Charkoudian and Ellen Wayne undertook research into whether differences in the relationship between participant's and mediator's gender and racial/ethnic backgrounds affected disputants' perceptions of fairness in mediation. They used a very small sample confined to five Northeastern states of America, looking at 70 cases, about half of which were co-mediated. They looked at mediations in which the mediator/s and parties' gender, race, or ethnicity did not match, and other mediations in which one party shared the gender or race of the mediator. Their study found gender matching between parties and mediator/s significantly impacted participant perception. In cases where a single party shared the mediator's gender identity the isolated party reported feelings of unfairness, believing that the mediator listened less to them and was therefore more likely to take sides. The findings led Charkoudian and Wayne to believe that matching co-mediators and participants' gender offered a way of decreasing any perceived power imbalance. Much of the research into gender matching has assumed the parties are cisgender and heterosexual so considerable further research is required.

Using co-mediation offers mediators a way to introduce two mediators from different genders or cultural backgrounds. It can be particularly useful in heterosexual marital disputes to have a male and female mediator as there is a tendency for parties to believe that the mediator of the same gender will automatically agree with the party who shares their gender and take their side.

In my own experience it is simplistic to think that most people would choose to work with someone of a perceived cultural sameness. I have had clients choose to work with me as a white woman rather than with someone who more obviously would seem to be 'like them'. One man of an Afro-Caribbean heritage told me that he would have felt very uncomfortable saying negative things about people from his own culture if the mediator shared that culture. A woman from an Asian community told me that she would not trust that a male of female mediator from her own culture would hold the confidentiality, as she felt that if a community elder asked them about what had been said in a mediation the mediator would feel obliged to tell them out of respect for one's elders. I cannot comment on the truth or prevalence of these perceptions, but it is important to remember that for everyone who welcomes a mediation from a similar cultural background there are others who would see it as a negative. I know that if I perceive a person to be very similar to myself in race, culture, class, etc. there is a danger that I will be lazy and assume that we think the same way about lots of things. This may mean that I do not explore and deconstruct sufficiently what the person means and how their perceptions differ from my own. This can lead to the danger that I may too quickly assume that I understand. I believe I work better with those where there is a perceived cultural difference. As a naturally curious person, I am keen to understand how others experience the world in their unique way and will want to explore differences and similarities.

Training and Development Considerations

Cultural Competency Training

As Margery B. Ginsberg and Raymond Wlodkowski (2009:14) warned us, it is important to remember that: '[U]nless educators understand their own culturally mediated values and biases, they may be misguided in believing that they are encouraging divergent points of view and providing meaningful opportunities for learning to occur when they are in fact repackaging or disguising past dogmas. It is entirely possible to believe in the need for change and therefore learn new languages and techniques, and yet overlay new ideas with old biases and frames of reference. It is possible to diminish the potential and the needs of others at the most subconscious levels and in the most implicit ways without any awareness of doing so. Mindfulness of who they are and what they believe culturally can help them to examine the ways in which they may be unknowingly placing their good intentions with a dominant and unyielding framework – in spite of the appearance of openness and receptivity to enhancing motivation to learn among all students.'

If we are concerned with developing and offering cultural competency training, we must first recognise that it is not just the word 'culture' but also the word 'competence' which means something different to every person. Competence is usually taken to mean having the ability to do something well, successfully, or efficiently. Cultural competency is the term used to define a combination of attitudes and skills that promote clear and effective communication, congruent behaviours, attitude, and policies promoting greater understanding and better communication between individuals and groups from different cultures. Cultural competency training aims at developing individuals who 'value diversity and respect individual differences regardless of race, religious beliefs, or ethnocultural background' (Purnell:2005:xv). To that list I would add class, sexual and gender identity.

Holt and George (2014) describe a culturally competent professional as one who has made substantial progress, but continually works towards a number of goals:

1. developing an awareness of personal, professional, and cultural biases that may adversely impact minority groups, immigrants, and refugees.
2. developing an awareness of the definitions and dynamics of racism, discrimination, and cultural oppression.
3. acquiring knowledge about the history..., culture, norms, and traditions of diverse groups.
5. developing relevant interpersonal skills and effective methods for working with diverse groups. This includes gaining an understanding of how race, culture, and language affect interactions with professionals.
6. taking action in the service and advancement of equality and justice.

Professionals working with marginalized and oppressed groups should contribute to addressing injustice and discrimination in the lives of their clients.

This emphasises that cultural competency is not something which can be taught on a short course. It is an attitude based on philosophical values and beliefs. It is an embedded understanding which needs to be checked on through self-reflection, it is an ongoing process.

Bryant and Peters (2014:47) identified the most urgent need for cultural competency training within the legal professions as being the development of introspection and self-awareness. They recognised that other professions already place these skills high on their requirement of professional competencies, noting that, 'psychologists are encouraged to recognize that, as cultural beings, they may hold attitudes and beliefs that can detrimentally influence their perceptions of and interactions with individuals who are ethnically and racially different from themselves' (American Psychological Association, 2017).

Bryant and Peters (ibid) suggested five habits which lawyers needed to adopt, starting with the need to be aware of 'the significance of culture in the ways in which we make sense of the world...[t]hrough our cultural lens. We make judgments about people based on what they are doing and saying. We may judge people to be truthful, rude, intelligent, or superstitious based on the attributions we make about the meaning of their behaviour. Because culture gives us the tools to interpret meaning from behaviour and words, we are constantly attaching culturally based meaning to what we see and hear, often without being aware that we are doing so.'

The five habits that they invite lawyers to develop are:

1. Degrees of Separation and Connection
   This is aimed at avoiding the unexplored assumptions held by a lawyer and calls on them to identify the similarities and differences between their clients and themselves and to assess their impact on the working relationship.
2. Rings in Motion
   Focuses on the interactions between the client, decision-makers, opponents, and lawyers.
3. Parallel Universes
   Focuses on helping the lawyer identify alternative explanations for a client's behaviour through the use of what they term 'parallel universe thinking' by generating multiple interpretations of a client's behaviour, rather than assuming that their first interpretation would be true.
4. Red Flags and Remedies
   The authors offer specific skills and tips for this 'habit';
   - Being careful in the use of 'scripts' (e.g. for explaining confidentiality) in cross-cultural encounters.
   - Paying special attention to the beginning of communication to ensure that these rituals are culturally appropriate (e.g. by consulting with an interpreter familiar with the client's culture).
   - Using active listening techniques such as rephrasing client information to ensure clear understanding.
   - Gathering information about the client's cultural context; for example, asking the client how the problem would be handled in his country of origin.
   - Looking for red flags that the interaction is not working, such as signs of disengagement, boredom, or silence of the client or distraction or negative judgment by the lawyer.
5. The Camel's Back
   Focuses on the need for the lawyer to recognise when an interaction has reached 'breaking point'. This includes the lawyer developing self-awareness so they can recognise early when this is most likely to happen, e.g. when they are tired, frustrated, under stress, under time pressure, etc.

These prompts are very useful in thinking about cultural competency within the mediation profession. Stallard (2002:472) expresses the view that within the legal process mediation is well placed to address cultural challenges, 'The advantage of alternative dispute resolution in a cultural context is that it examines the interests underlying the parties' positions in order to evaluate the needs, concerns, and desires of each side. Researchers realize that cultural constructions of personhood, conflict (specifically, its genesis, management, and resolution), and rationality are factors crucial to understanding how different cultures interpret and respond to conflict situations.' Voyvodic of The University of Windsor, Michelle LeBaron, Associate Professor at George Mason University's Institute for Conflict Analysis and Resolution, and Zena Zumeta, President of the Mediation Training and Consultation Institute in Ann Arbor, Michigan, are amongst those who have challenged the level of cultural competence within the legal professions, calling on them to practice more self-reflection and acknowledge systemic power and privilege. Although considering mediation to be further along than some other areas of legal practice they stress the need for continued development to ensure that it is a process which is flexible and adaptable enough to function well for people from a wide range of cultural backgrounds.

LeBaron and Zumeta (2003:463) stress that mediation processes must reflect a 'range of values about how disputes are named, understood, and addressed' and that whether working in court-attached mediations or privately mediators should be trained in applying cultural competences in their work. As I do, they do not see the need for this to include considerable knowledge of different cultural groups, but it does require an understanding of 'culture as a powerful underground river that shapes expectations, understandings, and actions in mediation' (2003:465). They, and Voyvodic, identify the starting point for a mediator to develop cultural competence as being through self-reflection and insight into their starting points, assumptions, and biases whilst further developing skills in flexibility, adaptability, and being comfortable with ambiguity. This may remind some readers of the existential importance of being able to at least work with uncertainty, if not to embrace it, and the need for phenomenological investigation in which assumptions have been bracketed.

Howard Gadlin (2003) developed a series of questions which may help in the self-reflection practice:

- How do my own various identities (race, gender, sexual orientation, class, etc.) affect the way I interpret the experiences of people I consider are like me, and those who I perceive as being unlike me?
- How can I make myself aware of the ways in which these varying identities affect my own understanding of my mediator role, and what, if anything should/could I do to limit these effects (or expand my awareness, so I am not limited by them?
- Is it important to me that any settlement is in writing? How does this fit with the cultural or personal needs of the disputants?

Many of the recommendations for Culture Competence training as suggested by LeBaron, Zumeta, and Gadlin are good practice for all mediation training not just those with an emphasis on culture. They identify areas which I have currently drawn attention to as being existential and phenomenological, although they do not use either word. They call for training in identifying meaning, developing insight into one's own assumptions, developing the skills and attitude to establish a sensitive and adaptable yet professional mediation practice. They speak of the need to identify and work with different worldviews stating, 'culturally competent mediators make room for various starting points, recognising the need to translate worldviews and currencies back and forth among parties who may have conflated cultural differences...' (LeBaron and Zumeta (2003:470). They stress the need for mediators to develop their emotional, imaginative, and spiritual skills and to recognise and address power imbalances, through taking seriously their responsibility to behave ethically. As Francis (2017:63) reminds us, 'trainers in dispute resolution must know themselves, have deep knowledge of the conflict resolution techniques, culture, cultural communications, and be mindful...the teacher who is brave enough to teach dispute resolution must be a highly skilled facilitator.'

Psychologically Informed Training

Most accredited mediation training programmes are heavy on process, and many are focused on problem-solving skills, although some include an understanding of power dynamics and the psychology of conflict within their overall training. I believe that a training which is grounded in a psychological approach, and therefore embedding psychological understanding in the very breath of every part of the programme, is a good preparation to work with all cultures.

Part two of this book was dedicated to describing such a psychologically informed approach, so I shall not go over it again here. The training I and colleagues run each year in Oxford, whilst accrediting successful students to mediate in all manner of disputes, holds at the heart of the programme the belief in the importance of understanding the psychology at the heart of the dispute, and in every individual involved in the conflict. By meeting everyone in a dispute as a unique individual with their own take on the world, and therefore on the dispute, the psychologically trained mediator will be a curious explorer working with all involved to find a culturally appropriate resolution which meets the disputants' values and beliefs in a 'good enough' way for them to leave the dispute behind and move on with their lives.

Such training aims to develop culturally competent, and culturally fluent and fluid mediators who can identify and work with the cultural needs of all those involved in the dispute and work in a safe yet flexible way, working towards a meaningful settlement. Such a mediator may allow more extended social interchange during the pre-mediation period prior to bringing parties together on a mediation day. This allows the mediator more time to understand the personal and cultural elements which may be at play through creating a non-pressured space for individual disputants to convey **their** experience through the use of their personal narrative, use of metaphor, storytelling, or any other means which allows them to honour the complexity of their personal perceptions and interpretations, rather than presenting a factual account of the nature of the dispute. Such a way of telling 'their truth' would be very unlikely to be tolerated in a court or in an arbitration process. By allowing space and time the mediator can access what is really important to the party. They can explore their needs rather than wants, by working to stay with and deconstruct aspects of their story, particularly those parts which at first sight may be deemed irrelevant to the mediation. A culturally competent and fluent mediator will understand that there will be a reason (even an unconscious one) why a party is telling something to the mediator.

Through understanding and being alert to cultural understanding of power, psychologically informed mediators should not assume they understand with whom the power lies. The almost silent party may be the holder of the ultimate power of agreeing or sabotaging any agreement.

Part of the assessment process for the Psychologically Informed Mediation course in Oxford requires the mediation student to write a self-evaluation, because as mentioned earlier, we cannot attempt to understand and know others until we attempt to understand and know ourselves.

Chapter 15

Conclusion – To Return to the Existential and Phenomenological

The topic of this book is a complex and possibly contentious one. I apologise to those cultures which I may have omitted, either through lack of space, or my own ignorance. Also, to those cultures who may feel I have misrepresented them in some way. I am engaged on the start of a learning journey of my own in this field.

It was not my intention that this book be seen as a blueprint for how to work with cultural issues within the mediation context. It is intended to generate questions and discussion, and to raise the subject amongst mediators and mediation training providers. To my knowledge there are very few places where this discussion is active and ongoing, and I know of a very limited number of training courses which have an overtly psychological approach and in which the role of culture is an intrinsic and vital part of the curriculum.

There is much to be learnt about the role of culture, and the more we learn the more our lives are enriched. However, it must be accepted that there can never be a time when all mediators know everything about the cultural context and heritage of everyone they work with. We also need to acknowledge that cultural identifiers are always developing and changing. It is respectful to try to discover what we can about the cultures of those we work with, and essential to be culturally sensitive. However, as you may have already picked up, my personal view is that a mediator can work with all cultures if they adopt an open psychologically informed, culturally sensitive approach, based on a basic understanding of existential and phenomenological philosophical thinking and practice.

We have become a society which loves labels and seems to want to divide people into smaller and smaller identifiable groups and subcultures. I can see why this is important in raising the profile of certain groups who society has chosen to ignore and who now wish to be visible, acknowledged, and respected. However, there is a danger that a label provides a lazy way of categorising people.

As a child I hung out mainly with boys, climbed trees, and went on adventures. I was happy dressed as a cowboy with a Stetson hat and holster (having no idea of cultural appropriation) and had no interest in dolls, unless to operate on them in my imaginary hospital surgery! Fortunately, no-one jumped on my choices, thinking that I may believe myself to be male or wish that I was, or thinking that my tendency to operate on toys may be a sign of an unconscious wish to stab people! In my youth I fought hard not to be defined by my gender in a world which seemed to favour the male and to hold a stereotypical view of what was acceptable for women to do and not do. At the same time, I received criticism from some women's groups for my joy in having fun with make-up and fashion. It seemed to me that it was a time when we should have been encouraging all people to enjoy life by wearing whatever they wanted and exploring their own boundaries. I wanted the world to see each person as unique, with equal rights, worthy of equal respect (unless their behaviour did not merit it, and of course my response to what behaviour is ok and what isn't is culturally influenced), and accepting of all their aspirations. Today, I am more ready to consider my gender as an important part of the way I identify myself. This does not mean that I automatically feel closest to other women or have any expectation that a woman of the same age, race, and class as myself will necessarily share my values and beliefs.

It is vital to a healthy society that everyone, whatever their cultural heritage and in whatever way they choose to identify themselves is treated with equal respect and their personal experiences understood and validated. One of the themes I have written of in this book is that of authenticity, so it seems important to be honest about my personal stance on labels. I am not a great fan! In my professional work as a psychotherapist, I work with many clients who understand themselves to have been misgendered, either at birth, through their lived experience, or by society. I work with people who consider themselves heterosexual, homosexual, bisexual, pansexual, asexual, monogamous, polyamorous, or in other terms used to indicate their gender identification and/or sexual orientation. I have clients who identify themselves firstly by their race or colour, others by their own definition of their medical condition or disability. These identifiers are important to the individual's self-concept. For some people they are extremely positive and therefore to be celebrated, for others it may be more negative and driven by familial or societal ideas about what is considered to be 'normal', and therefore 'acceptable', and so potentially causing the client to feel shame or failure. Of course, labels, whether self-imposed or imposed by society will affect the way we see ourselves and how others see us, and therefore in many cases, how others behave towards us.

Recently in the psychotherapy profession there has been considerable debate about the extent to which a therapist is allowed to explore any identifying labels a client may initially use to describe themselves. This seems to stem not from a respect for people's rights to identify themselves, and a wish to fully understand their worldview, but more from a fear of being considered to be politically incorrect. Most of my clients are very clear about how they define themselves and I have experienced the struggles they have had to have their true selves validated. For others the need to belong and to join a community has led to them seeking labels which instead of freeing them and allowing them to expand their lived experience has confused and limited them. Belonging to certain groups or cults brings a sense of belonging and community which some individuals have found hard to access.

One example is that of a fourteen-year-old boy who came into therapy to support him in embarking on gender reassignment, including hormone treatment and surgery in his desire to become female. Most of the transgender clients I have worked with have felt very uncomfortable in their designated gender from a very early age and have made successful transitions. When exploring with this client when the belief that he was not male had started it became apparent that it was fairly recent. He told me that he had never really thought about his gender until the last year, accepting himself as male without question. He only began questioning this when his friends started regularly watching pornography. At first the nature of the videos they watched was straightforward heterosexual consensual encounters, which he found sexually arousing, but the nature of the material changed, focusing more on erotic asphyxiation with the male partner strangling his female partner. My client told me that it was a common practice for his friends to ask their young girlfriends if they could engage in this practice with them. He described how he had been physically sick after watching some of the videos and was fearful that he would be expected to strangle his girlfriend when he started dating. The repulsion he felt towards the practice had led him to believe that he must not be a 'real man' and therefore to adopt a very binary approach to the subject leading him to believe that he must really be female. At that point he had started growing his hair and wearing more androgynous clothing although this had not felt comfortable to him. In therapy we explored what it really meant to be a man and how different men feel different things and act differently. The client saw that he did not need to join the crowd or exile himself and seek a different label but could live to his own values. This client is now in his final year of university, does not feel the need to claim any particular sexual orientation label, but has been in a happy relationship with a female for the last year.

Another example in which group labels can be limiting was with a female client in her twenties who identified as polyamorous and lived in a shared house with others who shared that identity. She came to therapy because she had started a relationship with a man outside of the house group. She feared that she had fallen in love with him but that she must end the relationship because he did not believe in polyamory. This seemed to me to be such a paradoxical situation. One might consider that a polyamorous approach would give the individual greater freedom to explore relationships, but for this client it appeared to limit her. I explored what this man's feelings were towards her and her beliefs. He had told her that he did not agree with her views and although he would remain monogamous in their relationship, he was not requiring her to do so, although he could not say whether he would feel he needed to leave the relationship if she did enter another sexual relationship at the same time as seeing him. She was not attracted to anyone else at the time and so the issue was largely theoretical. Her biggest concern was what the polyamorous group she lived with would think if she made a commitment to exploring the relationship. She felt very much part of this group and all the cultural aspects which came with belonging to that community. She felt the need to 'ask permission' of those in her house to continue with her relationship with someone outside the group. She feared the group may throw her out' and she would lose 'a culturally safe space' which had held her and be cast into a culture of heterosexual monogamy which felt alien to her. It interests me that while there are many positive aspects to belonging to a culture which may bring a sense of belonging and understanding, expand our knowledge, sensitivity, and self-esteem, cultural belonging can also have the potential to be limiting and evoke fear of loss and isolation.

Another example from my practice is that of a young woman who had grown up in a charismatic Christian community in America. She had embraced their religious beliefs and felt very much part of the culture until she started being attracted to other women early in her teens. This was unacceptable in the eyes of the community. She was sent off to a conversion camp with the intention that this would 'cure' her of her attraction to females. In the event, the horrific experience did not have the desired effect, and she continued to be attracted to women. Believing that she was sinful and would be cast out by the community, she concluded that her attraction to females meant that she must be in the wrong body and that therefore she must be male, and so she left home for university with the intention of beginning the process to transition to a male. She entered university with a new male name and was housed in halls of residence which were designated for students who labelled themselves as transgender. The group who lived in this house were very close and supportive, they all chose to wear non-gendered clothing, had their own language, and hung out together. As part of her course in the second year the students undertook studies outside of the home campus and she chose to study at Oxford University for the year and began seeing me for therapy. She was shocked by the more fluid and flexible ways in which the group of students she became close to chose to identify sexually, and how they were more accepting of difference of any kind. This was very confusing for her. She was already on hormone treatment, bound her breasts, and was booked for surgery to remove her breasts when she returned to the States. During the year we worked together she explored shifts in her understanding about sexuality in general and her own, we looked at how she seemed to have a strong desire to belong to a group and to take on the group culture and conform to the group rules and behaviours, whether they were explicit or implied. Our focus was on developing a greater sense of, and trust in self. Unfortunately, the therapy was interrupted when her father suddenly became very ill, and she returned to her hometown.

I am offering the above vignettes to show how easy it can be to take a simplistic view when on first meeting, someone identifies themselves to you as a member of a particular cultural group. If I do not explore the meaning this has for them, I run with my own understanding and assumptions about what it means to belong to that group. This is dangerous territory and can lead to me running ahead to find a solution which fits more with my poor unexamined assumptions than with the complexity of the worldview of the person I am working with. Mediation is not therapy, and I am not suggesting that a mediator should explore in depth the worldview and unconscious motivators of all the parties! My point is we, as mediators, must be prepared to go beyond first impressions, early assumptions, and quick logical thinking which lead to swift problem solving and apparent resolution, but instead we must be patient and curious, and pay as much attention to what is not being said as we do to what is being said.

If a mediator, therapist, or coach can bring a phenomenological approach to their work it allows for the client to be seen both in their uniqueness and their commonality with others, with the professional attempting to bracket all theoretical presumptions they may hold about what to expect from a person from a particular group or background. A mediator must tune into the needs of each party in the dispute. These will include many cultural transactional elements, such as shaking hands, proximity of seating, and all the other aspects highlighted throughout this book. By the way a person enters the room, greets the mediator, reacts to the other party, holds their body, gives eye contact, etc. they are offering phenomenological information about their self-concept and their needs. They may signal that they need to lead and take space, or that they are very uncomfortable to be at the centre of things. They may indicate the extent to which their individuality is more important than having a collective identity or vice versa. All these are giving the professional insights into what they need from them and from the process and may be very different from what they are verbalising. It is important to explore what their phenomenological way of being and their verbal and non-verbal statements tell us about their understanding about their culture and personal experiences, and the meaning they attach to it.

In mediation every person involved will have their own perspective on the conflict and the mediator needs to work hard and sensitively to explore all elements to get as near as possible to understanding this. It is tempting to ignore elements which we don't understand, deem irrelevant, are contradictory, or we feel uncomfortable about, but to get to a meaningful resolution, these are the very areas we, as mediators, must give time to.

I feel sad that we seem to increasingly feel the need for labels, and cannot embrace difference as something wonderful, reminding us of the complexity and richness of the human state. We have so much to learn from one another through engaging our curiosity and listening to people's individual lived experience, which will of course be culturally influenced, rather than trying to group or label people. At the same time, I understand the strength which being part of a cultural group brings. A mediator cannot afford to ignore all the elements which make up the party's sense of self and their unique perceptions on the meaning of the dispute.

As we have seen, mediation practices exist throughout the world and in many different cultural settings. Whatever the context, I believe the mediator's main task is not to make assumptions or to label people, expecting them to conform to any cultural labels or expectations. Mediators must not assume that because we can identify a party's cultural heritage and allegiances, or even because they state them themselves, we can automatically understand where a person 'is coming from'. Instead, we must remain curious and sensitively explore the uniqueness of everyone involved in the mediation. It requires respect, patience, and curiosity to stay with being uncertain and not knowing, It can make us feel vulnerable fearing that tentative exploration may make us appear less professional or knowledgeable, but if we can do so we are more likely to enable parties to find a resolution which is meaningful for them culturally and personally, and therefore more likely to be adhered to, which at the end of the day is what everyone in mediation is hoping for.

I am ending with a quote from LeBaron and Zumeta (2003:471), 'Mediation is no substitute for efforts to address the systemic inequities and injustices that must be ameliorated if fairness and justice are to be part of our multicultural mosaics. But it can be a space in which people from diverse cultural and worldview perspectives find scope to be themselves, to unravel disputes in ways that make sense to them with the assistance of culturally competent third parties.' As mediators we have a lot of work to do to create a safe and welcoming mediation space for all. My aim is to at least open up discussion on how this may be achieved.

Bibliography

American Psychological Association. (2017). *Multicultural Guidelines: An Ecological Approach to Context, Identity, and Intersectionality*. Retrieved from: http://www.apa.org/about/policy/multicultural-guidelines.pdf

Anderson, A., Downs, S.D., Faucette, K., Griffin, J., King, T., & Woolstenhulme, S. (2007). How Accents Affect Perception of Intelligence, Physical Attractiveness, and Trust-worthiness of Middle-Eastern-, Latin-American-, British- and standard-American English-Accented Speakers. *Intuition: The BYU Undergraduate Journal in Psychology*, 3, 5–11.

Arnold, M. (1993). In Collini (Ed.) *Culture and Anarchy and Other Writings*. Cambridge: Cambridge University Press, p. 41.

Atwood, G.E., & Stolorow, R.D. (2016). Walking the Tightrope of Emotional Dwelling. *Psychoanalytic Dialogues*, 26(1), 103–108.

Avruch, K. (2004). Culture as Context, Culture as Communication: Considerations fro Humanitarian Negotiations. *Harvard Negotiation Review*, 9, 391.

Bandura, A. (1977). *Social Learning Theory*, Englewood Cliffs, NJ: Prentice Hall.

Barrett, J.T., & Barrett, J.P. (2004). *A History of Alternative Dispute Resolution*, San Francisco, CA: Jossey-Bass.

Baruch, R.A., Bush, B., & Folger, J.P. (2004). *The Promise of Mediation: The Transformative Approach to Conflict*, London: John Wiley & Sons.

Baruch, R.A., Bush, B., & Folger, J.P. (2007). Transformative Mediation and Third-Party Intervention: Ten Hallmarks of a Transformative Approach to Practice. *Conflict Resolution Quarterly*, 13(4).

Becker, E. (1973), *The Denial of Death,* London: Souvenir Press.

Bourdieu, P. (1972). *Outline of a Theory of Practice*, Cambridge: Cambridge University Press.

Brown, S.E. (2002). What is Disability Culture? *Disability Studies Quarterly*, 22(2), 34–50.

Bryant, S., & Peters J.K. (2014). Five Habits for Cross Cultural Lawyering. In Kimberly Holt Barrett &William H George, eds, *Race, Culture, Psychology & Law* Thousand Oaks, California: Sage.

Buber, M. (1996). *I and thou* (Kaufmann, W., Trans.). New York, NY: Simon & Schuster.

Bugental, J.F.T. (1987). *The Art of the Psychotherapist: How to Develop the Skills That Take Psychotherapy Beyond Science*. New York: Norton.

Bujo, B. (2000). *African Theology in its Social Context*, Eugene Oregon: Wipf & Stock Pub.

Bujo, B. (2001). *Foundations of an African Ethic: Beyond the Universal of Western Morality*, Redwood City, CA: PublishDrive.

Bibliography

Burton, J. (1990). *Conflict, Resolution and Prevention*, London: St Martin's Press.
Bush, R.A.B., & Folger, J.P. (1994). *The Promise of Mediation, The Transformative Approach to Conflict,* San Francisco, CA: Jossey-Bass.
Cameron, K.S., & Quinn, R.E. (2021). *Diagnosing and Changing Organizational Culture*, San Francisco, CA: Jossey-Bass.
Cantone, J.A., Martinez, L.N., Willis-Esqueda, C., & Miller, T. (2019). Sounding guilty: How accent bias affects juror judgments of culpability. *Journal of Ethnicity in Criminal Justice,* 17(3), 228–253. doi:10.1080/15377938.2019.1623963
CEDR. (2018). *The Eighth Mediation Audit*. www.cedr.com
CEDR. (2023). *The Tenth Mediation Audit*. www.cedr.com/foundation/mediation-audit/
Chaplin, T., & Aldao, A. (2012). Gender Differences in Emotional Expression in Children, *Psychological Bulleting*, 139(4), 735–765.
Christies, P., & Lovemore, M. (1993). *African Management: Philosophies, Concepts and Applications*, London: Knowledge Resources.
Cobb, S. (1992). *The Pragmatics of Empowerment in Mediation: Towards a Narrative Perspective*, Report for the National Institute of for Dispute Resolution, Washington, DC: NIDR.
Cobb, S. (1993). Empowerment and Mediation. In J.P. Folger & T.S Jones (Eds) *New Directions in Mediation: Communication research and perspectives* (pp. 48–77), Thousand Oaks, C.A: Sage.
Cobb, S. (1994). A Narrative Perspective on Mediation: Towards the Materialization of the Storytelling Metaphor. In J.P. Folger & T.S. Jones (Eds) *New Directions in Mediation; Communication, Research and Perspectives* (pp. 50–51), Thousand Oaks, CA: Sage Publications.
Cobb, S. (2000). Negotiation Pedagogy: Learning to Learn. *Negotiation Journal*, 16, 315–391.
Cobb, S. (2013). *Speaking of Violence: The Politics and Poetics of Narrative in Conflict Resolution (Explorations in Narrative Psychology)*, Oxford: Oxford University Press.
Cobb, S., & Rifkin, J. (1991). Neutrality as a Discursive Practice: The Construction and Transformation of Narratives in Community Mediation. In A. Sarat & S. Silbey (Eds) *Studies in Law, Politics, and Society* (Vol. 11, pp. 69–91), Greenwich, CT: JAI Press.
Cobb, S., & Rifkin, J. (1991). Practice and Paradox: Deconstructing Neutrality in Mediation. *Law & Social Inquiry*, 16(1), 35–62 (28 pages) www.jstor.org/stable/828547
Collins, S.A. (2000). Men's Voices and Women's Choices. *Animal Behaviour*, 60(6), 773–780. Retrieved from http://webhost.lclark.edu/clifton/behav/Discuss4b.PDF
Costantino, C.A., & Merchant, C.S. (1996). *Designing Conflict Management Systems: A Guide to Creating Productive and Healthy Organizations*, San Francisco CA: Jossey-Bass.
Dai Xiaodong, & Chen Guo-Ming. (2023). *Conflict Management and Intercultural Communication – The Art of Intercultural Harmony*, Abingdon: Routledge.
Davidheiser, M. (2008). Race, Worldviews, and Conflict Mediation: Black and White styles of Conflict Revisited. *Peace and Change: A Journal of Peace Research*, 33(1), 60–89.
Davis, L.J. (1995). *Enforcing Normalcy: Disability, Deafness, and the Body*, Versoo Books.
Deal, T.E., & Kennedy, A.A. (2000). *Corporate Cultures,* New York: Basic Books.
De Beauvoir, S. (1947). *The Ethics of Ambiguity,* New York: Philosophical Library.
Derwing, T.M., & Munro, M.J. (2009). Putting Accent in Its Place: Rethinking Obstacles to Communication. *Language Teaching*, 42(4), 476–490.
Dreyfus, H., & Rabinow, P. (1982). *Michel Foucault: Beyond Structuralism and Hermeneutics 65,* Brighton: Harvestor.

Deurzen van, E. (1996). *Everyday Mysteries,* London: Routledge.
Deurzen van, E. (2012). *Existential Counselling & Psychotherapy in Practice*, London: Sage.
Deutsch, M. (1991). Subjective Features of Conflict Resolution: Psychological, Social and Cultural Influences. In R. Vayrynen (Ed.) *New Directions in Conflict Theory: Conflict Resolution and Conflict Transformation*, London: SAGE.
Dixon, J.A., Mahoney, B., & Cocks, R. (2002). Accents of Guilt? Effects of Regional Accent, Race, and Crime Type on Attributions of Guilt. *Journal of Language and Social Psychology*, 21(2), 162–168. doi:10.1177/02627x02021002004
Dominguez-Urban, I. (1997). The Messenger as the Medium of Communication: The Use of Interpreters in Mediation. *Journal of Dispute Resolution*, 1, 1–52.
Durchslag, H.B. (2020). *The Collective Unconscious in the Age of Neuroscience – Severe Mential Illness and Jung in the 21st Century,* London: Routledge.
Ekman, P., Friesen, W.V., O'Sullivan, M., Chan, A., Diacoyanni-Tarlatzis, I., Heider, K., Krause, R., LeCompte, W. A., Pitcairn, T., Ricci-Bitti, P.E., Scherer, K., Masatoshi, T., & Tzavaras, A. (1887). Universals and Cultural Differences in the Judgments of Facial Expressions of Emotion. *Journal of Personality and Social Psychology*, 53(4), 712–717.
Ekman, P., Friesen, W.V., & Ellsworth, P. (1972). *Emotion in the Human Face: Guidelines for Research and an Integration of Findings.* Pergamon Press.
Ekman, P., & Keltner, D. (1997). Universal Facial Expressions of Emotion: An Old Controversy and New Findings. In U.C. Segerstråle & P. Molnár (Eds) *Nonverbal Communication: Where Nature Meets Culture* (pp. 27–46). Lawrence Erlbaum Associates, Inc.
Elkins, D.N. (1998). *Beyond Religion: A Personal Program for Building a Spiritual Life Outside the Walls of Traditional Religion,* Wheaton, IL: Quest Books.
Evans, S., Neave, N., & Wakelin, D. (2006). Relationships Between Vocal Characteristics and Body Size and Shape in Human Males: An Evolutionary Explanation for a Deep Male Voice. *Biological Psychology*, 72(2), 160–163.
Fanon, F. (1986), *Black Skin, White Masks*, London: Pluto Press.
Folberg, J., & Taylor, A. (1984). *The Mediation Process: A Guide to Resolving Conflict without Litigation,* San Francisco, CA: Jossey-Bass.
Foster-Harris, W. (1881). *Basic Patterns of Plot,* Norman, OK: University of Oklahoma Press.
Foulkes, P., & Docherty, G. (2006). The Social Life of Phonetics and Phonology. *Journal of Phonetics*, 34(4), 409–438.
Francis, V. (2017) Infusing Dispute Resolution Teaching and Training with Culture and Diversity (February 7, 2017). SSRN: https://ssrn.com/abstract=2915904 or http://dx.doi.org/10.2139/ssrn.2915904
Frankl, V.E. (1984). *Man's Search for Meaning,* London: Simon & Schuster.
Frankl, V.E. (2000). *Man's Search for Ultimate Meaning*, London: Simon & Schuster.
Freud, S. (1909). Analysis of a Phobia of a Five-Year-Old Boy. In *Pelican Freud Library's Case Histories 1 'Dora' and 'Little Hans'* (pp. 149–287), London: Penguin Group.
Freud, S. (1930). *Civilization and Its Discontents*, Penguin Freud Library, London: Penguin.
Freud, S. (1973). *Introductory Lectures on Psychoanalysis*, Penguin Freud Library, London: Penguin.
Frumkin, L.A., & Stone, A. (2020). *Not All Eyewitnesses Are Equal: Accent Status, Race and Age Interact to Influence Evaluations of Testimony*, Walton Hall, Milton Keynes: School of Psychology and Counselling, Faculty of Arts and Social Sciences, The Open University.

156 Bibliography

Fuertes, J.N., Potere, J.C., & Ramirez, K.Y. (2002). Effects of Speech Accents on Interpersonal Evaluations: Implications for Counselling Practice and Research. *Cultural Diversity and Ethnic Minority Psychology*, 8(4), 346–356.

Gadlin, H. (2003). *Cross Cultural Issues in ADR*. Paper presented at the Association of American Law Schools Annual Meeting Workshop on Dispute Resolution: Raising the Bar and Enlarging the Canon, Washington, DC, Jan. 2–5, 2003.

Geertz, C. (1973). *The Interpretation of Cultures,* New York: Basic Books.

Ginsberg, M.B., & Wlodkowski, R.J. (2009). *Diversity and Motivation: Culturally Responsive Teaching in College* (2nd ed.). Jossey-Bass.

Glasl, F. (1999). *Confronting Conflict,* Bristol: Hawthorn Press.

Gluszek, A., & Dovidio, J.F. (2010). Speaking with a Nonnative Accent: Perceptions of Bias, Communication Difficulties, and Belonging in the United States. *Journal of Language and Social Psychology*, 29(2), 224–234. doi:10.1177/0261927X09359590

Gold, J.A. (2005). ADR Through a Cultural Lens: How Cultural Values Shape Our Disputing Processes. *Journal of Dispute Resolution*, 289, 292–93.

Goleman, D. (1996). *Emotional Intelligence*, London: Bloomsbury Publishing PLC.

Greatbatch, D., & Dingwall, R. (2001), *Selective Facilitation: Some Preliminary Observations on a Strategy Used by Divorce Mediators,* London: Routledge.

Habermas, J. (1979). *Communication and the Evolution of Society*, Boston: Beacon Press.

Hanaway, M. (2012). *Co-mediation: Using a Psychological Paired Approach to Conflict*, Henley-on-Thames: The CH Group.

Hanaway, M. (2021), *Psychologically Informed Mediation: Studies in Conflict and Resolution*, Abingdon: Routledge.

Hanaway, M. (2024). *The Unterwelt* (unpublished paper, currently in development).

Handy, C.B. (1978). *Gods of Management: The Four Cultures of Leadership*, London: Souvenir Press.

Harter-Uibopuu, K. (2002). Ancient Greek Approaches Toward Alternative Dispute Resolution. *Willamette Journal of International Law and Dispute Resolution,* 10(1), 7–69.

Heery, M. (2002). Inside the Soul of Russian and American Psychotherapy Trainings. *Journal of Humanistic Psychology*, 42(3), 89–101.

Heery, M., & Bugental, J.F.T. (2005). Meaning and Transformation. In E. van Deurzen & C. Arnold-Baker (Eds) *Existential Perspectives on Human Issues: A Handbook for Therapeutic Practice* (pp. 253–364), Basingstoke, England: Palgrave.

Heidegger, M. (1962|) *Being and Time,* Oxford: Oxford University Press.

Hemert van, Dianne , A.; van de Vijver, Fons , J.R.; Vingerhoets, Ad , J.J. M. (2011). Culture and Crying. *Cross-Cultural Research*, 45(4), 399–431. doi:10.1177/1069397111404519. ISSN 1069-3971. S2CID 53367887.

Higley, D.J., et al (1996). CST Testosterone and 5-HIAA Correlate with Different Types of Aggressive Behaviors. *Biological Psychiatry: A Journal of Psychiatric Neuroscience and Therapeutics*, 40(11), 1067–1082.

Hofstede, G. (1984). National Cultures and Corporate Cultures. In L.A. Samovar & R.E. Porter (Eds) *Communication Between Cultures*, Belmont, CA: Wadsworth.

Hofstede, G., Neuijen, B., Ohayv, D.D., & Sanders, G. (1990). Measuring Organizational Cultures: A Qualitative and Quantitative Study Across Twenty Cases. *Administrative Science Quarterly*, 35(2), 286–316.

Hofstede, G. (1991). *Cultures and Organizations: Software of the Mind*, New York: McGraw-Hill.

Bibliography 157

Hofstede, G. (2001). *Culture's Consequences. Comparing Values, Behaviors, Institutions, and Organizations Across Nations* (2nd ed.), London: Sage.

Holt, K.B., & George, W.H. (Eds) (2014). *Race, Culture, Psychology & Law*, Thousand Oaks, California: Sage.

Husserl, E. (1913), *Ideas Pertaining to a Pure Phenomenology and to a Phenomenological Philosophy – First Book: General Introduction to a Pure Phenomenology* (K. Kersten, Trans.), The Hague: Nijhoff. (Original work published 1982)

Irani, G.E., & King-Irani, L. (1996). *Recognizing the Other, Forgiveness, and Reconciliation: Lessons from Lebanon*, Beirut: Lebanese American University.

Irani, G.E. (1999). Islamic Mediation Techniques for Middle East Conflicts. *Middle East Review of International Affairs (MERIA)*, 3(2).

Irani, G.E. (2000). Rituals of Reconciliation: Arabic-Islamic Perspectives. *Mind and Human Interaction: Windows Between History, Culture, Politics, and Psychoanalysis*, 11(4), 226–45.

Irani, G.E. (2002). Acknowledgement, Forgiveness and Reconciliation in Conflict Resolution: Perspectives from Lebanon. *Chronos*, 5, 195–220.

Irani, G.E. (forthcoming). Acknowledgment, Forgiveness, and Reconciliation in Conflict Resolution: Perspectives from Lebanon. In G.E. Irani & L.E. King-Irani (Eds) *Lessons from Lebanon*.

Johnson, G., & Scholes, K. (2001). *Exploring Public Sector Strategy*, London: Financial Times/Prentice Hall.

Jones, T.S., & Brinkett, R. (2008). *Conflict Coaching: Conflict Management Strategies and Skills for the Individual*, London: Sage.

Jung, C.G. (1991), *The Archetypes and the Collective Unconscious*, London: Routledge.

Keen, S. (1991). The Enemy Maker. In C. Zweig & J. Abrams (Eds) *Meeting the Shadow* (pp. 198–199), New York: TarcherPerigee.

Killmann, R.H. (2023). *Mastering the Thomas-Killmann Conflict Mode Instrument -TKI*, California: Kilmann Diagnostics.

Kinzler, K.D., Shutts, K., Dejesus, J., & Spelke, E.S. (2009). Accent Trumps Race in Guiding Children's Social Preferences. *Social cognition*, 27(4), 623–634. doi:10.1521/soco.2009.27.4.623

Kluckhohn, C., & Kelly, W.H. (1945). The concept of culture. In, R. Linton (Ed.). *The Science of Man in the World Culture* (pp. 78–105), New York.

Ko, S.J., Judd, C.M., & Stapel, D.A. (2009). Stereotyping Based on Voice in the Presence of Individuating Information: Vocal Femininity Affects Perceived Competence but Not Warmth. *Personality and Social Psychology Bulletin*, 35, 198–211.

Koopman, P.M. (1993). in Christies, P., & Lovemore, M. (1993). *African Management: Philosophies, Concepts and Applications*, London: Knowledge Resources.

Kövecses, Z. (2004). Introduction: Cultural Variation in Metaphor. *European Journal of English Studies*, 8(3), 263–274.

Krauss, R.M., Freyberg, R., & Morsella, E. (2002). Inferring Speakers' Physical Attributes from Their Voices. *Journal of Experimental Social Psychology*, 38, 618–625.

Kring, A.M., & Gordon, A.H. (1998). Sex Differences in Emotion: Expression, Experience, and Physiology. *Journal of Personality and Social Psychology*, 74(3), 686–703. CiteSeerX 10.1.1.379.5826. doi:10.1037/0022-3514.74.3.686. PMID.

Kroeber, A.L., & Kluckhohn, C. (1952). *Culture: A Critical Review of Concepts and Definitions*, Cambridge, MA: Peabody Museum Press.

Kuper, A. (1999). *Culture: The Antropologist's account* (pp. x–xi), Cambridge, MA: Harvard University Press.

Ladd, P. (2003). *Understanding Deaf Culture: In Search of Deafhood*, Clevedon, Brisol: Multilingial Matters Ltd.

Lakoff, G., & Johnson, M. (2003). *Metaphors We Live By*, Chicago: University of Chicago Press.

LeBaron, M., & Zumeta, Z.D. (2003). Windows on Diversity: Lawyers, Culture, and Mediation Practice. *Conflict Resolution Quarterly*, 20(4), 463.

Lehane, D. (2010). *Shutter Island*, New York: Harper Collins.

Luban, D. (1987). *The Quality of Justice* (Presented to Institute of Legal Studies), Wisconsin: University of Madison.

Malatesta, C.Z., & Haviland, J.M. (1982). Learning Display Rules: The Socialization of Emotion Expression in Infancy. *Child Development*, 53(4), 991–1003.

Marshall, T. (1999). *Restorative Justice: An Overview*, London: Home Office.

Martin, J. (1992). *Cultures in Organizations: Three Perspectives*, New York: Oxford University Press.

Masuda, T., Ellsworth, P.C., Mesquita, B., Leu, J., Tanida, S., & Van de Veerdonk, E. (2008). Placing the Face in Context: Cultural Differences in the Perception of Facial Emotion. *Journal of Personality and Social Psychology*, 94(3), 365–381.

Matsumoto, D., Yoo, S.H., Nakagawa, S., & Multinational Study of Cultural Display Rules. (2008). Culture, Emotion Regulation, and Adjustment. *Journal of Personality and Social Psychology*, 94(6), 925–937.

Matsumoto, D. (1990). Cultural Similarities and Differences in Display Rules. *Motivation and Emotion*, 14(3).

May, R. (1991). *The Cry for Myth*, New York. W.W. Norton and Co.

Mindell, A. (1995). *Sitting in the Fire, Large Group Transformation using Conflict and Diversity,* San Francisco CA: Harper Collins.

Mindell, A. (2017). *Conflict: Phases, Forums, and Solutions,* North Charleston: World Tao Press.

Mischel, W. (1968). *Personality and Assessment*, New York: Wiley.

Moore, C. (1986). *The Mediation Process*, San Francisco: Jossey-Bass.

Moore, M. (1997). Theory of Transactional Distance. In D. Keegan (Ed.) *Theoretical Principles of Distance Education* (pp. 22–38), New York: Routledge.

Morris (2002). Critiquing the Critics: A Brief Response to Critics of Restorative Justice. *British Journal of Criminology*, 42(3), 596–615.

Newman, C., & Monaghan, A. (2005). *Butterworth Mediators on Mediation: Leading Mediator Perspectives on The Practice of Commercial Mediation*, Haywards Heath: Tottel Publishing.

Nietzsche, F. (1974). *Thus Spoke Zarathustra*, London: Penguin.

Paladino, M.P., & Mazzurega, M. (2020). One of Us: On the Role of Accent and Race in Real-Time in-Group Categorization. *Journal of Language and Social Psychology*, 39(1), 22–39. doi:10.1177/0261927x19884090

Pruitt, D.G. (1998). Social Conflict. In D.T. Gilbert, S.T. Fiske, & G. Lindzey (Eds) *The Handbook of Social Psychology* (4th ed., pp. 470–503). McGraw-Hill.

Rand, A. (2000). *The Art of Fiction: A Guide for Writers and Readers*, London: Penguin.

Randolph, P. (2013). Compulsory Mediation. https://mediate.com/compulsory-mediation/ (January 11, 2013).

Reich, W. (1967). *Reich Speaks of Freud*, London: Condor.
Reich, W. (1973). *The Discovery of the Orgone* (Vol. 1), New York: Farrar, Straus and Giroux.
Rifkin, J., & Cobb, S. (1991). Practice and Paradox: Deconstructing Neutrality in Mediation. *Law and Social Inquiry Journal*.
Rifkin, J., Millen, J., & Cobb, S. (1991). Towards a New Discourse for Mediation: A Critique of Neutrality. *Mediation Quarterly*, 9(2), 151–164.
Russo, M., Islam, G., & Koyuncu, B. (2017). Non-native Accents and Stigma: How Self-fulfilling Prophesies Can Affect Career Outcomes. *Human Resource Management Review*, 27(3), 507–520.
Samuels, A. (1993). *The Political Psych,* London: Routledge.
Sartre, J.-P. (1960). *Critique of Dialectical Reason,* Paris: Editions Gallimard.
Savage, C.A. (1997). Culture and Mediation: A Red Herring. *American University Journal of Gender, Social Policy & the Law*, 5, 273.
Schein, P. (2017). *Organizational Culture and Leadership*. Hoboken, NJ: Wiley.
Schneider, M.A. (1993). *Culture and Enchantment*, Chicago: The University of Chicago Press.
Scott, W.R. (2014). *Institutions and Organizations: Ideas, Interests, and Identities*. Los Angeles, CA: SAGE Publications.
Shantz, C. (1987). Conflicts Between Children. *Child Development*, 58, 283–305.
Spangler, B. (2003). Transformative Mediation. In G. Burgess & H. Burgess (Eds.) *Beyond Intractability*, Boulder: Conflict Information Consortium, University of Colorado. www.beyondintractability.org/essay/transformative-mediation
Stallard, A. (2002). Joining the Culture Club: Examining Cultural Context When Implementing International Dispute Resolution, 17 OHIO ST. J. ON DISP. RESOL. 463, 471 (2002) (quoting E. FRANKLIN DUKES, RESOLVING PUBLIC CONFLICT: TRANSFORMING COMMUNITY AND GOVERNANCE 167 (1996)).
Strasser, F., & Randolph, P. (2004). *Mediation- A Psychological Insight into Conflict Resolution*, London: Continuum.
Sun Tzu. (2009). *The Art of War,* London: Pax Libororum.
Suttie, I. (1936). *The Origins of Love and Hate,* Harmondsworth: Penguin.
The Week Staff Writers unnamed author. *Is Eye Witness Testimony Too Unreliable to Trust?* https://theweek.com/articles/480511/eyewitness-testimony-unreliable-trust
Tillich (1952). *The Courage to Be,* New Haven: Yale University Press.
Totton, N. (2006). *The Politics of Psychotherapy*, Maidenhead: Open University Press.
Tutu, D. (2000). *No Future Without Forgiveness*, Sutton: Rider Press.
Tylor, E.B. (2012). *Primitive Culture; Researches into the Development of Mythology, Philosophy, Religion, Art, and Custom,* Cambridge: Cambridge University Press.
Vorontsova, I. (2021). *Metaphors for Thinking in Modern Mandarin Chinese: A Corpus Study*. Master of Arts thesis, Vancouver: The University of British Columbia.
Wang, X. (2019,) The Symbol of the Iron House: From Survivalism to Existentialism. *Existential Psychology East-West*, 2, 7.
Wells. G., (1978). Applied Eyewitness-Testimony Research: System Variables and Estimator Variables. *Journal of Personality and Social Psychology*, 36(12), 1546–1557.
Wester, S., Vogel, D., Pressly, P., & Heesacker, M. (2002). Sex Differences in Emotion: A Critical Review of the Literature and Implications for Counseling Psychology [PDF]. *The Counseling Psychologist*, 30(4), 630–652.

Whitworth, N. (2021). *Accent, Identity and Prejudice.* www.leedsbeckett.ac.uk/blogs/carnegie-education/2021/05/accent-identity-and-prejudice/

Winslade, J., & Monk, G. (2000). *Narrative Mediation: A New Approach to Conflict Resolution,* San Francisco, CA: Jossey-Bass.

Yalom, I. (1980). *Existential Psychotherapy*, New York: Basic Books.

Yalom, I. (2013). *Love's Executioner and Other Tales of Psychotherapy*, London: Penguin.

Yarn, D.H. (Ed.) (1999). *Dictionary of Conflict Resolution*, San Francisco, CA: Jossey-Bass.

Yuki, M., Maddux, W.W., & Matsuda, T. (2007). Are the Windows to the Soul the Same in the East and West? Cultural Differences in Using the Eye and Mouth as Cues to Recognize Emotions in Japan and the United States. *Journal of Experimental Psychology*, 43(2), 303–311.

Index

Note: Page locators in **bold** and *italics* represents tables and figures, respectively.

accent prestige theory 54
accommodating approach to conflict 9
actions not words stage of conflict 8
Africa, cultural history of mediation in 109–111
'African Management' 109
Africa Peace and Conflict Network 94
agency 62–64
aggression 8, 14–15
alterity 67
alternative dispute resolution (ADR) 5–6, 22, 24, 30; in Russia 116; in the United States 111–112; *see also* mediation
Al Wasata 115
ambiguity 73–74
Anderson, A. 54
Annan, K. 110
arbitration 29, 32–33
Arb-Med 29
archetypes 126
Arnold, M. 95
Atwood, G. E. 60
authenticity 66, 75–76
avoiding approach to conflict 9
Avruch, K. 95

Becker, E. 65, 68
'Being and Time' 62
Belt and Road Initiative (BRI) 112
Berry, A. 36
Berry, J. 36
Bet-the Company Culture 102
body language 69–70, 123, 129–130; mediator 134–137
Bourdieu, P. 96
brain response to conflict 10–11
Bretano, F. 79
British accents 54–56

Brown, S. E. 99–100
Bryant, S. 142–143
Bugental, J. 66, 67, 73
Bujo, B. 110–111
Bush, A. B. 37–39
Bushido code 115–116

Cameron, K. S. 102
Cantona, E. 72
Cantone, J. A. 54, 55
Centre for Effective Dispute Resolution (CEDR) 139
Charkoudian, L. 140–141
Chen Guo-Ming 17
China, cultural history of mediation in 112–113
China Council for the Promotion of International Trade Mediation centre (CCPIT) 113
Christies, P. 109
Civil Justice Council (CJC) 29
Civil Procedure Rule (CPR) 29–30
civil rights movement 111
Ci-Yue Chui 96
clarity in decisions 38
Cobb, S. 33–34
Code of Hammurabi 108
Cold War, the 114
collaborating approach to conflict 9
collectivist cultures 76
Collins, S. A. 55
co-mediation 43–44, **44**; choosing the wrong co-mediator for 46–47; communication in 47; danger of manipulation in 47; different perceptions in 45; ego in 47; emotional support in 44–45; modelling behavior in 45–46; offering diversity 45; practical considerations with 44; supervision and

162 Index

continuing professional development with 46; tensions and challenges of 46–47; value for money of 46
Communication Theory 96
competing or defeating approach to conflict 9
Competing Values Framework 102
compromising approach to conflict 9–10
compulsory mediation 29–30
confidentiality in mediation 22–23
conflict: definitions of 11–13; different responses to 7; emotional aspects of 14–15, 18–20, 25–26; physical reaction to 10–11; positive versus negative 16; problems with ignoring 6–7; psychological aspects of 13–15, 19–20, 23–24; as relational 16–18, 59–60; social aspect of 15–18; stages of 7–8; strategies and behaviors for handling 8–10
Confucius 108, 112
Congress of Vienna 114
Constantino, C. A. 13
continued struggle or battle 12
court-mandated mediation 29–30
'Critique of Dialectical Reason' 67
cultural bias 52–57
cultural competency training 141–145
cultural differences in mediation: body language 69–70, 123, 129–130; language 123–129; listening and language skills for 132–134; presence, proximity, and mediator body language 134–137; use of interpreters 130–132
Cultural Dimensions Theory 96
cultural history of mediation 108–109; in Africa 109–111; in China 112–113; in Europe 113–114; in India 114; in Islamic countries 114–115; in Japan 115–116; in Russia 116; in the United States 111–112
cultural values 124
Cultural Web view 102
culture 147; Competing Values Framework and 102; complexity of 103; Cultural Dimensions Theory 96; cultural identifiers and 103–107, *104*; Cultural Web view 102; definitions of 93, 94–96; disability 99–101; families and 105–106; Feedback/Rewards Systems and Risk Orientation 102; Hofstede's framework of 96, **97–98**; identity versus 93, 98–99; organisational 101–103; religious beliefs and 106; role models and 106; subcultures and 106–107; worldview and 94–95
culture matching 140–141

Dai Xiaodong 17
Davidheiser, M. 94–95
Davis, L. J. 99
Deal, T. E. 102
death 64–66
debate and polemics stage of conflict 7
de Beauvoir, S. 63, 64–65, 67, 73
Deng Xiaoping 112
Derwing, T. M. 55–56
diamond of divergence 43
diamond of pain 43
Differentiation Perspective 102
Disability Culture 99–101
Docherty, G. 54

Eigenwelt 76
Ekman, P. 71
embodiment 70–73
e-mediation 30–31
emotional aspects of conflict 14–15, 18–20, 25–26
emotional dwelling 60
emotional support in co-mediation 44–45
emotions 70–73
empathy 60
empowerment 37–38
Epston, D. 33
'Ethics of Ambiguity, The' 63
Europe, cultural history of mediation in 113–114
evaluative/problem-solving style of mediation 27, **28**, 31–32
existential dimensions 75–77
existentialism 60, 61; death, temporality, and finiteness 64–66; emotions, experience, and embodiment 70–73; freedom, responsibility, and agency 62–64; meaning and meaningless 68–70; relatedness and isolation 66–67; uncertainty 73–74
experience 70–73, 147–151
external conflict 12

facilitative/transformative style of mediation 27, **28**, 32
Fanon, F. 8, 125
Feedback/Rewards Systems 102
fight-flight-freeze response 10, 25

finiteness 64–66
Folger, J. P. 37–39
Foulkes, P. 54
Fragmentation Perspective 102
Francis, V. 145
Frankl, V. E. 63, 68
freedom 62–64
Freud, S. 15, 60
Freyberg, R. 54
Friesen, W. V. 71
Frumkin, L. A. 52
Fuertes, J. N. 54

Gadlin, H. 144
Geertz, C. 94, 96
gender reassignment 149
George, W. H. 142
Geworfenheit 62
Ginsberg, M. B. 141
Glasl, F. 7–8
global responses to mediation 117–122
Gold, J. A. 95
Goleman, D. 10
Grotius, H. 113

Habermas, J. 34
Halsted, A. 139
Hanaway, M. 43, 46
Handy, C. B. 102–103
hardening stage of conflict 7
Harvard Model 27
Heads of Agreement 42
Heery, M. 73
Heidegger, M. 61, 62, 66, 72–73, 75, 78, 105
Higley, D. J. 15
Hofstede, G. 93, 96, **97–98**
Holt, K. B. 142
Husserl, E. 34, 78, 79

identity versus culture 93, 98–99
images and coalitions stage of conflict 8
India, cultural history of mediation in 114
individualist cultures 76
individual session, psychologically informed mediation 86–87
Industrial Revolution 114
Integration Perspective 102
internal conflict 12
International Commercial Court (ICC) 113
interpreters 130–132

Islamic countries, cultural history of mediation in 114–115
isolation 66–67
Iulia, V. 124

Japan, cultural history of mediation in 115–116
Johnson, G. 102
Johnson, M. 124
joint session, psychologically informed mediation 87, 90
Jones, D. 54
Judd, C. M. 54
Judicial Arbitration and Mediation Services (JAMS) 111
Jung, C. 107
Jungian shadow 77

Kant, E. 113
Kennedy, A. A. 102
Kierkegaard, S. 61, 126
Killmann, R. H. 8–10
Klein, M. 15
Kluckhohn, C. 93
Ko, S. J. 54
Koopman, P. M. 109
Kövecses, Z. 124
Krauss, R. M. 54
Kroeber, A. L. 93
Kuper, A. 93

Lakoff, G. 124
language differences in mediation 123–129; listening and language skills for 132–134; use of interpreters and 130–132
League of Nations 114
LeBaron, M. 103, 144, 152
Lehane, D. 74
listening 87–90, 132–134
litigation versus mediation 5, **6**, 23
lived experience *see* experience
loss of faith stage of conflict 8
Luban, D. 34

Magee, P. 36
Mallon, C. 99
Mandela, N. 110
Marshall, T. 35–36
Martin, J. 102
Martinez, L. N. 54, 55
Matsumoto, D. 70–71

Index

May, R. 67, 125, 126
McGovern, S. 54
meaning 68–70
meaninglessness 68–70
Med-Arb 32–33
mediation 27; Arb-Med 29; compulsory or court-mandated 29–30; confidentiality in 22–23; cultural differences in (*see* cultural differences in mediation); current responses to use of 117–122; defined 3; differences between litigation and 5, **6**, 23; evaluative/problem-solving 27, **28**, 31–32; existential concepts in (*see* existentialism); facilitative 27, **28**, 32; fees for 22; forms of 5–6; future of 121–122; history of 108–116; Hofstede's framework of culture and 96, **97–98**; impact of lived experience on 70–73, 147–150; legal training in 23–24; Med-Arb 32–33; narrative 33–35; negotiation in 3–5, *5*; neutrality in 24–25; online 30–31; phenomenological concepts for 78–80; psychologically informed (*see* psychologically informed mediation); restorative justice (RJ) 35–36; success rate of 22; transformative 27, **28**, 32, 36–39
mediation day 41–43, 85–87
mediation process: co-mediation in 43–47, **44**, mediation day in 41–43, 85–87; pre-mediation 40–41, 81–85
mediation profession 138–139; cultural competency training for 141–145; cultural representation in 139–140; culture matching in 140–141; psychologically informed training for 145–146; structural considerations for 139–141
Mediation Service of South Africa (IMSSA) 110
mediation time warp 43
mediators: advantages of sole mediation for 47; body language of 134–137; choosing the wrong co- 46–47; major skills of 25; managing interruptions 42; neutrality of 24–25, 41; training for 23–24
Merchant, C. S. 13
Merleau-Ponty, M. 78
Mesopotamia 108
Miller, T. 54, 55
Mindell, A. 6, 16, 19
Mitwelt 76
modelling 45–46
Monk, G. 35

Morris 36
Morsella, E. 54
Muhammed 114–115
Munro, M. J. 55–56
musalaha 115
myths 125–127

Nakagawa, S. 70–71
Napoleonic Wars 114
narrative mediation 33–35
National Library of Medicine 65
negotiation 3–5, *5*
neutrality of mediators 24–25, 41
Ngubane, B. 100
Nietzsche, F. 61, 66, 73
nonbeing 64
nongovernmental organisations (NGOs) 120, 121

Online Dispute Resolution (ODR) 30–31
organisational culture 101–103
Otherness 67

perceived incompatible goals 13
Person Culture 102–103
Peters, J. K. 142–143
phenomenology 78–80
physical response to conflict 10–11
polyamory 149–150
Potere, J. C. 54
Power Culture 102–103
pre-mediation 40–41; psychologically informed mediation 81–85
presence 134–137
Promise of Mediation, The 38
proximity 134–137
psychological aspects of conflict 13–15, 19–20, 23–24
psychologically informed mediation 39, 43–44; alternative perceptions in 57–58; assumptions made in 52–55, **53**; authenticity in 58; cultural differences and 58–59; existential concepts in (*see* existentialism); flexibility of 87; individual sessions 86–87; introduction to 51–60; joint session 87, 90; opening joint session 85–86; pre-mediation phase 81–85; skills needed in 87–90; speech patterns and accents and 54–56; training programmes for 145–146
Pufendorf, S. 113

Index

questioning 89
Quinn, R. E. 102
Quran, the 108, 115

Ramirez, K. Y. 54
Rand, A. 17
Randolph, P. 13, 29
Reich, W. 15
relatedness 40–41, 66–67
relational nature of conflict 16–18, 59–60
responsibility 62–64
restorative justice (RJ) 35–36
Risk Orientation 102
Role Culture 102–103
Rousseau, J.-J. 113
Rumi 67
Russia, cultural history of mediation in 116

Samuels, A. 15–16
Sartre, J.-P. 61, 66, 67, 75, 76, 78, 126
Savage, C. A. 95
Schein, P. 101
Scholes, K. 102
Scott, A. 54, 98
Servant Leadership 126
7/11 Rule 53–54
Shantz, C. 12, 13
Sharia law 114–115
Shaw, G. B. 54
silence 88–89
skill-based empowerment 38
social aspect of conflict 15–18
Soviet Union, the 116
Stallard, A. 143–144
Stapel, D. A. 54
stategies of threats/limited destructive blows/fragmentation of the enemy stage of conflict 8
Stolorow, R. D. 60
Stone, A. 52
storytelling 34
Strasser, F. 13
sulh 115
Sun Tzu 23, 59, 60
Suttie, I. 15

Tahkim 114–115
Tao Te Ching 108
Task Culture 102–103
Taylor, E. 94
temporality 64–66
Thirty Years' War 113
Tillich 64
time-distribured social episodes 12
together into 'the abyss' stage of conflict 8
Totton, N. 14, 16
Tough-Guy, Macho Culture 102
transformative mediation 36–39
Treaty of Westphalia 113
trust in co-mediation 46
tuning in 87
tuning out 90
Tutu, D. 110

Uberwelt 76
Umwelt 76
uncertainty 73–74
United Nations 114
United States, cultural history of mediation in the 111–112
Unterwelt 76–77

values, cultural 124
van Deurzen, E. 78

Wayne, E. 140–141
Wells, G. 52
White, M. 33
Willis-Esqueda, C. 54, 55
Winslade, J. 35
Wlodkowski, R. 141
worldview 94–95

Xuefu Wang 61

Yalom, I. 58, 61, 65, 66, 67
Yarn, D. H. 13
Yoo, S. H. 70–71

Zumeta, Z. 103, 144, 152

Printed in the United States
by Baker & Taylor Publisher Services